Parties and Political Change in South Asia

Over the past seven decades and more, political parties have become an essential feature of the political landscape of the South Asian subcontinent, serving both as a conduit and product of the tumultuous change the region has experienced. Yet they have not been the focus of sustained scholarly attention. This collection focuses on different aspects of how major parties have been agents of – and subject to – change in three South Asian states (India, Pakistan and Sri Lanka), examining some of the apparent paradoxes of politics in the subcontinent and covering issues such as gender, religion, patronage, clientelism, political recruitment and democratic regression. Recurring themes are the importance of personalities (and the corresponding neglect of institutionalisation) and the lack of pluralism in intraparty affairs, factors that render parties and political systems vulnerable to degeneration.

This book was published as a special issue of *Commonwealth & Comparative Politics*.

James Chiriyankandath is Senior Research Fellow at the Institute of Commonwealth Studies, University of London, and Co-Editor of the journal *Commonwealth & Comparative Politics*. Having previously worked at the universities of Hull, London Guildhall and London Metropolitan, he has taught, researched and published on the politics of South Asia (especially India) for over two decades.

Parties and Political Change in South Asia

Edited by
James Chiriyankandath

Routledge
Taylor & Francis Group

LONDON AND NEW YORK

First published 2015 by Routledge

2 Park Square, Milton Park, Abingdon, Oxon, OX14 4RN
605 Third Avenue, New York, NY 10017

Routledge is an imprint of the Taylor & Francis Group, an informa business

First issued in paperback 2020

British Library Cataloguing in Publication Data
A catalogue record for this book is available from the British Library

ISBN 13: 978-1-138-82156-9 (hbk)
ISBN 13: 978-0-367-73920-1 (pbk)

Typeset in Times New Roman
by RefineCatch Limited, Bungay, Suffolk

Publisher's Note
The publisher accepts responsibility for any inconsistencies that may have
arisen during the conversion of this book from journal articles to book chapters,
namely the possible inclusion of journal terminology.

Disclaimer
Every effort has been made to contact copyright holders for their permission to
reprint material in this book. The publishers would be grateful to hear from any
copyright holder who is not here acknowledged and will undertake to rectify
any errors or omissions in future editions of this book.

Contents

Citation Information   vii

1. Parties and political change in South Asia   1
   James Chiriyankandath

2. Losing the connection: party-voter linkages in Pakistan   7
   Shandana Khan Mohmand

3. Elite formation within a political party: the case of the Dravida
   Munnetra Kazhagam   32
   C. Manikandan and Andrew Wyatt

4. Class, nation and religion: changing nature of Akali Dal
   politics in Punjab, India   55
   Pritam Singh

5. Incumbency, internal processes and renomination in
   Indian parties   78
   A. Farooqui and E. Sridharan

6. Women candidates and party nomination trends in India –
   evidence from the 2009 general election   109
   Carole Spary

7. Parties, political decay, and democratic regression in Sri Lanka   139
   Neil DeVotta

8. Elite patronage over party democracy – high politics in
   Sri Lanka following independence   166
   H. Kumarasingham

Index   187

Citation Information

The chapters in this book were originally published in *Commonwealth & Comparative Politics*, volume 52, issue 1 (February 2014). When citing this material, please use the original page numbering for each article, as follows:

Chapter 1
Parties and political change in South Asia
James Chiriyankandath
Commonwealth & Comparative Politics, volume 52, issue 1 (February 2014) pp. 1–6

Chapter 2
Losing the connection: party-voter linkages in Pakistan
Shandana Khan Mohmand
Commonwealth & Comparative Politics, volume 52, issue 1 (February 2014) pp. 7–31

Chapter 3
Elite formation within a political party: the case of the Dravida Munnetra Kazhagam
C. Manikandan and Andrew Wyatt
Commonwealth & Comparative Politics, volume 52, issue 1 (February 2014) pp. 32–54

Chapter 4
Class, nation and religion: changing nature of Akali Dal politics in Punjab, India
Pritam Singh
Commonwealth & Comparative Politics, volume 52, issue 1 (February 2014) pp. 55–77

CITATION INFORMATION

Chapter 5
Incumbency, internal processes and renomination in Indian parties
A. Farooqui and E. Sridharan
Commonwealth & Comparative Politics, volume 52, issue 1 (February 2014) pp. 78–108

Chapter 6
Women candidates and party nomination trends in India – evidence from the 2009 general election
Carole Spary
Commonwealth & Comparative Politics, volume 52, issue 1 (February 2014) pp. 109–138

Chapter 7
Parties, political decay, and democratic regression in Sri Lanka
Neil DeVotta
Commonwealth & Comparative Politics, volume 52, issue 1 (February 2014) pp. 139–165

Chapter 8
Elite patronage over party democracy – high politics in Sri Lanka following independence
H. Kumarasingham
Commonwealth & Comparative Politics, volume 52, issue 1 (February 2014) pp. 166–186

Please direct any queries you may have about the citations to
clsuk.permissions@cengage.com

Parties and political change in South Asia

James Chiriyankandath

Institute of Commonwealth Studies, School of Advanced Study, University of London, London, UK

Over the past seven decades and more political parties have become an essential feature of the political landscape of the South Asian subcontinent, serving both as a conduit and product of the tumultuous change the region has experienced. Yet they have not been the focus of sustained scholarly attention. This collection focuses on different aspects of how major parties have been agents of – and subject to – change in three South Asian states (India, Pakistan and Sri Lanka), examining some of the apparent paradoxes of politics in the subcontinent. Recurring themes are the importance of charismatic leaders and their families (and the corresponding neglect of institutionalisation) and the lack of pluralism in intraparty affairs, factors that render parties and political systems vulnerable to degeneration.

In the seven decades since South Asia emerged from two centuries of British colonial rule the subcontinent has witnessed considerable and often tumultuous, political change – military coups and popular uprisings, terrorism, rebellions, secessionist movements, civil wars, and the internal reorganisation or breakup of states. During this time political parties across the region have served both as a conduit and a product of these changes. Indian parties attracted significant attention from, especially American, political scientists in the 1960s and 1970s (Baxter, 1969; Erdman, 1967; Kochanek, 1968; Sisson, 1972; Weiner, 1967).[1] In subsequent years the character and role of political parties in South Asia, did not receive the same degree of scholarly interest except for the rise of parties based on religious, ethnic or caste identity (Chandra, 2004; Graham, 1990; Katzenstein, 1979; Malik & Singh, 1994; Nasr, 1994; Subramanian, 1999). As coalition and minority governments became the

1

norm at the national level in India after 1989 (Chiriyankandath, 1997), the changing party system also became more a focus of study (Chhibber, 1999; Mehra, 2013; Wyatt, 2010). In the last decade there has been a revival of interest in parties as for the first time there are governments elected on the basis of, at least nominally, competitive multiparty political systems in all the seven states of the subcontinent (DeSouza & Sridharan, 2006; Enskat, Mitra, & Spiess, 2004; Hasan, 2002; Suri, Hällhag, Kadirgamar-Rajasingham, Tjernström, & Gomez, 2007). Much still remains to be done in exploring the place of parties in South Asia – apart from Nasr's (1994) work on the Jama'at-i Islami in Pakistan no substantial study of any subcontinental party outside India has yet appeared.

A large number and bewildering variety of parties are found across the region: in 2013 the Election Commission of India recognised 1443, including six recognised as national and 37 as state parties;[2] the Election Commission of Pakistan listed 254;[3] the Department of Elections in Sri Lanka lists 64;[4] the Bangladesh Election Commission lists 40;[5] 139 parties registered in the run up to the November 2013 Constituent Assembly polls in Nepal;[6] and even in tiny Bhutan and the Maldives, where political parties were only legalised in the past decade, there were five contesting the 2013 legislative election in Bhutan and eleven the 2009 poll in the Maldives.[7] Although less than a hundred of the nearly two thousand parties are represented in national legislatures, the proliferation of parties has contributed to making government by coalition more common, especially in India, where the number of parties in the Lok Sabha (House of the People) increased from a mere 12 in 1957 to 37 in 2009.

South Asian parties include several of the oldest in the post-colonial world, foremost among them the 129-year-old Indian National Congress that led India to independence in 1947. Despite numerous splits and breakaways, most notably in 1969 and 1978, it has ruled the country for all but 13 of the past 67 years (albeit at the head of a coalition for the last 10). Congress's chief rival, the Bharatiya Janata Party, though founded in 1980, traces its organisational roots to the Hindu nationalist Rashtriya Swayamsevak Sangh (National Volunteer Organisation) established in 1925 and the Hindu Mahasabha formed in 1913. In Pakistan the ruling Pakistan Muslim League (Nawaz Sharif), though only formed in 1988, in its nomenclature and rendition of history claims the heritage of the All India Muslim League that was founded in 1906 and brought the country into being.[8] Its main opponent, the Pakistan People's Party, was launched by Zulfiqar Ali Bhutto in 1967 and led by the Bhutto family from its foundation. Both the main parties in Sri Lanka, the opposition United National Party and the Sri Lanka Freedom Party (the main component in the ruling United People's Freedom Alliance), were formed by leading figures in the erstwhile Ceylon National Congress within three years either side of the independence of the island in 1948. The contributors to this collection focus on different aspects of how these major parties have been agents and subjects of change.

The contributors use the prism of party politics to examine some of the apparent paradoxes of politics in South Asia. Shandana Mohmand's contribution interprets the behaviour of voters, local leaders and candidates through a longitudinal study of the politics of a village in Pakistani Punjab from the late 1960s to the early 2010s, affording a unique insight into how the changing political dynamics in a rural locality linked to party competition at the national level. Some aspects of the story she tells – of politically influential families and women endowed with political clout by virtue of their family backround – represent recurring themes in discussions of subcontinental political parties.

Leading families are a ubiquitous feature of many major parties in South Asia, including several of those studied in this collection. C. Manikandan and Andrew Wyatt's detailed analysis of the changing nature of leadership in one of India's oldest regional parties (fd. 1949), the Dravida Munnetra Kazhagham in the southern state of Tamil Nadu, shows the important role played by the sons, daughter and other relatives of the octogenerian Muthuvel Karunanidhi, the veteran party leader and former chief minister. Pritam Singh's complementary survey of how the politics of the Shiromani Akali Dal, the oldest Indian regional party (fd. 1920), have changed mentions in a footnote the father and son who serve as the Akali Dal chief minister and deputy chief minister of Indian Punjab, Parkash Singh Badal, another octogenerian party leader, and Sukhbir Singh Badal (several of their relatives are also, or have previously, served as ministers and legislators).

The salience of family and kinship in the leadership of South Asian political parties is inescapable – the writer Patrick French even forsees the Indian Lok Sabha perhaps turning into a 'Vansh Sabha' (house of dynasties) (French, 2011, pp. 105–123). There have been two or more leaders of national political parties (and heads of government) from one or two families in India (the Nehru-Gandhis), Pakistan (the Bhuttos), Sri Lanka (the Senanayakes and Bandaranaikes), Bangladesh (Mujibur Rahman and his daughter Hasina Wazed, Ziaur Rahman and his widow Khaleda Zia), and Nepal (the Koiralas). A consequence has been that the region, despite returning some of the lowest numbers of women to legislatures, has had the largest number of female heads of government and leaders of governing parties – seven since 1960. Yet, as Carole Spary shows in her analysis of the nomination of women candidates in the 2009 Lok Sabha elections, Indian political parties remain disinclined to risk nominating women except in constituencies where personal strengths and family connections favour particular female candidates.

The process by which political parties nominate candidates is one that has not received much attention in South Asian election studies but here Spary's contribution is accompanied by another by Adnan Farooqui and E. Sridharan investigating how five Indian political parties chose their candidates in the 2004 and 2009 Lok Sabha elections. Its main finding, that parties are highly centralised in picking candidates does not come as a surprise, given the central role played by charismatic leaders, the neglect of institutionalisation and, often, a lack of pluralism within party forums. Farooqui and Sridharan refer to how the Bahujan Samaj Party expected candidates to 'buy' their nomination by making large financial contributions. Criminality, corruption and wealth form an important element in political selection in India, something highlighted by the Association for Democratic Reforms (ADR) which found in 2009 that while 15 per cent of candidates to the Lok Sabha had criminal charges pending, twice the percentage – 30 per cent – of those elected did so (ADR, n.d., pp. 21–22). Similarly, although only 16 per cent of the candidates were 'crorepatis' (i.e. people with declared assets of over a crore or ten million rupees) this included 58 per cent of those returned with a third of MPs declaring assets worth over 50 million rupees (ADR, n.d., pp. 22; Gowda & Sridharan, 2012, p. 236).

The last two contributions to the issue, by Neil DeVotta and Harshan Kumarasingham, complement each other in tracing the descent of post-colonial Ceylon from 'a model dominion', the phrase used by the historian of the Commonwealth Nicholas Mansergh and quoted by Kumarasingham, to an authoritarian polity in which, as DeVotta says, 'one family [that of President Mahinda Rajapaksa] dictates all politics'. Rendered especially vulnerable by its path to independence being mediated by a rarefied Anglophile political class, Sri Lanka's two main political parties subsequently vitiated its democracy through competing in espousing Sinhala ethnic chauvinism and helping push the beleaguered Tamil minority to violent seperatism.

If the experience of South Asia's southernmost state was an illustration of how parties can become agents of political degeneration, the preceding contributions in this collection show how they can serve as channels of political change, that, while sometimes negative, is potentially also constructive: in linking local to national politics (Mohmand), providing a focus for regional aspirations and ethnic and religious identity within a federal polity (Manikandan and Wyatt, and Singh), and widening the scope of democratic representation (Farooqui and Sridharan, and Spary). Over the past six and a half decades parties have become an essential feature of the South Asian political landscape. How they develop will help determine the ways in which that landscape changes in the years to come.

Acknowledgements

The editor would like to thank the reviewers of this collection, as well as the participants in the panel on 'Political parties and change in South Asia' at the 22nd European

Conference on South Asian Studies in Lisbon, 25–28 July 2012 – Binayak Bhatta-charya, Neil DeVotta, Harshan Kumarasingham, Shandana Mohmand, Bettina Robotka and Pritam Singh. Andrew Wyatt (the panel's co-convenor) played an invaluable part in bringing it all together.

Notes

1. While he did not publish a volume on political parties, the British political scientist W. H. Morris-Jones was another pioneer in this field (see Morris-Jones, 1957, pp. 166–199, 1987, pp. 166–229).
2. Election Commission of India, Tables 1–3. Retrieved November 7, 2013, from http://eci.nic.in/eci_main/ElectoralLaws/OrdersNotifications/ElecSym19012013_eng.pdf
3. Election Commission of Pakistan, List of Political Parties Enlisted on Our Record. Retrieved November 13, 2013, from http://ecp.gov.pk/Misc/ListPolPartiesWith addresses.pdf
4. Department of Elections, Political Parties. Retrieved November 13, 2013, from http://www.slelections.gov.lk/pp.html
5. Election Commission Bangladesh, Registered Parties. Retrieved November 13, 2013, from http://www.ecs.gov.bd/English/RegisteredPoliticalPartyEng.php
6. Number of parties contesting in Nepal's November election doubles. *Xinhua News*, 17 October 2013. Retrieved November 13, 2013, from http://news.xinhuanet.com/english/world/2013-10/17/c_132807077.htm
7. Election Commission of Bhutan. Retrieved November 13, 2013, from http://www.election-bhutan.org.bt/?page_id=59; and Inter-Parliamentary Union, Retrieved November 13, 2013, from http://www.ipu.org/parline-e/reports/2199_e.htm
8. Pakistan Resolution. Retrieved November 13, 2013, from http://www.pmln.org/pakistan-resolution/

References

Association for Democratic Reforms (ADR). (n.d.). *Lok Sabha 2009 national election watch report*. Retrieved November 13, 2013, from http://adrindia.org/research-and-reports/lok-sabha/2009/pdf-of-national-level-analysis

Baxter, C. (1969). *The Jana Sangh: A biography of an Indian political party*. Philadelphia: University of Pennsylvania Press.

Chandra, K. (2004). *Why ethnic parties succeed: Patronage and ethnic headcounts in India*. Cambridge: Cambridge University Press.

Chhibber, P. K. (1999). *Democracy without associations: Transformation of the party system and social cleavages in India*. Ann Arbor: University of Michigan Press.

Chiriyankandath, J. (1997). 'Unity in diversity'? Coalition politics in India. *Democratization*, 4(4), 16–39.

DeSouza, P. R., & Sridharan, E. (Eds.). (2006). *India's political parties*. New Delhi: Sage.

Enskat, M., Mitra, S., & Spiess, C. (Eds.). (2004). *Political parties in South Asia*. Westport, CT: Praeger.

Erdman, H. L. (1967). *The Swatantra Party and Indian conservatism*. Cambridge: Cambridge University Press.

French, P. (2011). *India. A portrait*. Delhi: Allen Lane.

Gowda, M. V. R., & Sridharan, E. (2012). Reforming India's party financing and election expenditure laws. *Election Law Journal, 11*(2), 226–240.

Graham, B. D. (1990). *Hindu nationalism and Indian politics: The origins and development of the Bharatiya Jana Sangh*. Cambridge: Cambridge University Press.

Hasan, Z. (Ed.). (2002). *Parties and party politics in India*. Delhi: Oxford University Press.

Katzenstein, M. F. (1979). *Ethnicity and equality: The Shiv Sena and preferential policies in Bombay*. Ithaca, NY: Cornell University Press.

Kochanek, S. A. (1968). *The Congress Party of India: The dynamics of one-party democracy*. Princeton, NJ: Princeton University Press.

Malik, Y. K., & Singh, V. B. (1994). *Hindu nationalists in India: The rise of the Bharatiya Janata party*. Boulder, CO: Westview Press.

Mehra, A. K. (Ed.). (2013). *Party system in India: Emerging trajectories*. New Delhi: Lancer.

Morris-Jones, W. H. (1957). *Parliament in India*. London: Longmans, Green & Co.

Morris-Jones, W. H. (1987). *Government and politics in India* (4th ed.). Huntingdon: The Eothen Press.

Nasr, S. V. R. (1994). *Vanguard of the Islamic revolution: Jama'at-i Islami of Pakistan*. Berkeley: University of California Press.

Sisson, R. (1972). *The Congress Party in Rajasthan: Political integration and institution-building in an Indian State*. Berkeley: University of California Press.

Subramanian, N. (1999). *Ethnicity and populist mobilization: Political parties, citizens and democracy in South India*. Delhi: Oxford University Press.

Suri, K. C., Hällhag, R., Kadirgamar-Rajasingham, S., Tjernström, M., & Gomez, J. (2007). *Political parties in South Asia: The challenge of change*. Stockholm: International Institute for Democracy and Electoral Assistance.

Weiner, M. (1967). *Party building in a New Nation*. Chicago: University of Chicago Press.

Wyatt, A. (2010). *Party system change in South India. Political entrepreneurs, patterns and processes*. London: Routledge.

Losing the connection: party-voter linkages in Pakistan

Shandana Khan Mohmand

Institute of Development Studies, University of Sussex, Falmer, UK

How do political parties in Pakistan aggregate votes and connect to voters, especially in rural areas? Most explanations for party-voter linkages in rural Pakistan can be grouped into four broad categories: (a) political parties are made up of powerful landlords who use economic power to collect votes from dependent voters; (b) parties are conglomerations of clientelist networks; (c) parties are large aggregations of kinship networks; and (d) parties function by building links with specific types of constituencies across large parts of the country, and voters forge links with political parties based on ideology and party identification. These are, at best, only partial explanations. How is it that they can all co-exist? The answer lies in the level of analysis employed. I argue that when viewed in aggregated form at a macro-level of analysis, such as that of national politics, these varied explanations of party-voter linkages appear to be distinct and sometimes mutually exclusive. However, when disaggregated and examined at a micro-level of analysis, that of village-level politics, it becomes obvious how it is possible for all of these linkages to not only co-exist but often even work together. I adopt this micro-level of analysis through a longitudinal study of one village in Pakistan's most populous and politically most important province, Punjab. Using the case study of Sahiwal, I argue that the reason for the varied explanations is that the link between political parties and their voters is rarely direct. Instead, it is mediated by different types of local actors. As the national political arena changes, different actors gain precedence, leading to multiple explanations of what is really going on in rural Pakistan between political parties and their voters.

Introduction

There is only one week to go until the election of 11 May 2013, and the villages of Sargodha district in Punjab are abuzz with political activity. Despite the ongoing harvest, village life is focused around village squares and *daaras*,[1] where men seated on string beds talk politics. Who will they be voting for, what did they think of the last politician that made his/her way through the village, how convinced were they by the message conveyed at the village corner meeting, all of these form the staple of conversations in village after village that I visit. Many of these conversations revolve, in particular, around a local politician of the *Mekan* kinship group who has injected a real sense of drama into an already electric environment. The Pakistan Muslim League – Nawaz (PML-N) – the most powerful party in the province and favoured to win the election at the centre – has issued a party ticket for a provincial seat to a large landlord and a relative of the party chief. This is not unusual in any way, and is quite typical of how party candidates are recruited by many of Pakistan's parties. However, in this case, the chosen politician is not locally popular. He was elected from this constituency in the 2002 election and was the runner-up in 2008. Yet, he has no real performance record. According to most people I speak with, he has a 'feudal mentality' and has not delivered. To top it off, he lives and works in Lahore, the provincial capital, and is considered an outsider by the voters in this constituency of Sargodha district.

Opposing him is the local *Mekan* politician, a member of one of the area's largest kinship groups (or *biraderi*s). He ran for the first time in 2008, as an independent candidate unattached to any political party, and despite receiving only 2800 votes in that election, he has built a reputation over the five years since then as a 'worker'. He is easily accessible and well connected. His family has been part of the local government system and two brothers are high-ranking bureaucrats, and he has used his contacts in the state to deliver. This has swung support strongly in his favour within the constituency. Encouraged by this, he approached the PML-N for a ticket for the 2013 election, but was refused in favour of the landed relative, even though the latter had contested the previous two elections on a rival party's ticket.

The *Mekan* candidate has decided to go ahead anyway, contesting again as an independent. His following has grown quickly in strength and has made him a stronger contender for the provincial seat than the landlord candidate of the PML-N. A few days before my visit, a member of the party's leadership stopped by the constituency for an election rally and was told by the PML-N's district-based youth wing that they were bound to lose this seat. Furthermore, the party's rally was boycotted by the sizeable *Mekan biraderi*. The party has today suddenly issued a statement to 'open' the seat. This means that the party is no longer backing its own candidate, nor opposing the local man (who, it is now rumoured, has been invited to join the PML-N in the case of a win). The conversations at the *daara*s are infused with excitement.

8

Local will, it seems, has prevailed over what in Pakistan is called the *jaagirdar-ana nizam*, or a 'feudal system' of politics. The *biraderi*s of the constituency[2] have managed to come together against a veteran, landed politician who has provided little and has remained inaccessible to his voters. Instead, a man with far less experience but an apparent will to deliver is now set to win, and that too as an 'unofficial' member of the party that is expected to win in both the province and the centre. This will pull in even more votes and ensure that he wins – as he did.

This story from the election of May 2013 confirms the general perception that political parties in Pakistan are internally weak and fluid organisations that recruit members by looking for local bigwigs that can pull in a ready electorate using whatever means and power are available to them. Landlords are able to do this quite readily and are, therefore, obvious choices for party tickets. However, if another candidate clearly demonstrates that s/he has the ability to organise a larger vote bank, then the party (usually simply the party leadership) has no problems in dropping an old acquaintance for a new one. At the same time, however, both the 2008 and 2013 elections have shown that politics in Pakistan – for decades defined as 'personalised politics' is based around locally powerful individuals – has quite decidedly shifted to political parties as the primary and most important actors. Political parties may need local bigwigs, but political hopefuls increasingly need party tickets to be able to pull in a winning vote.

Party-voter linkages

Political parties in Pakistan issue manifestos and have some noticeable leaning – though quite 'diffuse and erratic' (Kitschelt & Wilkinson, 2007, p. 3) – towards the left or the right of the political spectrum in terms of their programmatic packages. However, this is not the basis on which they recruit members or organise their vote banks. Kitschelt and Wilkinson argue that a central concern in the study of political parties and how they function is to understand, ' . . . the substantive alignments that rally citizens around rival contenders or the strategic appeals made by leading politicians in each camp' (2007, p. 1). They point out that institutional arguments based around the study of formal electoral institutions have not been able to adequately explain how political parties connect to their voters in many parts of the world. What is required instead is an understanding of 'the mechanisms of citizens' and politicians' strategic conduct that link their asset endowments and preferences to individual strategies and collective outcomes of political action manifesting themselves in diverse principal-agent relations of accountability and responsiveness' (Kitschelt & Wilkinson, 2007, p. 6).

In this paper, I seek to advance the understanding of how political parties function and of party-voter linkages in line with this argument, and ask: how do political parties in Pakistan aggregate votes and connect to their voters, especially those who live in rural areas? There are various confusing, and sometimes contradictory, answers offered. These include: (a) through the 'feudal' mode of politics, (b) through clientelism, (c) through kinship networks, and (d) through party identification. I look at each of these in turn in the second section, and argue that while they all help explain how political parties organise the vote in rural Pakistan, they are each, at best, only partial explanations. How is it that they can all co-exist? The answer lies in the level of analysis employed. I argue that when viewed in an aggregated form at a macro-level of analysis, such as that of national politics, these varied explanations of party-voter linkages appear to be distinct and sometimes mutually exclusive. However, when disaggregated and examined at a micro-level of analysis, that of village-level politics, it suddenly becomes obvious how it is possible for all of these linkages to not only co-exist but often even work together.

I adopt this micro-level of analysis in the third section and explain party-voter linkages and how these have changed over time through a case study of a village in Pakistan's most populous and politically most important province, Punjab. Sahiwal provides the perfect case for such a longitudinal analysis because it was the focus of two detailed studies in the 1960s (Ahmad, 1977) and the late 1970s (Rouse, 1988). I re-studied[3] the village in 2006–2007, and again briefly just before the May 2013 election, with the aim of analysing what had changed here since the previous studies. Together, these three studies are able to present a unique, longitudinal, micro-level view of the impact of national political changes – represented by alternating periods of authoritarianism and democratisation – on the residents of a village, and on their political and socio-economic relationships with one another, captured at three points in time over more than four decades.

Using the case of Sahiwal, I conclude in the fourth section that the reason for the varied explanations is that the link between political parties and their voters is rarely direct. Instead, it is mediated by different types of local actors, ranging from landlords and brokers, to kin groups and local party leaders. As the national political arena and its political parties change, different actors gain precedence at the local level, leading to multiple explanations of what is really going on in rural Pakistan between political parties and their voters. Because the case village is dominated by a family of landlords, this paper also deals centrally with the popular notion of the landlord control of politics and political parties in Pakistan, and refutes the idea of a 'feudal' hold on politics by large landlords. It argues instead that landlords continue to play a central role in politics not because of their lingering economic power but because of the nature of political parties and the fact that they do not connect directly to their voters in rural Pakistan.

10

Competing explanations of party-voter linkages in Pakistan

As already stated most explanations for party-voter linkages in rural Pakistan can be grouped into four broad categories. Each of these is dealt with in turn below.

The 'feudal' mode of politics

One of the most popular views of Pakistan's political parties states that they function by recruiting powerful local landlords on whom rural voters are socio-economically dependent. This is often referred to as the 'feudal' mode of politics, and according to this explanation, citizens in rural Punjab and Sindh, in particular, vote not as they would like to, but rather, as they are told to (Alavi, 1983, 1990; Gardezi, 1983; Sayeed, 1980; Waseem, 1994). These landlords may be electoral candidates themselves, or they may be local power holders that political parties work with, who are able to use their control over land and people's livelihoods to tell them how to cast their vote.

In Punjab, the province on which I focus in this paper, the preponderant power of landed groups in politics has its origins in the nature of colonial rule. Through the process of establishing and expanding its revenue and administrative structure in rural Punjab, the colonial state created socio-economic inequality that was premised on landownership, and then encouraged this to be stitched together with political dominance by patronising a political party formed entirely of landlords, the Unionist Party. This fusion of economic, social and political power at the point of production was labelled 'feudalism' by scholars such as Alavi (1983) and Herring (1979). The political power and influence of these landlords in Punjab kept both the Congress and the Muslim League from gaining any substantial support in the 1937 election for the Provincial Legislative Assemblies[4] (Oren, 1974). Things changed dramatically in the 1946 election when the Muslim League swept the Muslim seats of the province, based to a large extent on the fact that many of the Muslim members of the Unionist Party had joined the League, bringing with them their rural constituencies and votes, for fear of the Congress party's commitment to land reforms in India. Jinnah and his Muslim League were ambiguous on this issue, and so Pakistan looked like a much better prospect for these landlords (Talbot, 1980).

Pakistan, therefore, came into being in 1947 led by a political party that was dominated in the Punjab by conservative landlords. For years after partition, the Muslim League depended on landlords to organise and control the countryside (Herring, 1979; Sayeed, 1980). Despite limited land reforms, the political power of the rural landed elite was further entrenched under Pakistan's first military regime led by General Ayub Khan. In 1959 the regime introduced the party-less Basic Democracies system of local government elections,[5] which created a restricted franchise that put political power entirely in the hands of the landed classes. Soon afterwards, however, the power of the landlord in rural Punjab suffered a serious setback.

Ayub's 'politics of exclusion', pursued by the regime through the 1960s, and his doctrine of 'functional inequality' (Jalal, 1994, p. 159) resulted in rising unrest and opposition, that many scholars claimed was based on class-based conflict and economic considerations (Ahmad, 1972; Alavi, 1973; Gough, 1977). In 1968 discontent erupted into a movement that was led by 'labour militancy and student radicalism' and which demanded universal adult franchise and parliamentary democracy (Jalal, 1994, p. 160). The movement brought down Ayub's military regime and led to Pakistan's first democratic election. The radicalism of the movement was adopted by the newly created Pakistan People's Party (PPP) as it campaigned under Zulfikar Bhutto for its first election 'by galvanising the common man behind his programme of Islamic Socialism and promise of *roti, kapra, makan* ("bread, clothing, housing")' (Jones, 2003, p. 2). Though Bhutto vacillated in his public speeches on the extent of socialism or revolution that he supported, his election campaign statements such as '[the] present movement would not be successful until the worker owns his factory and the tenant the land he cultivates'[6] earned him a large constituency within urban labour and the rural peasantry (Jones, 2003, p. 239). The PPP rode to an almost 60 per cent victory at the national level in the 1970 election in West Pakistan and a 76 per cent landslide victory in Punjab based on the crucial 'mass support by the powerless, non-privileged, non-landholding classes in the countryside' (Jones, 2003, p. 399).

Much of this was a result of the successful rural campaign of the radical 'Punjab Left' faction within the PPP, whose workers campaigned in villages directly with tenants and agricultural labourers, and whose most vehement stance was the exclusion of all 'undesirable' landed elements from the PPP. Though the Punjab Left was not entirely successful in keeping the PPP free of landed groups – especially given that Bhutto himself was a large landlord, and many large landholders from his native Sindh had joined the PPP early on – it did manage to keep them out in Punjab to the extent that by the time of the election, almost half of the party leaders were political newcomers.

After coming to power the party also instituted land, tenancy and homestead reforms, which were strengthened by a change in attitude of various state departments. For example, when 'soon after the 1970s elections, rural lords reacted to the PPP's promise to give land to the tillers by allying with local state functionaries to carry out a series of tenant evictions' landlords found that the judiciary had become very receptive to litigations by tenants concerning evictions and coercion (Jalal, 1994, p. 162), and that out of the cases of evictions registered in Punjab, 70 per cent of the judgements ordered the restoration of tenants (Herring, 1983, p. 117).

Baxter points out that 'no member of the rural elite can find much pleasure in the results of the 1970 elections ... [because] as a group the rural elite was badly beaten and this by a group largely comprising unknowns' but he also warned that 'only another election held on the terms of those in 1970 can determine the future of the landed aristocracy – and whether the PPP has redeemed its pledge to end "feudal" power in politics' (1974, p. 28). However, the next election was not held on the same terms. By the time the 1977 election rolled around, the 'Punjab Left' had lost its centrality within the PPP because of internal party dynamics, and Bhutto attempted to pacify growing discontent by recruiting the support of larger landlords and moderate middle-roaders in both urban and rural areas (Jalal, 1994; Jones, 2003). The military regime of General Zia-ul-Haq that followed Bhutto consolidated the landed elite's return to politics by repressing or outright banning political parties. Landowners were also allowed to recover some of the land lost under Bhutto, and many tenancy claims based on the tenancy reforms of the 1970s were now thrown out of the courts.The changes of the 1970s were further undone by the party-less 1985 election, the result of which was 'a parliament dominated by landed interests' (Jalal, 1994, p. 180). Political parties returned to the political arena after Zia's death in 1988 but continued to include, and, in fact rely on, the local power of landlords. When General Pervez Musharraf instituted Pakistan's third military regime in 1999, he once again attempted to weaken the PPP and the PML-N,[7] both of whose leaders – Benazir Bhutto and Nawaz Sharif – spent the entire Musharraf era in exile. And like Zia, Musharraf introduced party-less local government elections, which, yet again, strengthened the old local power blocks and networks. Keefer, Narayan and Vishwanath (2003, p. 14) estimate that up to 70 per cent of seats at the local level were won by the 'rural gentry', while Bari and Khan (2001) point out that a majority of elected *nazim*s (district mayors) owned land in access of 25 acres and that there was a positive correlation between the size of land ownership and the probability of success in elections for the district *nazim* (p. 59).

Given this history, 'feudalism' continues to serve as the favourite 'whipping boy of Pakistan's intelligentsia' (Ahmad, 1998). Gazdar argues that the landed have a 'monopolistic control on electoral politics' (2003, p. 3). The media too continues to advance this idea. Take, for example, the media's coverage of the February 2008 election through headlines such as the BBC's 'Feudal shadow over Pakistan elections' (Hasan, 2008), *Dawn's* 'Pakistan's Feudal Demon' (Salahuddin, 2008), or *Daily Times'* 'Feudal Politics' (Ali, 2008). In the 2013 election, the unexpectedly disappointing performance of a relatively new party, ex-cricketer Imran Khan's Pakistan Tehreek-i-Insaaf (PTI), was blamed by many media analysts and commentators on the continuing hold of 'feudal' politics in Punjab.

Zaidi finds that most elected representatives are extremely asset-rich (2004, p. 4935). Coupled with Pakistan's high land inequality – its gini coefficient[8] for land is 0.83, compared to 0.62 for India and 0.49 for China (Bardhan, Mitra, Mookherjee, & Sarkar, 2009; World Bank, 2002) – such arguments have given rise to the explanation that the rural elite can use its landed power to control and manipulate the vote in rural Pakistan to have itself elected to seats in parliament. At the same time, however, other studies point out that this explanation is incomplete. Keefer et al. (2003) argue that, 'anthropological evidence shows that rural inhabitants were less reliant on landowners in the 1990s than earlier, reducing the leverage of landowners over the voters in their areas' (p. 15). The 'feudalism' explanation is also strongly countered by the fact that farms of larger than 12.5 acres have reduced significantly in number while those under 2.5 acres have increased dramatically between 1972 and 2000 (Agricultural Census of Pakistan, 2000).

Wilder further points out that things have changed for the landed elite, and that they are no longer able to rely on their economic wealth to get votes. Instead, they have had to start catering to demands for private and club goods from their constituents in return for their vote. Writing for the Guardian during the 2013 election, Jason Burke asked 'why feudal ties no longer bind for voters' in rural Punjab, and answered by pointing out how economic power and personal status could no longer pull in votes and that now even landed politicians had to campaign and appeal personally to their constituents. Referring to this new trend, he quotes one landlord politicians as saying, 'Politics has become such a dirty game. It's getting so hard' (Burke, 2013).

Political parties as clientelistic networks

A second explanation for party-voter linkages holds that political parties in Pakistan operate as conglomerations of clientelistic networks. Kitschelt points out, 'in a global comparison, Pakistani parties rely quite heavily upon clientelistic inducements while offering few programmatic inducements to voters ... [and] average voters respond more readily to targeted material inducements than to programmatic policy appeals' (2009 pp. 22–23). According to this explanation, rural Punjabi voters exchange their vote for goods and services, and at each election, evaluate either a candidate's delivery record or their potential for delivering during the next term, and then vote accordingly. Due to this most candidates spend their time in office providing targeted goods to supporters (Keefer et al., 2003; Wilder, 1999).

This is partly a consequence of Pakistan's regular alternation between authoritarian and democratic rule since its creation. As explained above,

14

under each round of military rule in Pakistan, political parties were created, disbanded, exiled and manipulated to serve the needs of an authoritarian regime to an extent where they came to be little more than aggregations of multiple clientelistic networks. Authoritarian regimes and clientelistic politics based on traditional rural power holders have a particularly synergistic relationship. Both Archer (1990) and Hagopian (1994) argue that clientelism helps maintain regime stability by reducing ideological organisation and conflict. Another factor that contributes both to the predominance of local intermediaries over political parties in Pakistan and to their organisation as clientelistic networks is the way in which essential services are delivered to the rural population. The Pakistani state rarely delivers universal, non-discretionary, and rule-based services to villages (Keefer et al., 2003). ' ... Because Pakistan's rural constituencies are particularly poor, particularly spread out and thoroughly organized into voting blocs, the relative political benefits of providing narrowly targeted rather than broadly available public goods, are high' (World Bank, 2002, p. 74). Most politicians understand the fact that their success

> depends on their personal reputation for providing goods, jobs and government access to individuals with whom they have had contact ... Such legislators have little interest, as a consequence, in providing public goods that benefit a broad range of the public. (Keefer et al., 2003, p. 17)

By pulling in such local leaders, political parties organise extensive networks of patronage (Cheema & Mohmand, 2006; Zaidi, 2005).

In Pakistan clientelistic linkages between politicians and voters were particularly strengthened by the politics of the 1980s and 1990s. General Zia brought back local government elections in 1979 on a non-party basis after considerable measures had been taken to repress political party activity within districts. This meant that local candidates had only local networks to rely on in order to win their seats for the District Councils. Furthermore, since Zia had only this tier of electoral politics on which to rely for legitimacy he gave District Councils considerable power to raise and spend money, turning them quickly into an attractive source of political patronage. The two rounds of local government elections held in 1979–1980 and 1983 introduced an era of fierce local electoral competition between individual local power holders operating without political parties (Cheema & Mohmand, 2003). When national elections were held a few years later in 1985 on a similar non-party basis, this local system of personality-based, clientelistic politics was transplanted to the national stage. As one minister put it during the 1985 National Assembly's first budget session, 'We don't have one party, or ten parties ... we have two hundred parties. Each member of the assembly considers himself responsible only to himself' (Cheema & Mohmand, 2003, p. 10).

After Zia's regime ended in 1988, the over-reliance of political parties on the individual power and networks of local influentials continued (Cheema, Khwaja, & Qadir 2006). Jalal argues that Zia had encouraged the personalisation of politics, weakening of party organisations and the fluidity and mobility of local vote blocs to keep his rural landed allies happy, who wanted access to political power without the imposed discipline of an external party structure (1999, p. 322). However, Wilder points out that landlords were no longer able to rely on their economic wealth to get votes since their landholdings had been reduced by land reforms, sales and land fragmentation. At the same time, repeated elections had made the rural electorate realise that they possessed something of value to the rural elite – their vote, which could be exchanged for material benefits. The landed elite now had to start catering to demands for private and club goods and services from their clients. Jones notes that they used their social access to elite circles 'to rebuild their influence, getting local petitioners jobs, transfers, promotions, more canal water, agricultural loads, fertilizer, tubewell connections, etc.' (2003, p. 454).

Wilder's research shows that the tendency to vote in response to targeted material inducements – popularly known as *thana katcheri kee siyasat* (literally, politics of access to the police and courts) – became stronger with each successive election through the 1990s (1999, p. 197). This played out particularly strongly during the four elections of the 1990s when the fluidity of vote bases became evident, and voters swung in large numbers between the PPP and the PML-N looking for services. However, this explanation of party-voter linkages too is incomplete. Wilder quotes a politician as follows:

> Every MNA [Member of the National Assembly] has a constituency of approximately half a million [voters]. There is a limit to the number of jobs an MNA can create, how many postings and transfers he can arrange, how many villages he can electrify and develop, etc. (1999, p. 209)

It seems that while clientelism is a powerful explanation of how parties connect to their voters in rural Punjab, its explanatory value may be exaggerated.

Political parties as kinship networks

Another view of party-voter linkages holds that political parties are aggregations of kinship-based networks. According to this explanation kinship groups, or *biraderi*s, mostly support members of their kin as electoral candidates without taking into account other considerations about the candidate or political party (Alavi, 1972, 2001; Talbot, 1998; Wilder, 1999). Political parties organise internally by carefully analysing the social structure of each constituency and then allotting tickets to members of the dominant *biraderi* in that area. Candidates then garner the support of local leaders in their constituencies that are from the same or related *biraderi*s.

This practice has an old history. In fact, Talbot (1998) argues that *biraderi*-ism was an integral part of politics in the Punjab even before the creation of Pakistan, and that, in fact, one of the reasons why Jinnah's Muslim League managed to win only one seat in the 1937 election was because it did not use 'traditional channels of political mobilisation in the countryside', such as *biraderi* networks (1998, p. 63). By the next election, however, Jinnah appears to have learnt the trick, and his party fought the 1946 election by organising around *biraderi*s and the influence of landed groups (Talbot, 1998, p. 73). The party won a resounding victory that sealed the deal on Pakistan's birth.

This norm continued past independence to the first set of local government elections held under the Basic Democracies system in 1959–1960 during General Ayub's military regime. Inayatullah (1963) argues that *biraderi*-ism was the major principle of political organisation in villages during these elections. Bhutto's dramatic 1970 electoral victory did not just render the political power of the landed elite ineffective, but 'also claimed to have finally "shattered" the *biraderi* system, at least insofar as its customary political functions are concerned' (Jones, 2003, p. 331). *Biraderi*-based organisation was particularly central to politics in the 1980s under general Zia-ul-Haq. Gilmartin argues that the 'importance of *biradari* [*sic*] grew hand in hand with the increasingly heavy hand of state control under Zia' (1994, p. 36). The personalisation of politics that occurred during this military regime, explained earlier, also included an increasing use of kinship-based local networks as an electioneering tool, and the results of the party-less 1985 election was determined by 'ties to clan, tribe, or *biradari* [*sic*] and feudal social bases' (Rais, 1985 in Wilder, 1999, p. 183). Even in the 1993 elections Waseem (1994) and Wilder (1999) claim that most of the candidates of the two main parties, the PPP and PML-N, represented the dominant *biraderi*s of their constituencies. Waseem (2006) claims that even in the election of 2002 held during General Musharraf's regime, rural Punjabi citizens voted predominantly on the basis of caste and *biraderi*.

Yet again, however, this explanation is incomplete, and its importance may also be exaggerated. The main problem with it is that it provides a rather static view of politics in Pakistan. Consider this explanation of electoral success by one politician: 'where I have won I had Rajput *biraderi* support. Where Mr. Akram Ansari has won, he had Ansari *biraderi* support. The Ansari *biraderi* is in the majority so he has won' (Wilder, 1999, p. 184). If this were indeed the logic on which party-voter linkages are primarily organised, electoral results would be more predictable than they have been in recent years. Central Punjabi politics is characterised by the existence of marginal seats that are fiercely contested, and where voters have been recorded to have an

17

anti-incumbency bias (Wilder, 1999, p. 209; Cheema & Naseer, 2008). Another problem with this explanation is that rural Punjab is organised into highly fragmented, heterogeneous communities in which multiple *biraderis* co-habit next to one another, and in which it is difficult to imagine that candidates can win elections based entirely on the primacy of lineage solidarity. *Biraderi*-ism is not only a strong explanation of party-voter linkages, but it is also an over-simplified view of a more complex phenomenon.

Party identification and the growing dominance of political parties

Each of the foregoing explanations has demonstrated that rural politics in Punjab is not based on the logic of strong party identification, and does not provide incentives for political parties to articulate consistent programmatic packages. From the point of view of both voters and brokers, ideological, class- or party-based identification is trumped by the need to access essential goods and services. As one local leader remarked to me, 'I am a PPP supporter at heart but the PPP candidate here is very weak and I need a road.' Yet, analyses of the two most recent elections of February 2008 and May 2013 insist that political parties have emerged as the primary political force in Pakistan.

This is not the first time that this has happened in Pakistan. For a brief period in the 1970s politics in rural Punjab had come to be organised along class lines, led by the brand new PPP's socially transformative agenda. Jones summarises the impact of PPP's 1970s campaign by pointing out that, ' ... the political map of Punjab had altered and the countryside was no longer a place where vast bodies of politically inert folk would passively support their traditional leaders' (2003, p. 243). The military regime of Yahya Khan, under whom the 1970 election was held,[9] had expected that '*biraderi*, century-old rural relations, traditions, the hold of certain establishment families and not mere crowds at public meetings will be the deciding factor at the polls' (*Morning News* (Dhaka) article in Jones, 2003, p. 257). But the crowds at the PPP's public meetings converted their support into votes for a political party across much of the country on election day and all other traditional forms of political organisation and alignment were defeated. A popular adage of the time was that even a lamppost would have won had it had a PPP ticket.

The 1970s marked a historical watershed in the study of Punjabi politics. Jones argues that the PPP's 1970 election campaign marked the point of transition from 'the passing age of elite politics' to a 'new age of mass politics' in Pakistan (2003, p. 7). Though the link that was developed in 1970 between the party and the voter was broken soon after when it was reduced to the type of personalised, clientelistic relationships outlined above under the Zia regime, Wilder argues that landlords now appear to understand that 'while parties [still] need strong candidates in rural constituencies, strong candidates increasingly need strong parties to win' (Wilder, 1999, p. 218). Interestingly, Wilder (1999) argues that the rise of clientelism in the 1980s and 1990s revived political parties, and in rural Punjab politics came to be focused more and more around parties rather than simply around powerful local personalities. The reason for this was simple – 'politicians only have access to patronage if they win an election, and in particular, if they end up in the winning party' (Wilder, 1999, p. 193). Patrons thus had to belong to or be linked with parties, and though clientelism played out strongly through the four elections of the 1990s,[10] it led to political parties slowly taking centre stage again.

Through the 1990s, a two-party system developed in Pakistan in which all electoral competition was centred on the PPP and the PML-N, with various smaller parties aligned to one or the other. Parties were now important to the extent that even General Musharraf had to create one to support and legitimise his military regime after he overthrew the PML-N in a dramatic coup in 1999. Called the Pakistan Muslim League – Quaid (PML-Q), the party was formed of splinter groups of the PPP and PML-N, and it won the 2002 election as a result of various political manipulations aimed against the other two parties. However, the PPP and the PML-N made a comeback after 9 years of General Musharraf's military regime in the 2008 election. The PPP formed the government at the centre – six weeks after the assassination of its leader, Benazir Bhutto – and the PML-N in Punjab. An exit poll revealed that the parties had developed very particular constituencies that stretched across the entire country. The PPP's vote bank, similar to that in the 1970s, was still largely amongst lower income and very poor groups, and amongst the majority of rural, illiterate and female voters. In other words, the PPP was still the party of the poor and the marginalised. The PML-N, on the other hand, appeared to have established a fairly stable urban, educated, middle and upper class and male constituency (Gallup Pakistan, 2008).

Though the labels of 'feudalism' and clientelism were all thrown about by the media in its coverage of the election, the fact that the two main parties overcame extensive political manipulations to contest the elections under a sitting military President – General Musharraf, who was not only opposed both of the parties, but more importantly, whose loyal cadre of local government officials were organising the polls in each district – brought to the fore analysis about a resurgence of party-based identity and voting. The 2008 election is believed to have been won by a mix of an anti-Musharraf vote, party identification and a strong belief that because of Bhutto's recent assassination the PPP was the winning horse, thus driving voters in its direction. Gilani's (2008) analysis of elections in Pakistan has led him to conclude that party competition is now quite intense and, that, especially in central Punjab, the outcome of many electoral seats is often based on a very small swing vote.

The 2013 election further solidified this trend with the emergence of a third serious contender for power at the centre, Imran Khan's PTI, whose support base is very strongly based on identification with the party's ideology and programmatic package. The party ran a strong campaign to get out the vote – incentivised by the belief that its largest vote bank lies within Pakistan's young voters. This worked, and while the average turnout for the eight elections held between 1977 and 2008 was 40 per cent, with the highest being 47 per cent in the 1977 election (International IDEA),[11] a record 50 million voters lined up on 11 May 2013 to vote, bringing the turnout to about 55 per cent. This despite the fact that the Taliban were reported to have distributed pamphlets in various cities threatening violence against those who came out to vote. Ironically, not many new voters cast their vote for the PTI, choosing in many cases to vote instead for the country's older parties based on a number of reasons. In both urban and rural areas, the conversation had shifted decidedly to the role, rhetoric and ideologies of political parties.

However, the election may have ended up introducing a fifth emerging explanation of party-voter linkages in Pakistan – regionalism. Each of the three parties emerged with support mainly from one of Pakistan's four provinces – of PPP's 31 total seats in the National Assembly, 29 were won in Sindh; 117 of PML-N's 125 seats came from Punjab; and of PTI's 28 total seats, 17 were in Khyber Pukhtunkhwa. The ethnic support base of Pakistan's political parties is not a new idea, but the 2013 election confirmed that the effort of various parties over the last two decades to become national in character and support has certainly not worked.

Summary

How really do political parties connect to voters in rural Punjab – through pure clientelism, through landed candidates, through kinship and ethnicity, or through programmatic packages? Which of the explanations above best describes party-voter linkages in Pakistan, and why do they all continue to exist alongside one-another and continue to generate literature? The answer appears to be ambiguous, and I argue that this is because of the level of analysis at which these relationships are usually operationalised in the literature. While as determinants of national politics biraderi-ism, landlord-ism or clientelism's role may seem ambiguous and their importance exaggerated, they become more useful analytical concepts when employed to examine relationships between political actors at a more nuanced micro-level of analysis, such as that offered by a single village. In the next section I turn now to such an analysis to explore in detail the types of interactions parties have with voters, and how these change over time, so that we can start to assess these various competing explanations.

Mediated party-voter linkages in Sahiwal[12]

I arrive in Sahiwal in Punjab's Sargodha district a week ahead of the May 2013 election. I know the village well, having worked here over a long time in 2006–2007 as part of my doctoral dissertation on local politics and brokers (Mohmand, 2011). I know already that Malika,[13] the largest landlord in the village, is visiting from Lahore, the provincial capital where she lives. I head straight to her beautiful *haveli*,[14] only to find that she is preparing to head out to an election rally. Nawaz Sharif, the head of the party that Malika has supported for decades, the PML-N, is campaigning in Sargodha city today, and as one of his key local allies Malika is expected to be there to show support. Malika has held political office in the past and will do so again now. She is not running directly for an electoral seat this time but she tops the party list of women who will be nominated to reserved seats in parliament once the elections are over.[15] She invites me along to the rally but I have other people I want to visit in the village.

Chief among these is Fatah, an ex-agricultural tenant of Malika's family, who has spent much of his life politically opposing the social, economic and political power that Malika's family has exercised for over a century in Sahiwal as its only landlords. He has built a sizeable political support base within the village, and I am wondering whether the strong wave of popularity that the PTI is riding in Punjab, and the stiff competition it is expected to give the PML-N, has provided Fatah with a unique opportunity to further his political goals. Could Fatah's traditional opposition to the landlords make the PTI an ideal new ally, especially given the PTI's strong anti-'feudalism' campaign? To make sense of these evolving political relationships, however, it is important to take a brief look first at Sahiwal's political history.

Landlord-ism and the rise of party politics in Sahiwal

Sahiwal was given to Malika's husband's ancestors by the British colonial government as a grant of 4572 acres in 1860, and the family has dominated village life, economy and politics ever since. The village was managed by the family as one unit until 1920, when a feud between two grandsons of the original grantee allegedly led one to instigate the murder of the other. Since then the village has been divided into two. When Ahmad (1977) arrived in Sahiwal in 1964 to study it as part of his doctoral dissertation, Sahiwal was still owned and headed in its entirety by two descendants of the original grantee, Haji sahib and Khan sahib. Both were absentee *maaliks*[16] who controlled their village and their lands through *munshi*s, or managers, and who cultivated their lands through sharecropping arrangements with resident tenant farmers. When Rouse (1988) started her research in 1978, the lordship had passed on to Haji sahib's son,

Naib, who was still the village's largest landlord and political leader when I arrived in 2006. However, in 2008 Naib passed away, and economic and political power came to rest on his wife, Malika, despite the fact that Naib had two younger brothers.

During Ahmad's time, the control that the *maalik* family exercised over the village was reflected in its electoral politics. Every household in Sahiwal, whether of the *zamindar, kammi* or *musalli quom*,[17] counted itself as part of the electoral faction of either Haji sahib or Khan sahib, based largely on whose land they tilled, or from whom they drew their *seip*.[18] Factionalism ran so strong that 'many members of a lineage group working for one landlord may not even speak to members of their same lineage group working for the other landlord, much less participate with them in social events' (Ahmad & Alavi, 1974, p. 153). Ahmad recalls being told that this even included brothers, cousins, or uncles if these belonged to the opposing faction (1977, p. 103). In fact, the members of each faction even prayed apart in two separate mosques, in which the *maulvis*[19] 'broadcast propaganda for their respective masters every Friday before prayer time' (Rouse, 1988, p. 837).

This played out particularly strongly during the party-less local government elections held under the Basic Democracies system of Ayub Khan in 1959–1960. Villagers had no contact with political actors outside the village at this time, and the two *maaliks* each put up their own manager as a candidate, since local governments were too low a tier of government for the landlords to have been interested in contesting them (1974, p. 165). No one opposed their candidacy and everyone came out to vote for them because it was obvious that votes were being cast not for the candidates but for the landlords. In Sahiwal of the 1960s, the economic relationship with the landlord and the fear of sanction trumped all other ties of kinship, class, friendship and reciprocal clientelism.

This changed suddenly and drastically in 1970 when political parties were introduced, and when one of these, the PPP, led a direct campaign in rural Punjab with its marginalised groups. Wilder (1999) and Jones (2003) both point out that the main division along which voters in the 1970 election were split was defined by land – those that had it voted against the PPP and those that did not have it voted for it, earning the PPP the label 'party of the poor'. This is exactly what happened in Sahiwal too. As one respondent, an agricultural labourer, put it to me during an interview in 2007, 'Pakistan was liberated in 1947 by Jinnah. We [the poor] were liberated in 1970 by Bhutto'.

The PPP's campaign in the run up to the 1970 elections transformed politics in the village. For the first time the *maaliks* of Sahiwal had to deal with an external political force in their own village, and they reacted to their loosening control over the village by putting aside their antagonism and bringing their supporters together in one political faction. This, they thought, would allow them to increase their control over the villagers. They could not have expected what happened instead in the 1970 elections. Rouse (1988, p. 875) explains:

> The PPP found a receptive audience among Sahiwal's working population. Party chapters were organised in Shahpur[20] and Sahiwal. The local chapter was headed by a man from an artisan *quom*. When elections were held in 1970, the PPP set up its own candidate for the local seat. The large landlords, for the first time in Sahiwal's history, set up a joint candidate in opposition to the PPP's candidate. Both landlords used all their capacity to convince villagers to vote for their candidate. The PPP candidate won. For the first time, villagers voted along class and not factional lines ... The landless voted overwhelmingly for the PPP candidate, as did the majority of the sharecroppers and small holders.

The PPP regime meant many things to the residents of Sahiwal. For the first time they had direct access to national-level state power through their PPP representatives and 'the overall environment was in their favour', as was a political party to which they now looked as a source of support with which to counter the power of the *maaliks*. As one of my respondents in the village put it, 'Bhutto's regime changed everything because for the first time people with just 2–4 acres could get into top political seats in the area.'

Naib quickly realised which way the wind was blowing. When Bhutto opened up the PPP to landlords before the 1977 election, Naib joined it 'to regain lost control over the political process' (Rouse, 1988, p. 876). In fact,

> In order to realise his political ambitions he had to pay allegiance to the PPP political platform, and this meant implementing Bhutto's land reforms to the letter. And this he did. No more evictions took place in his *patti*[21] as long as Bhutto remained in power. The division of inputs provided in the law was strictly and honestly adhered to. Naib went further than most; he even called a meeting of the tenants to inform them of their newly acquired legal rights. (Rouse, 1983, p. 317)

Naib's strategy worked. Both his father, Haji sahib, and his wife, Malika, were given PPP tickets for the 1977 election, and both won seats in the Punjab Provincial Assembly.[22] However, Zia's military coup almost immediately afterwards meant that they were in power for less than three months. The new military regime announced elections soon after taking over, for which the PPP again awarded Naib with a ticket for the National Assembly. His candidature was strongly opposed by the PPP party cadre within Sahiwal, which wanted seats to be allocated on the basis of elections within the party. What could have been a critical juncture in the politics of the village and its power relationships came to nothing when the national elections were eventually cancelled. Soon after when the PPP was banned Naib's affiliation with it also ended, as did 'his commitment to liberal causes' (Rouse, 1988, p. 880).

To replace the cancelled national election, Zia announced party-less local government elections in 1979. As before, the *maaliks* were not interested in running for a local government office and they nominated a loyal supporter instead as a candidate. The small peasants, artisans and labourers again put up their own candidate in opposition to the landlords. This was Fatah of the *mekan biraderi*, and he was one of Khan sahib's agricultural tenants. Fatah won, despite vigorous campaigning by the *maaliks* for their own candidate. Rouse notes that this victory was of 'enormous importance because this time the rural producers had no national political organization behind them' (1988, p. 881). However, Fatah was evicted from his lands, and was unable to contest this legally in a judicial climate that now explicitly favoured the landed again, despite the fact that he was now an elected official of the local government.

Factionalism and political party competition

By the time I arrived in Sahiwal, the *maaliks* were back in control of their village but something had certainly changed, both in terms of politics and the village economy. Fewer and fewer people were now working on the land, people were travelling to the nearby town for day jobs, and as the *maaliks* sold small pieces of their land to meet costs, various ex-tenants and artisans of the village bought these to mark their upward mobility. Twenty-two per cent of the village, or 127 households as compared to the earlier two, now owned agricultural land. All these changes meant that the allegiance of the people could no longer be acquired through economic sanctions and coercion alone.

Political parties had disappeared through Zia's regime in the 1980s as a form of organisation, and local governments filled the vacant political space. As the Zia regime strengthened District Councils and made them an attractive source of political patronage, the *maaliks*, who had until now shunned this level of politics, became involved. The need to maintain control of the village compelled the *maalik* family to diversify its involvement and investment in politics. This was, however, limited to Khan sahib's side of the family, now led by his son Sardar. It started with Sardar's election to Sargodha's District Council in 1987 under Zia, and continued until his nephew Nazim's election to the seat of the deputy mayor of the union and *tehsil*[23] councils in the local government elections of 2005 under Musharraf. The fact that *tehsil* councils had access to significant funds for local projects meant that during my work in the village in 2006–2007, Nazim was the most actively sought after member of the *maalik* family.

Naib's side waited until national-level politics restarted and then became involved once again. Though the PPP was banned, the Zia regime created a new configuration of the PML[24] during the mid-1980s, with Nawaz Sharif at its helm. Since this was now the predominant political force at the centre, Naib shifted allegiance to it. Malika made it back to the Punjab Provincial Assembly in the non-party-based elections that Zia held in 1985, using the family's local influence to gather sufficient votes. Through the multiple elections that followed in the next two decades, the family maintained its support for the PML-N, and the party rewarded the family's ability to pull in the vote through party positions and by sanctioning development projects for their constituency. Malika is the vice-President of the PML-N's Punjab women's wing and is credited with having had significant public grants released for Sahiwal for street paving, sanitation and the upgrading of its two schools.

At the same time, *biraderi*-based politics began to emerge as a form of political organisation in the village. No political party had ever again attempted to organise the rural poor as the PPP had done in 1970. Instead it seemed that this space was filled by localised collective action organised around kinship groups. Sahiwal is divided internally across many small factions that are largely *biraderi*-based. Of these the most significant is a class-based one organised, fittingly, by Fatah around Sahiwal's middle strata of traders. Since his eviction, Fatah's family had purchased land, acquired education, forayed into the urban job market and built into the politically influential network of the larger *mekan biraderi,* which is well represented in the local government politics of both the *tehsil* and Sargodha district, and within the central bureaucracy. The *mekan* candidate in the story recounted at the beginning of this paper is a leading member of this network. All this enabled Fatah to translate his traditional opposition to the power of the *maaliks* into an alternate channel for access to state services by Sahiwal's residents, one that was independent of the *maaliks*. As he explained to me, 'I started politics as an ideological voter and organiser in the 1970s under the PPP. But when that ended, I moved to the politics of factionalism and *biraderi.*'

Not all *biraderi* networks, however, are able to build external links such as those of the *mekans*. For them negotiating for public services continues to happen through the *maaliks*, and so they continue to support the family in election after election. What these factions do ensure, however, is that *maaliks* now have to negotiate their support before each election. At an *akhat*[25] we witnessed soon after Nazim's victory in the local government elections of 2005, a member of the Syed *biraderi* told him in a rather straightforward manner that the election had been won and he now needed to get on immediately with the business of bringing development schemes to the village.

Of course such support pays off only if the PML-N comes into power. When in 2002 the village supported the PML-N because of Naib and Malika but the PML-Q came to power instead because of General Musharraf's political manipulations, the village received nothing from the national or provincial government through its tenure. In 2008, however, PML-N formed the government in Punjab, with Malika appointed as an advisor to the Chief Minister, and in 2013 the party came to power in the centre, with Malika slotted for a seat in the National Assembly. Given the flow of patronage during these tenures, supporting the *maaliks* has certainly paid off for the residents of Sahiwal.

This show of strength had changed the minds of even the likes of Fatah. Until now Fatah had mobilised a significant vote bank against the *maaliks* in each election, of about 500 votes out of the village's total 2000 votes. 'I used to have these polled for the PPP', he explained,

> both because I am a PPP supporter at heart, and because it represented the opposite of the *maaliks*' choice, the PML-N. But now I'm joining Malika, because there are no longer any good PPP politicians here, because she asked me personally, and because Malika is a better politician than the men of her family. She has managed to unite the village through service provision in a way that the men never could.

Even more importantly, however, this was because 'our interests now coincide'. By this Fatah was referring to the decision that week by Malika's PML-N to 'open' the local provincial seat in favour of his *biraderi* member, the *mekan* candidate. I asked him about the PTI, which was offering an anti-incumbency, anti-'feudalism' platform to the rural electorate. Fatah was no longer interested. 'The PTI candidate is the nicest man and a very close friend. But I cannot vote for him because it is a question of *biraderi*' he explained. As if to explain to me how rural politics works, Fatah said,

> the marginalised of rural Pakistan will always be PPP at heart, but the party's leadership has squandered this support away. This has taught us to no longer look for parties, but rather for people who can help us out and give us what we need.

Conclusion

The history of Sahiwal's politics helps clarify the explanations of party-voter linkages offered above and illiustrates how they all work together as partial explanations of a larger, complex phenomenon. The landlord Malika is the most powerful political actor in the village, and viewed from the outside, seems powerful enough to be able to define the electoral choice of the voters of Sahiwal. She is also a member of a powerful political party, based on her local influence and her ability to pull in the vote. This is exactly what the popular perception of political parties in Pakistan is – large collections of locally powerful landlords with substantial vote banks. Internally, however, Malika's support base is built on many different *biraderi* networks, each of which negotiates with her separately – for access to a distant and unresponsive state with limited resources – in return for their vote. This can be interpreted as either of two things, depending on the vantage point. From Malika's perspective this is clientelism. Looked at from below, from the perspective of the voter, it is *biraderi*-ism and collective action.

It is possible to postulate that if at any point Malika is no longer able to deliver, or if her constituents find other sources of support and access to the state, or even more importantly, if an intermediary between state and citizens were no longer required, her economic power and status would do little to keep her in power. The fact that Malika and her family remain politically important is as much a testimony to their ability to adapt to changing conditions, as it is to the lack of a transformative agenda within Pakistan's political parties. The story of Sahiwal tells us that the power and authority of the landed elite are susceptible to the politics and agendas of parties, but Pakistan's constant alternation between authoritarianism and democracy has not allowed its political parties to develop coherent and consistent programmatic packages that are focused on transforming the lives of its marginalised population.

The precise details of local-level politics vary across Pakistan's provinces. However, as in the case of Punjab, what remains largely constant in each case is the fact that political parties are not directly connected to their voters. Instead, the relationship is mediated by different types of autonomous local actors, ranging from landlords and tribal leaders, to clientelist exchanges through brokers, kin groups and local party leaders. As the national political arena changes, different actors gain precedence at the local level, leading to multiple, competing explanations of what is really going on in rural Pakistan between political parties and their voters.

Acknowledgements

Most of the research for this study was conducted as part of a larger research project on 'Informal Institutions and State Capacity', funded by the Centre for the Future State at the Institute of Development Studies (IDS) and based at the Lahore University of Management Sciences (LUMS). I remain immensely thankful to Mick Moore at IDS for supporting this project, Ali Cheema for heading it at LUMS, and to an incredible team of research assistants and students from the university. Many thanks are due in particular to Syed Ali Asjad Naqvi and Hassan Javid for the immense support they offered in the field. I would also like to thank James Chiriyankandath and Andrew Wyatt for their comments on an earlier version of this paper.

Notes

1. A public meeting space maintained by large landlords around which the social and political activity of the village revolves.

2. The *Mekan biraderi* was supported in its electoral bid by other local *biraderi*s as part of a larger political network of both large and small kinship groups of the constituency.
3. This research was conducted as part of a larger research project on 'Informal Institutions and State Capacity' in rural Punjab, based at the Lahore University of Management Sciences (LUMS), which I coordinated along with Dr Ali Cheema, and on which we worked with an incredible group of research assistants and students from the university. Many thanks are due in particular to Syed Ali Asjad Naqvi and Hassan Javed for their meticulous note-taking in their conversations with many of the male respondents with whom I could not work directly.
4. The Unionist Party secured 95 out of the 175 seats in Punjab, while the Congress won 18 and the Muslim League managed to get only 1 urban seat (Oren, 1974).
5. Each village, if between 700 and 1000 residents over the age of 21, chose a Basic Democrat to be part of a Union Council. The heads of the Union Council were represented on the *Tehsil* Council, the heads of which sat on the District Council. Together, the 80,000 Basic Democrats composed the electoral college for the Presidential elections. This was Ayub's pattern of 'controlled democracy'.
6. Quoted in Jones (2003) from the periodical *Azad* (November 1970).
7. This included various measures, such as the selective disqualification of politicians based on new educational criteria, the registration of new corruption cases, and arrests and incarcerations on various charges.
8. Gini coefficient measures inequality on a scale from 0 to 1, on which 0 is perfect equality and 1 is perfect inequality.
9. After Ayub Khan had to step down during the movement of 1968, he handed power to another general, Yahya Khan, who announced and oversaw the 1970 election and the subsequent civil war in East Pakistan, before handing power to Bhutto in December 1971.
10. Four elections were held in quick succession between the military regimes of Zia and Musharraf, bringing into power first the PPP (1988), then the PML (1990), then the PPP (1993), and then PML again (1997).
11. http://www.idea.int/vt/countryview.cfm?CountryCode=PK
12. A pseudonym originally coined by Ahmad (1977) and then used by Rouse (1988), not to be confused with the *tehsil* Sahiwal.
13. All names have been changed. I use pseudonyms throughout this paper, many of which were originally coined by Ahmad (1977) and later used by Rouse (1988).
14. Mansion.
15. Sixty seats (17 per cent) are reserved for women in parliament and are distributed across parties in proportion to the share of seats that each party wins.
16. Literally owner, but with strong connotations of lordship over the entire estate.
17. Quoms are hierarchically arranged, endogamous status groups that involve a notion of occupational castes. Gough calls them 'castelike status groups' (1977, p. 9). Within each *quom*, there are sub-*quom*s or *biraderi*s that are also, often, ranked hierarchically. The three main *quom*s are *zamindar*, *kammi*, and *musalli*. At the top of the hierarchy are the agricultural castes or the *zamindar*s. In Sahiwal, most of these were involved in agriculture, mostly as tenants. After them come the *kammi*s, who are the village artisans and who in Ahmad's time would have supported the farmers in their work by making their implements (the *lohar),* repairing their ploughs (the *tirkhan),* making earthen pots (the *kumhar*s), winnowing the wheat (the *mehnti musalli*), and making their shoes (the *mochi*). At the bottom of the hierarchy are the *musalli*s, who were the

village sweepers and domestic and farm labourers. This classification was much truer in Ahmad's time than it is now, when the sons and grandsons of these artisans have diversified into other professions, but much of the associated social hierarchy remains.

18. An informal contract in which *kammis* would provide services to *zamindars* in exchange for in-kind payments.
19. Caretaker of a mosque.
20. A town close to Sahiwal.
21. Section of the total land owned by the family.
22. Naib recounted this to me in an interview during my own fieldwork in Sahiwal in 2007.
23. Pakistan's local government system, when operational, is based around three tiers: the district, *tehsil* and union. A union can encompass between 5 and 15 villages, depending on their size.
24. The predecessor of the current ruling party, the PML-N or PML-Nawaz.
25. A meeting of the village called by the *maalik* or *lambardar*, in order to discuss and decide on important matters, including the collective voting decision of the village, or of the vote bloc.

References

Agricultural Census of Pakistan. (2000). *Government of Pakistan*. Lahore: Agricultural Census Organization.
Ahmad, S. (1972). Peasant classes in Pakistan. *Bulletin of Concerned Asian Scholars, 4*(1), 60–71.
Ahmad, S. (1977). *Class and power in a Punjabi village*. New York: Monthly Review Press.
Ahmad, E. (1998). *Feudal culture and violence*. Karachi: Dawn.
Ahmad, S., & Alavi, H. (1974). A village in Pakistani Panjab: Jalpana. In C. Maloney (Ed.), *South Asia: Seven community profiles*. New York: Holt, Rinehart and Winston.
Alavi, H. (1972). Kinship in West Punjab villages. *Contributions to Indian Sociology, 6*, 1–27.
Alavi, H. (1973). Peasant classes and primordial loyalties. *The Journal of Peasant Studies, 1*(1), 23–62.
Alavi, H. (1983). Class and state. In H. Gardezi and J. Rashid (Eds.), *Pakistan, the roots of dictatorship: The political economy of a praetorian state* (pp. 40–93). London: Zed Books.
Alavi, H. (1990). Authoritarianism and legitimation of state power in Pakistan. In S. K. Mitra (Ed.), *The post-colonial state in Asia: Dialectics of politics and culture* (pp. 19–71). New York: Harvester Wheatsheaf.
Alavi, H. (2001). The two biradiris: Kinship in rural West Punjab. In T. N. Madan (Ed.), *Muslim communities of South Asia: Culture, society and power* (pp. 25–76). New Delhi: Manohar.
Ali, S. M. (2008). Feudal politics. *Daily Times*, Lahore.
Archer, R. (1990). *The transition from traditional to broker clientelism in Colombia: Political stability and social unrest*. Working Paper No.140. Notre Dame: Kellogg Institute.

Bardhan, P., Mitra, S., Mookherjee, D., & Sarkar, A. (2009). Local democracy and clientelism: Implications for political stability in rural West Bengal. *Economic and Political Weekly, XLIV*(9), 46–58.

Bari, S., & Khan, H. (2001). *Local government elections: 2001 – Phase III, IV & V.* Islamabad: Pattan Development Organisation.

Baxter, C. (1974). The people's party vs. the Punjab 'Feudalists'. In J. H. Korson (Ed.), *Contemporary problems of Pakistan* (pp. 6–29). Lieden: E.J. Brill.

Burke, J. (2013, May 5). Pakistan elections: Why feudal ties no longer bind for voters. *The Guardian*. London: Guardian News and Media Limited.

Cheema, A., Khwaja, A. I., & Qadir, A. (2006). Local government reform in Pakistan: Context, content and causes. In   P. Bardhan and D. Mookherjee (Eds.), *Decentralization and local governance in developing countries: A comparative perspective* (pp. 257–284). Cambridge, MIT Press.

Cheema, A., & Mohmand, S. K. (2003). Local government reforms in Pakistan: Legitimising centralisation or a driver for pro-poor change. *Pakistan Drivers of Pro-Poor Change.* Brighton: Institute of Development Studies and Collective for Social Science Research.

Cheema, A., & Mohmand, S. K. (2006). Bringing electoral politics to the doorstep: Who gains who loses? *Decentralisation task force meeting of the initiative for policy dialogue.* New York: Columbia University.

Cheema, A., and F. Naseer (2008). General elections in the Punjab: Certain outcomes or a surprise wave. Lahore: Lahore University of Management Sciences.

Gallup. (2008). *Election 2008: Exit poll – election day survey.* Islamabad: Gallup Pakistan.

Gardezi, H. (1983). Feudal and capitalist relations in Pakistan. In H. Gardezi & J. Rashid (Eds.), *Pakistan, the roots of dictatorship: The political economy of a praetorian state* (pp. 19–39). London: Zed Books.

Gazdar, H. (2003). The land question. *Pakistan drivers of pro-poor change.* Karachi: Collective for Social Science Research and Institute of Development Studies (Sussex).

Gilani, I. S. (2008). *The story of eight elections and the calculus of electoral politics in Pakistan during 1970–2000.* Islamabad: Gallup Pakistan.

Gilmartin, D. (1994). Biraderi and bureaucracy: The politics of Muslim kinship solidarity in 20th century Punjab. *International Journal of Punjab Studies, I*(1), 1–29.

Gough, K. (1977). Introduction. In S. Ahmad (Ed.), *Class and power in a Punjabi village* (pp. 7–23). New York: Monthly Review Press.

Hagopian, F. (1994). Traditional politics against state transformation in Brazil. In J. S. Migdal, A. Kohli, & V. Shue (Eds.), *State power and social forces: Domination and transformation in the third world* (pp. 37–64). Cambridge: Cambridge University Press.

Hasan, S. S. (2008). *Feudal shadow over Pakistani elections.* London: *BBC.*

Herring, R. J. (1979). Zulfikar Ali Bhutto and the 'Eradication of Feudalism' in Pakistan. *Comparative Studies in Society and History, 21*(4), 519–557.

Herring, R. J. (1983). *Land to the tiller: The political economy of agrarian reform in South Asia.* New Haven: Yale University Press.

Inayatullah. (1963). Perspectives in the rural power structure in West Pakistan. *People and society series.* Karachi: USAID Development Research and Evaluation Group.

Jalal, A. (1994). The state and political privilege in Pakistan. In A. Banuazizi & M. Weiner (Eds.), *The politics of social transformation in Afghanistan, Iran and Pakistan* (pp. 152–184). Syracuse: Syracuse University Press.

Jalal, A. (1999). *The state of martial rule: The origins of Pakistan's political economy of defence*. Lahore: Sang-e-Meel.

Jones, P. E. (2003). *The Pakistan people's party: Rise to power*. Karachi: Oxford University Press.

Keefer, P. E., Narayan, A., & Vishwanath, T. (2003). *The political economy of decentralization in Pakistan*. Washington, DC: World Bank.

Kitschelt, H. (2009). *Expert survey on citizen-politician linkages: Initial findings for Pakistan in comparative context*. Durham, NC: Duke University Press.

Kitschelt, H., & Wilkinson, S. I. (2007). *Patrons, clients and policies: Patterns of democratic accountability and political competition*. Cambridge: Cambridge University Press.

Mohmand, S. K. (2011). Patrons, brothers and landlords: Competing for the vote in rural Pakistan. *Institute of development studies*. Brighton: University of Sussex. Doctor of Philosophy.

Oren, S. (1974). The Sikhs, Congress, and the unionists in British Punjab, 1937–1945. *Modern Asian Studies, 8*(3), 397–418.

Rouse, S. (1983). Systemic injustices and inequalities: Maliki and Raiya in a Punjab village. In H. Gardezi & J. Rashid (Eds.), *Pakistan, the roots of dictatorship: The political economy of a praetorian state* (pp. 311–325). London: Zed Books.

Rouse, S. (1988). Agrarian transformation in a Punjabi village: Structural change and its consequences. *Sociology*. Madison: University of Wisconsin. Doctor of Philosophy.

Salahuddin, S. (2008). *Pakistan's feudal demon*. Karachi: Dawn.

Sayeed, K. B. (1980). *Politics in Pakistan: The nature and direction of change*. New York: Praeger Publishers.

Shafqat, S. (1997). *Civil-military relations in Pakistan: From Zulfiqar Ali Bhutto to Benazir Bhutto*. Colorado: Westview Press.

Talbot, I. (1998). *Pakistan: A modern history*. New York: St. Martin's Press.

Talbot, I. A. (1980). The 1946 Punjab elections. *Modern Asian Studies, 14*(1), 65–91.

Waseem, M. (1994). *The 1993 elections in Pakistan*. Lahore: Vanguard Books.

Waseem, M. (2006). *Democratization in Pakistan: A study of the 2002 elections*. Karachi: Oxford University Press.

Wilder, A. (1999). *The Pakistani voter: Electoral politics and voting behaviour in the Punjab*. Karachi: Oxford University Press.

World Bank. (2002). *Pakistan poverty assessment – poverty in Pakistan: Vulnerabilities, social gaps, and rural dynamics*. Washington, DC: World Bank.

Zaidi, A. (1999). *Issues in Pakistan's economy*. Karachi: Oxford University Press.

Zaidi, A. (2004, November 6). Elected representatives in Pakistan: Socio-economic background and awareness of issues. *Economic and Political Weekly, 39*(45), 4935–4941.

Zaidi, A. (2005, December 3). State, military and social transition: Improbable future of democracy in Pakistan. *Economic and Political Weekly, 40*(49), 5173–5181.

Elite formation within a political party: the case of the Dravida Munnetra Kazhagam

C. Manikandan[a] and Andrew Wyatt[b]

[a]Department of Politics and International Studies, Pondicherry University, Puducherry, India; [b]School of Sociology, Politics and International Studies, University of Bristol, Bristol, UK

The Dravida Munnetra Kazhagam (DMK) is a long-standing regional party in the south Indian state of Tamil Nadu and in common with many parties it has an elite segment that is highly influential. The authors identify and analyse the social composition of the DMK elite at the time of the 2011 assembly election. They argue that the DMK elite need to be understood as a group that is constituted by a set of formal and informal institutional rules. They consider the extent to which family connections or 'dynastic ties' alongside other informal rules govern admission to the party elite. They ask to what extent the party elite are drawn from society in general or if the elite are skewed towards a socially privileged segment of Tamil society. This paper disaggregates the party elite in terms of caste, gender and religion. They find that the wider DMK elite of the legislative party bear some microcosmic resemblance to Tamil society but that the elite are segmented so this resemblance is very partial at the more senior levels of the party. They also find that the party has a workable structure and a degree of internal pluralism that is not consistent with claims made in the general literature that parties in India are institutionally weak.

Introduction

The Dravida Munnetra Kazhagam (DMK) has been one of the leading parties in Tamil Nadu since the 1960s. The party was formed in 1949 in what was then known as Madras State and developed out of the Dravidian movement that championed south Indian culture and campaigned for social reform that would undermine the leading position of upper caste Brahmans in south

India. The Dravidian movement was notably antagonistic towards the Congress movement from the 1920s onwards and the DMK took up this theme arguing that the Congress Party governing in Delhi and Madras was beholden to north Indian interests. In 1967 the DMK was able to unseat Congress in the state assembly elections and form a government that was re-elected in 1971. The DMK itself was challenged when it split in 1972. The actor-politician M.G. Ramachandran formed his own party the Anna DMK, later renamed the All-India ADMK (AIADMK). These two Dravidian parties profoundly weakened the Congress Party in Tamil Nadu and no other parties have been elected to govern the state since 1967.

The ideology of the Dravidian movement pointed in the direction of social and economic reform (Hardgrave, 1965, p. 74), but the reforms introduced after the DMK came to power in 1967 were far from comprehensive (Harriss, 2002). In terms of economic equality the party attracted criticism for failing to significantly advance the interests of agricultural labourers and other lower class groups. Writing in 1970 Mythily Sivaraman argued that the DMK was a 'capitalistic party' that had mass support but conceded too much to rural landowners and the owners of big businesses (2013, pp. 145–146). The DMK did introduce measures that promoted the social mobility of its supporters from lower middle class and backward caste backgrounds, increasing the scope of government jobs reserved for the Backward Classes (BCs) and changing agricultural policy to favour those running small- and medium-sized farms (Subramanian, 1999, pp. 207–208). However the party equivocated in its response to untouchability and lost its only senior Dalit leader, Sathyavani Muthu, in 1974 (Barnett, 1976, p. 299).

The DMK may not have introduced a social revolution but it made an important contribution to reconstructing the political order in Tamil Nadu. The DMK appealed to the aspirations of those from more modest social backgrounds, and was able to reflect this social milieu in the culture of government. The party had an overtly plebeian orientation. When in power after 1967 the DMK expanded public control over Hindu temples, removed religious images from government offices, and promoted the Tamil language (Subramanian, 1999, pp. 190, 210, 222–223). It was able to undermine the position of the Congress Party. The Tamilnad Congress of the 1960s was by no means a reactionary party of privilege but it relied heavily on local notables, including some very wealthy landlords (Price, 1996; Weiner, 1967). The DMK sought to disrupt the political power of these notables and supplanted this group, with a new, younger group of legislators from more modest backgrounds. The inheritors of this DMK legacy include the elite that currently lead the party. The foremost figure among the DMK elite is the party leader, M. Karunanidhi. Karunanidhi, who has enjoyed extraordinary longevity, has done much to shape the party. He gained the leadership of the DMK in a sharply fought contest following the death of the founding leader, C.N. Annadurai, in 1969. Karunanidhi tightened his grip on the party in the 1970s (Subramanian, 1999, p. 235), and his personal leadership was not decisively challenged, despite the DMK losing three successive assembly elections to the AIADMK after 1977.

In this article we examine how the DMK elite is constructed. Our aim is to assess the contemporary party and the most recent moment at which the elite can be identified was in 2011 just before the state assembly elections held in April of that year. We begin by profiling the elite and linking it to the party as an organisation and a legislative presence. We then outline the rules by which individuals progress into the party elite, paying close attention to the impact of family connections. In the latter part of the paper we show how the DMK elite reflects key identities in Tamil society, paying close attention to gender, caste and religion. In the conclusion we reflect on our findings in the light of general literature on parties in India. We argue that the DMK has some institutional depth, a finding that is contrary to the general perception of Indian political parties dominated by their leaders. We also argue that while there is evidence of family connections shaping political careers the 'dynastic' aspect of political recruitment needs disaggregation.

The DMK elite

The elite within the DMK can be identified as members of six overlapping groups which number around 150 individuals.[1] The largest group were the 118 candidates for election to the Legislative Assembly nominated in March 2011.[2] The Members of Parliament (MPs) of the DMK who sit in both the Lok Sabha and the Rajya Sabha are a smaller group, but include some of the most senior members of the party. The district secretaries of the party are key leaders at the mid-level of the party, and many of them were members of the state cabinet when the party left power in 2011. The DMK has a number of senior party posts as well as an informal 'kitchen cabinet' or inner circle of individuals close to the party leader. The combined population of these overlapping groups we term the wider DMK elite. There is currently no prohibition on holding a party post and sitting in a legislature, which is why there is a good deal of overlap between these six select groups. Indeed the very opposite applies as the party leader has spoken positively of this overlap, stating that nominations for election are a reward for service to the party (Karunanidhi, 2008, p. 123).

The MLAs

A seat in the state legislative assembly is highly coveted by ambitious members of the DMK. Party members develop their profile within the local party in the hope of securing party posts as well as getting nominations in local elections and the state assembly. There is no shortage of aspirants in spite of the burden of raising campaign funds. Election to the assembly is in itself a sign of upward mobility (Price, 1996, p. 378). Duncan Forrester (1969) profiled MLAs from across the parties in Tamil Nadu in the mid-1960s and a number of his observations still hold good, including the observation that law-making is a second priority to constituency work, as MLAs serve as brokers between citizens and the state (pp. 39–42). The pattern of nomination in March 2011 demonstrated stability in the wider DMK elite. Karunanidhi announced a significant number of new candidates, claiming 58 out of the 118 nominated were competing for the first time (*Times of India*, 2011b). However our own researches show the 'new faces' only numbered 44, with 74 candidates having previously been elected to the assembly (and indeed only 95 DMK MLAs had been elected in 2006).

Members of parliament

The DMK was able to get 17 MPs elected to the 15th Lok Sabha. As the DMK supported the United Progressive Alliance (UPA) coalition government a generous proportion of these MPs (seven) were allocated posts in the cabinet. The DMK has been allocated numerous cabinet posts since 1999, and the more notable appointments in 2009 included the re-appointment of A. Raja, as Union Minister of Communications and Information Technology, and M.K. Azhagiri, son of the DMK President, as Minister of Chemicals and Fertilisers. The DMK also has a presence in the indirectly elected upper house, the Rajya Sabha, with seven members in 2011.

District secretaries

The district secretary is a highly influential office holder within the DMK. The district secretaries gain resources when the party is in government using a variety of methods. They can try to influence the district administration to assign jobs to favour seekers, and also seek contracts for contractors prepared to pay kickbacks. Their presence in government gives them privileged access to licenses for regulated activity like quarrying, which they can use for themselves or sell on. A determined district secretary can accumulate significant patronage resources to distribute within the party and to potential supporters. District secretaries have some input into the allocation of nominations prior to elections, as well as being ideally placed to claim a seat for themselves. For the most part the DMK district secretaries are lightly supervised by the party leader and enjoy a great deal of autonomy. The power and authority of the district secretary is recognised in the party rule that any important DMK visitor to a district, including a state cabinet minister, is expected to seek permission for the visit from the district secretary. Of the 35 district secretaries in 2011 no less than 28 stood as MLA candidates while three more had seats in the Lok Sabha. This left only four not holding or running for legislative office. District secretaries are also much more likely to be members of the state cabinet than other MLAs. When the DMK was last in power, between 2006 and 2011, 14 out of the 28 district secretaries who were MLAs were members of the cabinet.

State cabinet

Seats in the state cabinet are allocated for a number of reasons which include accessing public resources that can be used for party purposes, rewarding successful candidates (often on a seniority basis), and symbolic representation. The state cabinet in 2006 was listed in order of precedence beginning with the Chief Minister, who held additional portfolios, and it is striking that those at the head of the list held the more prestigious, and almost certainly lucrative, portfolios. The number of re-appointments to the state cabinet is notable, with long-serving legislators taking the more senior posts. With regard to symbolic representation the leading castes groups are given representation, religious minorities get some recognition, and women and Dalits are also offered places. Membership of the state cabinet is one marker of privilege in the DMK and the rate of re-nomination of MLAs in the cabinet is striking. No less than 29 ministers out of 31 were re-nominated in 2011, the two that were not offered seats retired from politics after long careers with the DMK.

Senior office holders

There were eight senior offices in the party in 2011, and these were held as follows: President (M. Karunanidhi), General Secretary (K. Anbazhagan), Treasurer (M.K. Stalin), Deputy General Secretary (Parithi Illamvazhuthi, Durai Murugan, and Sarguna Pandian), HQ Secretary (Arcot N. Veerasami), and Youth Wing Secretary (M.K. Stalin).[3] Of these seven individuals, six were sitting MLAs in April 2011. These senior office holders sit on several party committees including the High-level Policy Implementation Committee, Administrative Committee, and the Executive Committee and the General Council.

The Party leader and his inner circle

M. Karunanidhi is the key decision-maker in the DMK, and even though he does consult with lower level leaders in formal party meetings, much party business is transacted informally. Many decisions, including the nomination of candidates, are made by the party leader in consultation with members of his inner circle.

Party committees often meet to ratify decisions made elsewhere. The membership of the inner circle shifts over time but has included legislators like T.R. Baalu, Durai Murugan, A. Raja as well as various members of Karunanidhi's extended family (Jose, 2011). Decisions on the nomination of candidates are said to be made by a formal committee but in practice the party leader is lobbied for selection. Family members sometimes pass these requests on, or make special pleas for favoured candidates. When the list of DMK nominees for the 2011 assembly elections was announced it was claimed that no less than four junior family members had been able to secure places on the list for their protégés and supporters (*Times of India*, 2011a). Physical access to the party leader is tightly controlled. It has been mentioned to us that even state cabinet ministers cannot get easily get one to one appointments to meet their leader, and so family members have a considerable advantage over other party members when it comes to lobbying. The relative independence with which Karunanidhi's son, and likely political heir, M.K. Stalin is able to act also indicates that informal decision-making remains important at the senior level of the DMK.

Rules for progression

The DMK has a set of institutional and informal rules that determine progression within the party. These rules help sustain a party that is well organised and has a state-wide presence. Like the Akali Dal in Punjab, the party also has a degree of internal pluralism that sets it apart from other political parties in India where the central leadership is completely dominant, and in some cases keeps the lower levels of the party deliberately weak in order to maintain their personal position.[4] The DMK has a well-identified structure with branches at the village and ward level. These branches feed into a district organisation which is led by the district secretary.

Elections

The DMK has regular internal party elections (usually held every five years) which are used to decide who should hold posts in the party down to the very lowest level. These organisation elections can be very important for deciding who fills the post of district secretary. The eleventh round of internal elections held in 2000 resulted in very competitive elections and brought new leaders into the party, including, for the first time, two women district secretaries (*The Hindu*, 2000). The elections encourage district secretaries to be responsive to party members and demonstrate their effectiveness. However the process under which the party elections as a whole are held is opaque. The senior post-holders appear to serve at the pleasure of the party leader, with infrequent turnover, and candidates elected unopposed. M.K. Stalin, who now holds two senior posts, advanced up the formal party hierarchy a step at a time in the 2003 and 2008 elections.

Achievement

The DMK has a party culture which recognises the achievements of individuals who work for the party. The district secretary holds his or her post by establishing a reputation for effective leadership and so deters rival candidates. The district secretary, often dubbed a 'DMK strong man' (and currently they are all men), is expected to have the resources and determination to hold the organisation together during the difficult periods in which the party is out of office. The emphasis on efficacy is such that members of other parties who join the DMK can work their way up the party hierarchy, Thiruvannamalai district secretary E.V. Velu, formerly of the AIADMK, being a case in point (interview, J. Jeyaranjan, November 2009).

Party service

A related, but sometimes contradictory, norm is the recognition of service to the party. The esteem placed on commitment to the party is reflected in comments by the party leader '(t)hose who worked hard, who acted bravely, who sacrificed their self-interest and who considered party as their soul have been selected as our party's candidate' (Karunanidhi, 2008, p. 123). However the party leadership is prepared to depart from this principle, and permits lateral entry to defectors from other parties, several of whom are now powerful district secretaries. In 2011 the party nominated five recent defectors from AIADMK to contest the assembly elections (*Times of India,* 2011b).

Support of a senior party leader

As in many parties ambitious members are able to advance their careers by making connections with senior members of the party.[5] This takes on special significance when there are family links but there are other cases of senior politicians in the DMK sponsoring the career of younger politicians. A. Raja, for example, had a close relationship with the late Murasoli Maran, the leading DMK politician in New Delhi. As has been mentioned already, senior leaders, especially M.K. Stalin and M.K. Azhagiri, seek to place their supporters in lower level party posts and get nominations for their followers.

Dynastic links

Some ambitious politicians in the DMK have used family connections to advance their careers. Dynastic links offer possible gains from: name recognition (within the party and the constituency), access to campaign funds, an existing network of supporters, and active lobbying on the part of a senior relative for nominations. The use of family connections has not been without controversy within the DMK, but it is a recognised way of developing a political career. As we discuss below, the party can exploit family connections as well, a fact that was glossed by the party leader's eloquent claim that the party honours those who have died while holding office and is happy to further the careers of surviving relatives (Karunanidhi, 2008, p. 384).

The outstanding beneficiaries of dynastic preferment have of course been members of the party leader's family. Karunanidhi's family has prospered in the last two decades, with two of his sons, M.K. Stalin and M.K. Azhagiri, currently holding senior positions in the DMK. Stalin came to prominence in the early 1990s when it was thought Karunanidhi was preparing the way for him to take on the leadership. In the mid-2000s Azhagiri caught the attention of the party by asserting himself in the southern districts and helping the party to win numerous seats in the southern districts in the 2006 assembly elections. In 2004, Dayanidhi Maran, one of Karunanidhi's younger nephews, was elected to the Lok Sabha and immediately placed in the Union cabinet. In 2007 Karunanidhi's youngest daughter, Kanimozhi was elected to the Rajya Sabha and it became known that she was increasingly involved in the running of the party.[6]

The prominence of Karunanidhi's family naturally attracts media attention and so it is important to emphasise that other individuals do hold senior posts in the DMK. The achievements of competent party workers are celebrated and the party relies on its robust organisation when fighting elections. The picture is mixed, members of the leader's family are very well represented but others can progress to senior levels in the party. That said, it would appear there is a glass ceiling within the party; it is commonly assumed that the next party leader will be related to the current leader.

Money

The DMK expects its members to make various financial contributions to the party, and it is extremely helpful for an ambitious member of the party to be able to access resources. It is sometimes thought prudent to follow a lucrative pre-political career and so accumulate capital that can be spent developing a political persona.[7] Candidates are expected to contribute, at the very least, to the cost of their campaigns, and often to cover the entire cost which can run to several crores of rupees.[8] It is unsurprising that the assets declared by the candidates for the 2011 assembly elections reveal a group of very wealthy individuals. Only four declared assets of less than a million rupees, another 30 declared assets between a million and 10 million rupees, and the remaining 84 had substantial assets valued at over 10 million rupees.[9]

Caste

Caste background can work to the advantage, and disadvantage, of ambitious politicians in the DMK. The topic is controversial in the DMK, and caste pride is officially disdained by the party leadership (and ordinary members sensitive to the Dravidian origins of the party). Nevertheless the party has been known to make discreet, and occasionally very indiscreet, appeals to caste sensibilities, and a candidate from a numerically strong caste community would be considered an asset. A candidate may be able to gain from access to a caste-based network that is available for political use. The prevalence of candidates from the larger caste groups shown in the tables below attests to the advantages that can be gained from belonging to a numerous and powerful caste. Conversely, ambitious DMK members from disadvantaged caste groups can struggle to be taken seriously and the rebellious attitude of many DMK cadre in 2001 to an alliance with a Dalit party reflected this (Gorringe, 2005, p. 319).

Localism

A strong attachment to one's locality still matters within the DMK. Candidates are very much locally based and represent areas to which they have strong links, which echoes Forrester's earlier observation that MLAs regarded themselves as a 'tribune' of their area (1969, p. 44). For the most part the DMK does not introduce talented outsiders to contest seats. Chennai was something of an exception, as many DMK leaders made their base in the city in the 1950s.[10] A local base is seen as an electoral asset, and Karunanidhi claims to have advised his Congress allies, allocating seats from Delhi to take heed of this norm (2008, p. 379).

Caste, gender and quotas

As a party the DMK makes some institutional effort to encourage the representation of groups that are socially disadvantaged and/or under-represented in the party. At the very top of the party two out of eight of the senior posts were reserved, so there would be a female Deputy General Secretary and a Dalit Deputy General Secretary. An equivalent arrangement is supposed to hold at lower levels of the party with a post set aside for a Dalit and a woman in each district. The party leadership is aware of the expectation that it should nominate a respectable number of women as candidates for elected office, but so far the DMK has not got anywhere near the 33 per cent figure currently being debated in Parliament.[11] In addition the statutory reservation of seats in the Lok Sabha and the state assembly obliges the party to nominate a minimum number of Scheduled Caste (SC) and Scheduled Tribe (ST) candidates. The DMK makes some effort to incorporate representatives of religious minorities and women at higher levels of the party. So it is possible for a few talented and resourceful individuals from these backgrounds to make progress. As we shall see later the commitment of the party to effecting balanced representation is decidedly equivocal but nevertheless it does create some opportunities for individuals from a wider range of backgrounds to begin careers in politics.

Seniority

A principle of seniority is respected within the DMK. Long-standing members of the party have served in key party positions for decades. The composition of DMK cabinets reflects this as senior MLAs are routinely given prestigious cabinet posts when the party returns to power. K. Anbazhagan, the General Secretary of the party, and finance minister between 2006 and 2011, is 91 years old. Karunanidhi is 89 years old. When the DMK cabinet formed in 2006 it included six ministers who had served in the cabinet formed in 1989, and their precedence was reflected in the allocation of the most prestigious portfolios. The only exception was the relatively youthful Chief Minister's son, M.K. Stalin, then 53, who was placed fourth in the list of priority.

The DMK, in common with many Indian political parties, does not have fully transparent rules for progression (Chandra, 2004). The party leader exercises a great deal of discretion in the operation of the party. However the party does work with a set of expectations that ambitious members find workable, and holds the party together. The party leadership accords lower levels of the party a degree of autonomy in local affairs (Subramanian, 1999, p. 237). Likewise individuals rising within the party do not expect arbitrary interference in their careers from above. A candidate who wins election to the state assembly is very likely to be re-nominated.[12] However there are important exceptions to this as we shall see below.

Dynastic links and the MLA candidates

The family links between DMK candidates have attracted press comment, and the density of links between Lok Sabha MPs has been noted in academic literature on dynastic politics (Chandra & Umaira, 2011). The dominance of Karunanidhi's family has attracted a great deal of interest (Jose, 2011), and been a staple of AIADMK election propaganda (Wyatt, 2013, p. 10). The MLA nominations in 2011 attracted press coverage noting the prevalence of those with family connections in the DMK list. Seven 'father–son' candidates were identified with interest directed at the candidates who were contesting at the same time as their parents (*The Hindu*, 2011). However these reports were incomplete and we have gone through the candidate list seeking out connections between candidates in 2011 who are related to other family members who have held elected offices at the state or national level. We have identified 24 out of the 118 candidates with such connections, or 20 per cent of the overall total.[13] Some of these connections are very well established, and, as we discuss below, the level of dynastic connections was lower than among Lok Sabha candidates. What was notable was the prevalence of dynastic connections among younger candidates in general constituencies. No less than 6 out of the 10 candidates aged 40 or less had dynastic connections. This contrasts sharply with the reserved constituencies where only 1 out of the 11 candidates was related to a former or current DMK legislator. This is consistent with our overall assessment that Dalit politicians are relatively less influential in the party, whereas politicians from backward caste backgrounds are better able to lobby for their sons and daughters to be nominated.

It is interesting that 20 per cent of the MLA candidates with family connections is significantly lower than the high proportion of dynastic politicians among the DMK MPs in the current Lok Sabha.[14] Seven out of the 17 DMK MPs in the current Lok Sabha have dynastic connections, a high proportion (41 per cent) which has been commented on elsewhere (Chandra & Umaira, 2011). This significant divergence suggests that looking at the Lok Sabha to discern trends in dynastic politics needs to be balanced against studies of state-level developments. The dynamics of Lok Sabha elections are quite different from assembly elections. Candidates have to bear much higher campaigning costs across large constituencies and once elected the returns to office vary greatly. Some MPs gain cabinet posts which offer considerable extractive opportunities while back bench MPs have fewer ways of recouping campaigning expenses and accumulating funds for fighting a future election. We hypothesise that the high costs of campaigning reduce the number of applicants for Lok Sabha nominations and that applicants with dynastic connections are more credible, given their superior access to financial resources. This makes it more likely that parties will select them to contest Lok Sabha elections. The barriers to entry are somewhat lower for state assembly elections, reducing the advantages dynastic candidates have.

The pattern of dynastic recruitment in the current DMK has wider significance. Existing literature and press reports on the topic of dynastic politics in India more generally suggests politics is organised around family networks with junior relatives being engaged to extend the family enterprise (Chandra & Umaira, 2011). The dominance of the Karunanidhi family fits this narrative but the pattern varies and it is possible that factors external to the family condition dynastic recruitment. We suggest three categories of dynastic careers that can be applied to the 24 candidates with family links: actively managed, latent, and contingent or sympathy succession. There is evidence of *active manage-ment* among several leading families in the DMK where older generations have introduced younger relatives into politics, lobbying successfully for party posts and MLA nominations. An archetypal case is that of N. Periasamy who contested the Tuticorin seat a number of times. In 2006 he secured nomination for his daughter Geetha Jeevan and concentrated on his duties as district secretary. *Latent* dynasticism refers to circumstances in which the transition between generations is not straightforward and does not occur as planned, or a younger family member decides to return to politics at a later stage. In these circumstances the candidates have to take more initiative themselves to revive the political influence of the family and seek selection. A third category, the *sympathy* succession occurs when the party nominates a member of the immediate family to contest a by-election following the death of a parent. There is an element of uncertainty and contingency about such recruitment. The sudden death of a relative may hasten the advancement of a relative who was being prepared for office but it may well also be an appoint-ment made at the initiative of the party which feels it has much to gain electo-rally from honouring the family of a deceased party worker (Wolkowitz, 1987).

We identify nine candidates who are part of families that have succeeded in actively managing careers of junior relatives. As well as Karunanidhi, the senior MP T.R. Baalu secured a nomination for his son, T.R.P. Raja. Younger relatives of three serving district secretaries were nominated in 2011.[15] Another eight candidates had latent family connections where a period of time had elapsed between their own nomination and the last time their family members held office. The benefits of family connections were much less obvious in these cases with some links being fairly tenuous, the parent having left office several decades ago or their preceding relative having held a post in another party. We identified four candidates who began their legislative careers as 'sympathy' candidates nominated to contest by-elec-tions following the death of their incumbent relative.[16]

Gender background of the MLA candidates

The candidate list presented by the DMK in March 2011 was overwhelmingly male, with only 11 out of the 118 candidates being women. Further analysis shows that almost all the women among the DMK elite are on the periphery of that group. All of the 35 district secretary posts were held by men at the time of the 2011 election. The only woman to recently hold this post was Vasuki Murugesan, who died prematurely in December 2009. The leading female politician in the DMK is Kanimozhi, daughter of the party leader. She is currently serving a second term in the Rajya Sabha and though her formal political career has been relatively short Kanimozhi has influence within the inner circle (Jose, 2011). Three of the 11 women nominated (Poongothai Aladi Aruna, Geetha Jeevan, and A. Thamizharasi) did hold ministerial posts in the 2006–2011 DMK government. The portfolios they were initially assigned were low in the order of precedence. In 2009 Poongothai Aladi Aruna was assigned the slightly more prestigious Information Technology portfolio. Women's political careers have not prospered inside the DMK. Only 4 out of 11 female candidates had previously been elected to the assembly (once each and all in 2006) meaning they cannot make claims to prominence on the basis of seniority and would have considerable difficultly claiming to have cultivated a personal stronghold. The mean average times a female candidate had been elected were 0.4, compared with the mean average of 1.6 times for male candidates. The latter average figure conceals the profile of several party patriarchs who have been elected multiple times.[17]

The women candidates were more likely to have dynastic connections than male candidates, with 4 out of 11 having links to relatives elected to the legislative assembly or the Lok Sabha. In noting this we are aware this needs some interpretation (Spary, 2007). Wolkowitz has researched the careers of female politicians in Andhra Pradesh in considerable detail and noted the kinship link might encourage party leaders to nominate those candidates ahead of others (1987, p. 208, 212). In other words, the party sees an advantage in nominating a female candidate from a political family. Among the legislators we profile it is striking that 6 of the 11 women candidates were nominated in seats reserved for SC candidates. Wolkowitz makes the telling point that assigning reserved seats to women works to the advantage of party leaders who can claim they are giving symbolic recognition to women and to Dalits. Even more cynically it leaves more seats available for male higher caste candidates (Wolkowitz, 1987).

A full explanation for the gender imbalance within the DMK elite needs further research. In interviews conducted by the authors members of the party have been reluctant to discuss the topic. Observers close to the party offered the contentious view that political careers within the party should be based on merit and long service, qualifications that women members of the DMK are said to lack. Another commentator stated that politics in his locality had a rough and sometimes violent character; in other words street politics draws on certain types of gender socialised behaviour which favour men (interviews December 2009). It has also been observed that the DMK exudes a masculine ethos, both in martial rhetoric and the use of language that portrays the party as a brotherhood (Rajadurai & Geetha, 1996, p. 568; Vaasanthi, 2006, p. 248).

Caste background of the MLA candidates

The DMK does not make strong claims about the caste composition of its legislative party. When the candidate list was released in March 2011, the commentary from the party concentrated on the relative youth of its candidates. Hence we had to make a considerable effort to piece together the caste composition of the candidate list.[18] There are a number of reasons for this reticence on the part of the DMK. The Dravidian movement questioned the equation between caste and social privilege, and so appealing to the pride of an individual caste group is often considered unseemly in the political culture of Tamil Nadu (Wyatt, in press). As Racine comments, caste can be 'a politically incorrect topic' (2009, p. 450). In addition to political culture the caste demography of Tamil society, fragmented between many different groups and with few groups enjoying dominance in a large geographical area (Washbrook, 1989, p. 223), creates an incentive against overt appeals to caste at the state level. Courting a dominant caste group runs the risk of driving voters from other backgrounds to the opposing alliance (Subramanian, 1999, p. 142). Fragmentation in the state party system (Wyatt, 2009), has allowed a few parties to make particular appeals to one caste group, but larger parties still have an incentive to contest as catch all parties, making populist appeals that downplay loyalty to a single caste group.

Having gathered the data we have presented it in summary form in four tables. We have found that the overall list of candidates is a roughly microcosmic representation of Tamil society in terms of caste and religion. However the upper segments of the DMK elite are less representative, with Dalits and religious minorities being under-represented in relation to their proportion of the population. We have followed Racine (2009, pp. 460–461) in our grouping of the high-status caste groups, and presented them as Upper Caste and Mudaliars and Chettiars. In the Upper Caste category we include Naidus, Pillai and Reddiar candidates. The DMK did not nominate any Brahman candidates, which reflects the origins of the party in the Dravidian movement which was hostile towards Brahman social and political influence, and suggests the softening of anti-Brahmanism in the DMK in the 1960s was superficial (Subramanian, 1999, pp. 198–199). We note that the terms Mudaliar and Chettiar are often appropriated by lower status caste groups (Rajadurai & Geetha, 2002; Racine, 2009, p. 460).[19] We have been able to disaggregate the data on the 'backward castes' using the official BC and Most Backward Class (MBC) designations used by the state government (GoTN, 2013). Inclusion on the BC list is not a certain marker of disadvantaged status which is supposed to determine inclusion in the Other Backward Class list (Galanter, 1984). As the BC list allows access to affirmative action quotas in employment and education it has been granted to groups even where the evidence of social disadvantage is limited. The Kongu Vellala Gounders, a dominant caste in western Tamil Nadu, being a case in point (Vijayabaskar & Wyatt, 2013). The Thevar caste cluster also illustrates the point that dominant status can coexist with the official designation of disadvantaged status. In order to clarify this disjuncture between official classification and social status we also list the 118 MLA candidates in Table 2 according to the number of major caste groups. This shows the extent to which the dominant and influential backward castes are represented by the DMK.

The data in Table 1 show that when sub-divided the DMK legislators fall into cohorts that are roughly proportionate with the broad classification of caste demography in Tamil society. The forward castes are somewhat over-represented and the religious minorities, especially Christians are under-represented, but the number of backward caste and Dalit candidates conforms to the proportions of these groups among the population of Tamil Nadu. The microcosm of caste in Tamil society that is more or less represented in the DMK candidates for the 2011 assembly election begins to disintegrate once the data are disaggregated and it comes under even more stress once we examine the caste composition of the established elite within the DMK. What Table 1 does not show, but Table 2 reveals, is that the larger castes groups tend to dominate, whereas many of the smaller caste groups do not have a presence among this cohort of DMK candidates. That some groups are not represented is inevitable given that the several hundred caste groups in Tamil Nadu exceed the number of seats in the state assembly (234). Groups identified as eligible for reservation by the state government's BCs, MBs and Minorities Welfare Department number 248, and there are scores of groups not on those lists. It is significant that most of the smaller, less influential groups are not represented, and that the leading or locally dominant caste groups such as the Thevars, Kongu Vellalar Gounders, Vanniars and Nadars are well represented. The social privileges of the forward castes are also reproduced in the social profile of the DMK candidates with groups such as the Naidus and Reddiars securing a significant number of nominations.

The lopsided caste composition of the DMK elite is reflected in the cabinet which was appointed in 2006 and remained largely the same until 2011 (Table 3).

Table 1. Major social groupings among DMK candidates for the 2011 assembly elections.

	Forward castes		Backward castes					
	Upper castes	Mudaliars and Chettiars	Backward Classes	Most Backward Classes	SC/ ST	Muslim	No data	Total number of candidates
Number of candidates	14	3	56	17	23	4	1	118
Percentage	12	3	47	14	20	3	1	100

Source: Data compiled by the authors.

Table 2. DMK candidates from major caste groups, 2011 assembly elections.

Caste groups	Number of candidates	Percentage of total number of candidates
Forward castes		
Chettiar	2	2
Mudaliar	1	1
Naidu	7	6
Pillai	3	3
Reddiar	4	3
Backward castes		
Kongu Vellalar Gounder	11	9
Mutharaiyar	4	3
Nadar	7	6
Thevar	20	17
Vanniar	12	10
Dalits		
Arunthatiyar	2	2
Pallar	6	5
Paraiyar	8	7
Total	87	74

Notes: In spite of strenuous efforts we were unable to locate the precise community background of five of the 21 candidates from Dalit backgrounds who contested reserved seats. So, the figures for the three largest Dalit castes may be slightly higher than we state here.
Source: Data compiled by the authors.

Table 3. Major social groupings among DMK members of the state cabinet, 2006–2011.

	Forward castes	Backward castes		SC/ ST	Muslim	Totals
		Backward Classes	Most Backward Classes			
Number	6	14	6	3	2	31
Percentage	19	45	19	10	6	100

Source: Data compiled by the authors.

The forward castes and the backward castes dominated the cabinet. Dalit ministers were a token presence.[20] The DMK won 95 state assembly seats in 2006, which was 23 seats short of a majority, but the Congress Party gave 'outside' support which enabled the DMK to govern as if it had a majority. The relatively small DMK cohort increased the proportion of legislators likely to get cabinet posts. However the party leadership gave minimal consideration to the 20 DMK legislators elected from seats reserved for the SCs and STs. The cabinet formed in 2006 included 31 ministers, of these just three were held by Dalit members of the DMK. The disparity is remarkable with 37 per cent of those elected from general seats holding cabinet posts and just 15 per cent of the SC/ST legislators having a cabinet post. In terms of the order of precedence the inequality persists with the SC/ST legislators largely consigned to inconsequential portfolios.

The profile of the Dalit candidates within the DMK correlates with the social disadvantages faced by their communities (Gorringe, 2012). Many of the comments made in relation to gender apply also to Dalit candidates. Very few Dalits have been able to develop careers within the party. Only two individuals stand out in recent years, Parithi Illamvazhuthi and A. Raja (a Lok Sabha MP and a former Union cabinet minister).[21] V.P. Duraisami is another relatively long-serving MLA from an Arunthatiyar background. He had served two terms by 2011, holding the post of deputy speaker during his second term, and is now a Deputy General Secretary of the DMK, yet he remains relatively unknown at the state level. In short, very few Dalit legislators have developed lengthy careers.

As a cohort the reserved legislators were disrupted by the re-drawing of constituency boundaries for the 2011 election, which included some re-allocation of reserved seats. The DMK took the opportunity to nominate younger Dalit candidates in the newly reserved seats. The mean average election rate for an SC/ST candidate in 2011 was 0.8, compared with the mean average of 1.6 for all other candidates. The re-drawing of constituency boundaries prior to the 2011 election complicated matters but this begs the question of why the DMK would not re-nominate sitting Dalit legislators to general seats in the vicinity of their old reserved seat. The DMK, and almost all other parties in India, use the reserved seats to define a quota of Dalit candidates and rarely nominate Dalits to general seats (McMillan, 2005).[22] Most Dalit legislators who served a term between 2006 and 2011 were set aside prior to the 2011 election. As Table 4 shows only two Dalits hold the coveted post of district secretary and it hardly needs adding that the two districts in which the DMK has Dalit district secretaries are small and lack political prestige.

Table 4. Major social groupings among DMK district secretaries, April 2011.

| | Forward castes | Backward castes | | SC/ ST | Muslim | Totals |
		Backward Classes	Most Backward Classes			
Number	6	21	6	2		35
Percentage	17	60	17	5		100

Source: Data compiled by the authors.

48

It is difficult to avoid the conclusion that the DMK does not value Dalit members of the party and that as individuals they gain less from the informal rules, such as election winning and seniority, which enable other members of the DMK elite to establish themselves. The experience of the two leading Dalit politicians of the DMK mentioned above does confirm one of the informal rules for progression, that close links with the party leader, and his family, help advance a career within the party.[23]

Conclusions

This article examines the way in which the elite of a party has been constructed and researches an area of Indian party politics that has often been neglected (Sridharan & DeSouza, 2006, p. 33). The DMK elite, in the narrow sense of the inner circle around the party leader do indeed dominate many decisions within the party. Yet our findings also show that the DMK does have a middle level leadership which operates with a degree of autonomy from the senior leadership, showing the party is not an oligarchy. It is often commented that Indian parties are organisationally weak (Chhibber, 2013). Symptoms of this weakness are said to include a lack of internal democracy and a tendency towards 'dynastic rule' (Hasan, 2010, p. 251). Chandra and Umaira (2011) observe that one aspect of organisational weakness is a lack of clarity in the chain of command, with it being very difficult for outside observers to identify who holds a given post within the party. The case of the DMK does not quite conform to the characterisation of party weakness in India. It may well be that the DMK, with its visible organisation structure, is relatively unusual among parties in India. However the findings from this case suggest further research on other parties in India is necessary to test the assumption that party organisations are generally weak.

The research reported here reveals the extent of family connections within the DMK elite merits attention. The pre-eminence of the party leader's family is well known, and the media has begun to report on a number of middle level leaders in the DMK who have junior family members with political ambitions. It needs to be emphasised that while family connections do help some get MLA nominations, this is not an absolute trend. A good number of junior relatives have not been able to secure nominations, or posts within the DMK (*The Hindu*, 2012). The claim that the DMK has become a 'family enterprise' is an exaggeration (Hasan, 2010, p. 250), though the expectation of dynastic succession has certainly divided the party. The data reported here on state level officials are unusual as most other work has concentrated on the family background of MPs in the Lok Sabha (Chandra & Umaira, 2011; French, 2011, pp. 91–123) or the party leadership (Chhibber, 2013). The relatively higher rates of legislators with family connections in the Lok Sabha suggests different dynamics at work at the national and state level, and is part of a further research agenda that could be taken up by other scholars of party politics. Our research shows that family connections are linked to political careers in different ways. Some careers are actively managed, and powerful leaders manage to hand power over to younger generations relatively quickly. In other cases the connection is latent, and younger family members work to revive the fortunes of a political family. The equation of organisational weakness with dynastic politics needs further examination (Chandra & Umaira, 2011; Chhibber, 2013). The DMK has a relatively strong organisation and yet family connections are relevant to political progression in some cases.

The DMK has internal rules and a set of norms, which while not always consistent or consistently applied, are widely understood within the party. These rules shape competition within the party and keep it relatively stable. It is this set of conventions on which the elite of the party has been constructed. It needs to be emphasised that internal rules are supplemented, in the case of the SCs and STs, with legal quotas. The very limited representation of women among DMK legislators and party post-holders, and the small number of Dalits holding party posts, begs the question of what would happen to the representation of Dalits in the DMK in the absence of official quotas. It is very likely that even fewer Dalits would be offered nominations to contest assembly and parliamentary seats.

Unlike some other parties in India the DMK does not have an autocratic leadership. The party also maintains a degree of internal pluralism, even though this has been severely tested since the late 1980s (Subramanian, 2003). However it is important to recognise important inconsistencies in the operation of the formal and informal rules by which the party operates. That the party accommodates elements of social structure which create privilege means that individuals who sit at the edge of the wealthy, male, backward caste mainstream in the party struggle to establish their position within the DMK elite.

Acknowledgements

This article draws on numerous interviews carried out since November 2009. The authors are very grateful to those who gave up time to be interviewed and also to colleagues, friends and acquaintances who helped us gather this data. They are particularly grateful to S.V. Rajadurai and M. Vijayabaskar for extensive assistance with data collection, and very graciously taking time to comment at short notice on the final draft. The paper benefited from editor's comments and referees' comments. Likewise they appreciate helpful advice from participants at a UKIERI funded workshop in Edinburgh in September 2013. The usual disclaimers apply.

Notes

1. We derived this number as follows: MLA candidates (118), holder of senior party offices not nominated as MLA candidates (2), national members of parliament

(25) and district secretaries who were not nominated in 2011 and who were not elected to the Lok Sabha in 2009 (5). Most of the members of the party leader's inner circle have a position in one of these categories, but a few do not.

2. This group could be narrowed down to sitting members of the current legislative assembly, but this is a very small group, as the DMK sits in opposition, and would exclude influential ex-MLAs who are likely to be candidates in the 2016 assembly. Assessing the candidate list gives a better sense of the social profile of the party elite than looking only at those elected in an election in which the DMK did very badly.

3. These posts have since been re-organised, with new posts added.

4. The Telugu Desam Party under the leadership of N.T. Rama Rao being a case in point (Suri, 2013, p. 169).

5. The Tamil Nadu Congress illustrates this process well. Individuals seeking nominations for assembly seats in in March 2011 usually had powerful backers. Rahul Gandhi was determined to get members of the Youth Congress nominated. Other senior figures, including P. Chidambaram, K.V. Thangkabalu and G.K. Vasan, sought nominations for their supporters.

6. The prominence of the leader's family has caused numerous tensions in the party, most notably a split in 1993 when numerous middle level leaders protested against the direction being taken by the party. A particular grievance was the apparent preparations for Karunanidhi's son M.K. Stalin to succeed to the party leadership. There was disquiet that other talented leaders, including V. Gopalsamy (Vaiko), were to be passed over, encroaching on the pluralism within the party. The split was followed by the formation of the Marumalarchi DMK or renaissance DMK in 1994. The MDMK alleges the DMK has given up Dravidian principles in favour of dynastic rule.

7. The list of donations to the 2011 election fund declared to the Election Commission makes for fascinating reading. A total of 312 donations are recorded. The larger donations of Rs 100,000–500,000 from the district secretaries might be expected but a good number of lower level officials and party members without posts were recorded making donations of Rs 25,000.

8. A crore is the Hindi word for 10 million, a term widely used in official documents and the Indian press.

9. These data were gathered from the affidavits each candidate has to provide under Election Commission regulations. It is fair to assume that in many cases these assets were under-reported. Indeed our own cross-checking of a few of the 2011 affidavits revealed this to be the case.

10. In 2011 there were a few exceptions, as several high-profile incumbents gave up their seats in Chennai is search of potentially safer constituencies.

11. One long-standing observer of the DMK reported to one of us that there is strong resistance to changing the gender balance of power of the party, with the feeling being expressed that quotas would enable women to override the norm of giving long years of service to the party that male candidates are supposed to have done historically (interview, December 2009).

12. This contrasts with the AIADMK where re-nomination is much less assured and second rank leaders can find themselves abruptly demoted. This applies to lower levels of the party organisation as well; in 2000 no less than 36 of the 50 district secretaries of the AIADMK were dismissed (*Frontline* 2000).

13. One or two more names might be added to this list who have connections to DMK post holders but who have never been elected to the state assembly. Among the

candidates in 2011 M.R.K. Panneerselvam stands out, his father was a DMK district secretary, but the handful of other individuals identified are related to junior post-holders and it is far from clear that these links are a significant contribution to the careers of the more successful younger generation.

14. Six of the MPs are junior relatives of earlier legislators, and the seventh (T.R. Baalu) is the father of an MLA elected in the 2011 assembly elections.

15. These powerful district secretaries were Veerapandi Arumugam, I. Periasamy and N. Periyasamy. In addition K.N. Nehru's nephew was elected to the Lok Sabha in 2009 and N.K.K. Periasamy gave up his district secretary's post and MLA seat in 2006 (both were immediately taken up by his son, who was re-nominated in 2011).

16. There were another three candidates for whom we could not locate any data.

17. Karunanidhi holds the record of 11 successful contests, and other notable veterans in 2011 included K. Anbazhagan (9), Durai Murugan (7), K.K.S.S.R. Ramachandran (7) and Veerapandi Arumugam (6).

18. This data were gathered from numerous sources including press reports in English and Tamil, interviews with rank and file party members, well placed observers such as local journalists, and acquaintances living in the constituencies in which the candidates stood for election.

19. Accordingly we place most Mudaliar candidates in the backward caste category. Of the five candidates from Mudaliar backgrounds one is from the high status Thondaimandala Saiva Vellala Mudaliar caste, another is from the Sengunthar community, and the remaining three are Agamudayars. The latter two groups are listed on the Backward Class list.

20. The proportions given in Table 3 are not that different from the DMK state cabinet of the early 1970s when the number of backward castes was increased to 56% of the overall total (Subramanian, 1999, p. 219).

21. Parithi Illamvazhuthi left the DMK six months after the 2011 assembly election, and later joined the AIADMK.

22. C.T. Dhandapani, who died in 2001, was an unusual exception. He served as Urban District Secretary for Coimbatore and a DMK legislator elected from unreserved seats. We are grateful to D. Karthikeyan for this information.

23. A. Raja became close to M. Karunanidhi, who in return has been extraordinary loyal to Raja as the 2G spectrum case unfolded. Parithi was a close associate of Stalin, sometimes described as his 'right hand man'.

References

Barnett, M. R. (1976). *The politics of cultural nationalism in South India*. Princeton: Princeton University Press.

Chandra, K. (2004). *Why ethnic parties succeed: Patronage and ethnic head counts in India*. Cambridge: Cambridge University Press.

Chandra, K., & Umaira, W. (2011). India's democratic dynasties. *Seminar, 622*. Retrieved June 22, 2013, from http://india-seminar.com/2011/622/622_kanchan_&_wamiq.htm

Chhibber, P. (2013). Dynastic parties: Organization, finance and impact. *Party Politics, 19*(2), 277–295.

Forrester, D. (1969). State legislators in Madras. *Journal of Commonwealth Political Studies, 7*(1), 36–57.

French, P. (2011). *India: A portrait*. London: Allen Lane.

Frontline. (2000, April 29). *Trouble in the AIADMK.* Retrieved September 13, 2013, from http://www.frontline.in/static/html/fl1709/17090380.htm

Galanter, M. (1984). *Competing equalities: Law and the backward classes in India.* Delhi: Oxford University Press.

Gorringe, H. (2005). *Untouchable citizens: Dalit movements and democratisation in Tamil Nadu.* New Delhi: Sage.

Gorringe, H. (2012). Caste and politics in Tamil Nadu. *Seminar, 633.*

Government of Tamil Nadu. (2013). *Citizen charter 2013–2014 backward classes, most backward classes and minorities welfare department.* Retrieved June 21, 2013, from http://cms.tn.gov.in/sites/default/files/documents/bcmbcmw_2.pdf

Hardgrave, R. L. (1965). *The Dravidian movement.* Bombay: Popular Prakashan.

Harriss, J. (2002). Whatever happened to cultural nationalism in Tamil Nadu? A reading of current events and the recent literature on Tamil politics. *Commonwealth & Comparative Politics, 40*(3), 97–117.

Hasan, Z. (2010). Political parties in India. In N. G. Jayal & P. B. Mehta (Eds.), *The Oxford companion to politics in India* (pp. 241–257). New Delhi: Oxford University Press.

Jose, V. (2011). The last lear. *The Caravan, 3*(4). Retrieved June 29, 2013, from http://caravanmagazine.in/reportage/last-lear

Karunanidhi, M. (2008). *Nenjuku Neethi, Part-3.* Chennai: Thirumagal Nilayam.

McMillan, A. (2005). *Standing at the margins: Representation and electoral reservations in India.* New Delhi: Oxford University Press.

Price, P. (1996). Revolution and rank in Tamil nationalism. *Journal of Asian Studies, 55*(2), 359–383.

Racine, J. (2009). Caste and beyond in Tamil politics. In C. Jaffrelot & S. Kumar (Eds.), *Rise of the plebeians? The changing face of Indian legislative assemblies* (pp. 439–489). New Delhi: Routledge.

Rajadurai, S. V., & Geetha, V. (1996). DMK hegemony: The cultural limits to political consensus. In T. V. Sathyamurthy (Ed.), *Region, religion, caste, gender and culture in contemporary India* (pp. 550–586). Delhi: Oxford University Press.

Rajadurai, S. V., & Geetha, V. (2002). A response to John Harriss. *Commonwealth and Comparative Politics, 40*(3), 118–124.

Sivaraman, M. (2013). *Haunted by fire: Essays on caste, class, exploitation and emancipation.* New Delhi: LeftWord.

Spary, C. (2007). Female political leadership in India. *Commonwealth and Comparative Politics, 45*(3), 253–277.

Sridharan, E., & DeSouza, P. R. (Eds.). (2006). *India's political parties.* New Delhi: Sage.

Subramanian, N. (1999). *Ethnicity and populist mobilization: Political parties, citizens and democracy in South India.* New Delhi: Oxford University Press.

Subramanian, N. (2003). Beyond ethnicity and populism? Changes and continuities in Tamil Nadu's electoral map. In P. Wallace & R. Roy (Eds.), *India's 1999 elections and 20th century politics* (pp. 50–93). New Delhi: Sage.

Suri, K. C. (2013). From dominance to disarray: The Telegu desam party in Andhra pradesh. In S. Pai (Ed.), *Handbook of politics in Indian states* (pp. 166–179). New Delhi: Oxford University Press.

The Hindu. (2000, March 23). *The changing profile of DMK.* Retrieved September 13, 2013, from http://www.hindu.com/2000/03/23/stories/04232238.htm

The Hindu. (2011, March 19). *Another father-son pair in DMK list.* Retrieved 20 March, 2011, from http://www.thehindu.com/news/national/tamil-nadu/another-fatherson-pair-in-dmk-list/article1551170.ece

The Hindu. (2012, October 12). *How 'Stalin formula' keeps sons from rising in DMK youth wing.* Retrieved 25 July 2013, from http://www.thehindu.com/news/national/tamil-nadu/how-stalin-formula-keeps-sons-from-rising-in-dmk-youth-wing/article3989066.ece

Times of India. (2011a, March 17). *Stalin camp takes nearly 75%, Alagiri gets most of the remaining.* Retrieved 20 September 2011, from http://articles.timesofindia.indiatimes.com/2011-03-17/chennai/29137843_1_dmk-first-family-m-k-alagiri-rajya-sabha-mp-kanimozhi

Times of India. (2011b, March 18). *DMK gives tickets to youngsters.* Retrieved June 29, 2013, from http://articles.timesofindia.indiatimes.com/2011-03-18/chennai/29144226_1_dmk-k-anbazhagan-karunanidhi-and-general-secretary

Vaasanthi. (2006). *Cut-outs, caste and cine stars: The world of Tamil politics.* Delhi: Penguin.

Vijayabaskar, M., & Wyatt, A. (2013). Economic change, politics and caste: The case of the Kongu Nadu Munnetra Kazhagam (KNMK) in Western Tamil Nadu, South India. *Economic & Political Weekly, 48*(48), 103−111.

Washbrook, D. A. (1989). Caste, class and dominance in modern Tamil Nadu: Non-Brahmanism, Dravidianism and Tamil nationalism. In F. Frankel & M. S. A. Rao (Eds.), *Dominance and state power in modern India* (pp. 204−264). Delhi: Oxford University Press.

Weiner, M. (1967). *Party building in a new nation: The Indian national Congress.* Chicago: Chicago University Press.

Wolkowitz, C. (1987). Controlling women's access to political power: A case study in Andhra Pradesh, India. In H. Afshar (Ed.), *Women, state and ideology: Studies from Africa and Asia* (pp. 205−225). London: Macmillan.

Wyatt, A. (2009). *Party system change in South India: Political entrepreneurs, patterns and processes.* Abingdon: Routledge.

Wyatt, A. (2013). Populism and politics in contemporary Tamil Nadu. *Contemporary South Asia, 21*(4), 365−381. doi:10.1080/09584935.2013.803036.

Wyatt, A. (in press). Caste and vernacular politics in Tamil Nadu, South India. In T. Neyazi, A. Tanabe, & S. Ishizaka (Eds.), *Democratic transformation and the vernacular public arena in India.* Abingdon: Routledge.

Class, nation and religion: changing nature of Akali Dal politics in Punjab, India

Pritam Singh

Faculty of Business, Oxford Brookes University, Oxford, UK

The Akali Dal is the best organised political party in Punjab and has ruled over Punjab for a longer period than any other political party since the creation of the Punjabi-speaking state in 1966. It articulates aspirations of Punjabi regional nationalism along with trying to protect the interests of the Sikhs as a religious minority in India and abroad. As a part of shaping Punjab's economic future, it deals with the pressures of Indian and global capitalism. This paper is an attempt to track the multi-faceted pressures of class, religion and nationalism in the way Akali Dal negotiates its politics in Indian federalism.

Introduction

The Shiromani Akali Dal (Akali Dal henceforth) is the best organised and the second oldest (next only to Congress) political party in Punjab, and the oldest regional party in India. It is the only regional party in Punjab and, in that position, views various politico-economic issues from the perspective of their impact and implications for Punjab.[1] It is also the only political party in India that claims to protect the interests of the Sikh minority living in the other states of India and in other countries.

A comprehensive understanding of Akali Dal politics requires capturing these four aspects together regarding Akali Dal: the best organised political party in Punjab, the oldest regional political party in India, the only regional political party in Punjab and the only party that claims to protect the interests, especially religious, of the Sikhs all over the world. Let us briefly expand on these four aspects. Regarding organisation, the other four party groupings in

Punjab are: the Indian National Congress (henceforth Congress), Bharatiya Janata Party (BJP), the Left parties (CPI/CPM/CPIML) and Bahujan Samaj Party (BSP). The BJP is confined to a few Hindu-majority urban areas, the Left parties are confined to a few pockets that have had communist activity in the past and the BSP is confined mainly to a few areas that have some concentration of so-called low-caste sections of the population. The only political party that comes somewhere near Akali Dal in terms of influence all over Punjab is Congress but even Congress' all Punjab reach in political influence, which was more than the Akali Dal's in the 1960s, is not matched by the comparable organisational strength of Akali Dal. The Congress is not a cadre-based party as the Akali Dal is and its influence and organisational strength have been on the decline in comparison with the rising influence and organisational strength of Akali Dal. Regarding Akali Dal being the oldest regional political party in India, the important point to highlight is that unlike Akali Dal with its autonomous origins, many of the regional parties are offshoots of the Congress Party after India's independence and even those who have autonomous origins are not as old as Akali Dal. Compared to Akali Dal's birth in 1920, the other regional parties with autonomous origins are: Jammu & Kashmir National Conference (1932), Kerala's Indian Union Muslim League (1948) and the Tamil Dravida Munnetra Kazhagam (1949).[2]

The fact that it is the best organised party in Punjab highlights the need for explaining the reasons for acquiring that status and for exploring the significance of this for relative strength of the regional Akali party and the so-called national parties in Punjab. Its status as the oldest regional party in India highlights both the strong roots of region-based nationalism in Punjab as well as the structural dimensions of the Sikh location in Punjab and India. The critical importance of these aspects in the politics of Akali Dal points to the weakness of analytical frameworks that attempt to generalise about regional parties in India and place Akali Dal as just another regional party in an analytical framework theorising regionalism in India. This does not mean, however, that general conceptual categories of class, caste, nation, religion, region and gender cannot be applied to studying Punjab politics and the place of Akali Dal in that politics. What I am emphasising is that the specificities of each regional formation should not be downgraded to fit a generalised framework about regionalism. This paper is an attempt to employ the conceptual categories of class, nation and religion in understanding the nature of Akali politics in Punjab and India. This paper has not taken into account the aspect of caste and gender in Akali politics. Undoubtedly, the incorporation of caste and gender into the analysis would enrich our understanding of Akali politics but I have focused on engaging with three characterisations of Akali Dal that are dominant in the literature and which take class, nation and religion as the defining criterion to characterise Akali Dal.

A dominant tendency in characterising Akali Dal by using the category of class is to characterise Akali Dal as a party of rich agrarian bourgeoisie. Purewal (2000) could be considered as representing this characterisation of Akali Dal.

The characterisation of Akali Dal that has nation and region as the central categories of characterisation is based on a framework of differentiating Indian political parties into two baskets of 'national' and 'regional', and then putting Akali Dal into the regional basket along with all other regional parties. The source of theoretical inspiration for this characterisation of Akali Dal comes from work on regional parties such as that of Yadav and Palshikar (2009). The third characterisation of Akali Dal that assigns a key importance to religion follows primarily from the work of historian Bipan Chandra and characterises Akali Dal as the party of Sikh communalism (Chandra 1987). We discuss below the key phases in the historical evolution of Akali Dal since its birth in 1920 and then critically evaluate the three characterisations mentioned above in the light of the historical evolution of Akali Dal.

Early phase (1920–1947): coping with disadvantages of a minority status

Akali Dal owes its birth as a political organisation to the Sikh movement for control over its religious institutions during the British colonial rule in India (Grewal, 1996, 1998; M. Singh, 1978, 1988; Narang, 1983). Before the British annexation of Punjab in 1849 and the eventual merger of Punjab with the rest of colonially occupied India, Punjab existed as a sovereign state for 50 years under the rule of a Sikh emperor Ranjit Singh (Fisher, 1999; K. Singh, 1997; Singh & Rai, 2009). During the pre-Ranjit Singh era, the eighteenth century witnessed a long and bloody period of armed conflict between the Moghul rulers and the Sikh rebels. The control of many important religious shrines of the Sikh community, the most important being the birth place of Guru Nanak (1469–1539), the founder of the Sikh faith, had during this period passed on into the hands of a pacifist sect (called Udasi) amongst the Sikh community. This pacifist sect's control of Gurdwaras, the Sikh religious places, suited both the Moghul rulers as well as the Sikh guerrilla bands. The Moghul rulers by accepting or even supporting the pacifist Sikhs' control of the Gurdwaras wanted to discourage the rebellious tendency amongst the Sikhs while the guerrilla Sikh fighters knew that they could not logistically manage to run the gurdwaras while involved in armed combat against the rulers and tacitly agreed to let the pacifist sect keep managing the gurdwaras. The Sikh community was also respectful to the sect since its founder Sri Chand was one of the sons of Guru Nanak (S. Singh, 1983). Therefore, the control of gurdwaras by the sect was allowed to continue even during the Ranjit Singh era (1799–1849) (S. Singh, 1980).

The agreement of the mainstream Sikh community to the sect's management of gurdwaras came to an end when it became widely known in the early twentieth century that the management indulged in financial and religious malpractices (Kapur, 1986). A movement to replace that management by democratically elected representatives of the Sikh community achieved success and the volunteers who participated in the movement were called Akali (a worshipper of the Eternal God) (Fox, 1987; Kerr 1988). Bringing together all the Akali volunteers under one umbrella organisation resulted in the founding of Shiromani Akali Dal in December 1920. The major achievement of the Akali movement was the creation of a central management committee (SGPC i.e. Shiromani Gurdwara Prabhandhak Committee) to look after the gurdwaras (Kapur, 1986). The election to this committee was to involve the entire Sikh community leading to this committee being called the mini-parliament of the Sikhs. This historical association of Akali Dal with the founding of this committee has had a long-term impact on the public image and perception of Akali Dal as an organisation primarily concerned with politics of religious issues concerning the Sikhs. This perception is certainly historically grounded but it also acts as a barrier in building views of Akali politics that transcend this religious focus.

If in the early 1920s, the major focus of Akali activity remained with the issues concerning governance of Sikh gurdwaras, by the late 1920s and the 1930s, the shift was taking place towards politics aimed at protecting the collective interests of the Sikhs as a community. With the Sikhs constituting only 13 per cent share in colonial Punjab's population, the Akali Dal from its very inception was acutely aware of this minority status of the Sikh community and, therefore, of the vulnerability of the Sikhs to being marginalised in the political governance of Punjab (P. Singh, 2008). The emerging possibility of India being divided after the end of British Rule into a Hindu-majority Hindustan and a Muslim-majority Pakistan presented the Akali Dal with very tough scenarios regarding the political future of the Sikh community (Ahmed, 2012; Yong, 1994). With no possibility of carving out a Sikh-majority state due to demographic, geographical and political constraints, the Akali leadership could hardly manage to do anything more than seek vague promises from the Indian nationalist leadership to protect Sikhs in the Hindu-majority India.

It is clear that during this phase, the main concern of the Sikh leaders and masses was to avoid suffering the disadvantage of being a minority. Religious identity was the dominant aspect, although the class interests of the landed upper classes did play their role in designing various responses to proposals for political governance. Punjab also witnessed the emergence of a strong regional party – the Unionist Party – that comprised the landed elites of the three main religious communities of Punjab-Muslims, Hindus and Sikhs (Talbot 1988, 1994; Tiwana 1999). Akali Dal kept out of this regional grouping although some individual Sikh leaders associated with this regional grouping came into the fold of Akali Dal.

Post-colonial phase (1947–1966): advancing Sikh political interests and Punjabi language

In the post-colonial Indian Punjab, the in-migration of Sikhs from Pakistan/ West Punjab and the out-migration of Muslims from India/East Punjab led to the emergence of Sikhs, for the first time in their history, as a majority community in some central districts of Punjab, although taking Punjab as a whole, the Sikhs were still a minority. In 1951, the Sikhs were 35 per cent of the total population of the state (Brass, 1974, p. 301). Linguistically, Punjab was still a multi-lingual state because many districts that now form Haryana or are in Himachal Pradesh were not Punjabi-speaking areas.

The Akali Dal launched a movement for the creation of a Punjabi-speaking state (called Punjabi Suba) that started in 1955 and reached its height in 1960– 1961 (Sarhadi, 1970). Soon after India's independence, the Indian State was faced with similar demands in other parts of India for the reorganisation of states on linguistic grounds. Nehru, Patel and the other leaders of the ruling Congress Party were acutely aware of the partition of India in 1947 on religious grounds. They were, therefore, very suspicions of any identity which they thought could undermine their goal of forming a unified Indian identity. It is this mind-set and Indian nationalist vision which led them to initially oppose any demand for the creation of linguistic states. However, with the passage of time, the central leadership gave in to the demands for the creation of some new states, e.g. Gujarat and Andhra Pradesh. The central leadership could reconcile to the creation of these new states because they were not seen as threats to the territorial integrity of India.

The central leadership, however, viewed the demand for the creation of Punjabi Suba (Punjabi-speaking state) out of the existing multi-lingual state in a sharply different way. It not only rejected this demand, it suppressed the movement for Punjabi Suba by resorting to very repressive measures. The rejection of the demand for the creation of Punjabi Suba was due to two main reasons: Punjab was a border state between India and Pakistan, and the creation of a Punjabi-speaking state would have led to the creation of a territorial space with a Sikh majority. However, the death of Nehru, the most vocal opponent of Punjabi Suba (Gill, 1998, 1999), in 1964 and the rise to power of Lal Bahadur Shastri as prime minister of India created a new political environment that was conducive to the creation of Punjabi Suba. The rise of Sant Fateh Singh to eminence in Akali politics further facilitated the creation of this conducive environment because he emphasised the linguistic aspect of the demand. Eventually, Punjab was partitioned between a Punjabi-speaking state and Haryana in 1966 (P. Singh, 2008).

During this phase, Akali Dal articulated mixed aspirations of the Sikh community over questions concerning language, religion and nationalism in which the language aspect seemed to be dominant although tinged with various shades of religion. One very interesting aspect of Akali politics during this phase is that the Akalis viewed themselves primarily as active agents engaged in defensive action to protect the linguistic and cultural and, through that, the national interests of the Sikh community. Akali Dal did not visualise itself, during this phase, as a claimant to power in Punjab and confined itself to a merely oppositionist role. It participated in all the legislative assembly elections in Punjab from the very beginning but being very clear about always performing an opposition role. This political outlook was to undergo drastic change after the formation of Punjabi Suba when the Akali Dal saw itself as a natural claimant to power.

The mixture of religion and language has been so complex in Punjab that advancing the cause of Punjabi language by Akali Dal has been viewed by some 'secular' critics of Akali Dal (Chandra, 1987) as a disguised Sikh and, therefore, communal demand. This 'secular' charge against Akali Dal acquired some weight when even some Akali leaders themselves visualised the furtherance of Punjabi language as a Sikh issue (Sarhadi, 1970). However, the support extended by the Communist Party and some left-wing intellectuals to the demand for a Punjabi-speaking state in the last phase of the agitation for the state, and the clear enunciation by the Akali leader Sant Fateh Singh that their demand was for a Punjabi-speaking state irrespective of the percentage of population constituted by different religious communities in that state, did introduce some correctives to the communalisation of Punjabi language. This also contributed to Akali Dal being seen as a mixed champion of Sikh nationalism and Punjabi nationalism (P. Singh, 2008).

Seeking political power (1966–1975): frustrated ambitions and rising nationalist aspirations

With the creation of a Punjabi-speaking state in November 1966, there emerged a compact territorial space where the Sikhs were a majority. The 1971 census showed that Sikhs were 60.22 per cent of the total population of Punjab (Census of India data, cited by Robinson, 1987, p. 313). This raised the ambitions of Akali leadership to capture power in the new state, and the first assembly elections in the new state in 1967 led to the realisation of this ambition when a first non-Congress government led by the Akalis came to power (Deol, 1986; D. Singh, 1981). However, the Congress Party's success in engineering defections in Akali ranks and bringing down the government in August 1968 deflated Akali ambitions. The success of the Akalis in coming back to power in 1969 rekindled those ambitions which were again frustrated when the government was brought down through dissolving of the state assembly by the Governor in June 1971 (Government of India, 1988, p. 185). This cycle of rising and deflating ambitions led the Akali Dal to rethink their long-term strategy to deal with a governance structure in India where the Centre had hugely enormous powers. The Anandpur Sahib Resolution (ASR) seeking greater autonomy for states in India's federal structure was a product of this long-term thinking.[3] Akali Dal viewed itself as articulating the mixed aspirations of Sikh nationalism for power and that of Punjabi nationalism for regional autonomy within India's centralised structure of governance. The possibility of tensions between Sikh nationalist perspective and regional Punjabi nationalist perspective was not explored by simply assuming that what was good for Punjab was good for the Sikhs and vice versa. The ambiguity in Akali perspective over this commonality vs. tension between Sikh nationalism and Punjabi nationalism persists.

Defending democracy (1975–1977): resisting authoritarianism and protecting minority rights

The Akali Dal's vigorous role in opposing Indira Gandhi's Emergency rule in 1975 is a very fascinating subject that remains largely unresearched. The Akali Dal was the only political party that in an organised fashion launched a movement of resistance to oppose the Emergency. Indira Gandhi, alarmed by Akali success in organising volunteers to court arrests every day, offered an accommodation to Akali leadership that if they allowed her to rule at the Centre, she would agree to them ruling Punjab in a similar fashion as the DMK was ruling Tamil Nadu. Two independent accounts have confirmed that this offer was made by Mrs Gandhi to the Akalis. Mr Tarlochan Singh, a former Chairman of India's National Commission for Minorities and currently a member of India's Rajya Sabha (Upper House), in an interview with me on 5 April 2013 in Delhi, told me that he had arranged a meeting of Giani Zail Singh, the then Chief Minister of Punjab, and Parkash Singh Badal in Amritsar Circuit House in 1975 to place Mrs Gandhi's offer to Badal and Akali Dal. He said that though Badal was reluctant to meet but due to Badal's trust in him, he agreed to go ahead with the meeting. Badal did not commit to anything at the meeting and said that he would put forward the proposal to the top leadership of the party. The party leadership rejected the offer. Another very senior civil servant, now retired, also confided in me in Delhi in April 2013 that he was instrumental in arranging a meeting between Badal and Zail Singh, and that the Akalis refused to accept the offer.[4] Akali Dal could have accepted this easy route to almost permanent power in Punjab by agreeing to the Gandhi offer but it did not.

This Akali rejection of an accommodation with the Congress, especially under the circumstances of the Emergency rule, deserves some explanation to understand the deeper underlying currents that shape the Akali politics. Mr Tarlochan Singh offered one explanation of Akali rejection of Mrs Gandhi's offer. His view was that the Akalis were scared of their mass base being hostile to accepting an accommodation with the Congress.[5] This seemingly pragmatic explanation also suggests that there were deeper undercurrents in Sikh society against authoritarianism that compelled the Akali leaders not to succumb to power sharing with the Congress even if they might have been personally tempted to. My view is that Akali Dal did not accept accommodation for two reasons. One, a long-held belief that to be a Sikh is to fight against authoritarian rulers/oppression posed an almost paradigm barrier to accepting accommodation with Gandhi (see H. Singh, 1994 on Sikh heritage). Second, the Akalis seem to have an unarticulated belief in the value of democracy from the viewpoint of a minority. This belief was based on the realisation that a religious minority is likely to be more unsafe and insecure in an authoritarian situation than in a democratic framework. Democracy was seen as a system of checks and balances, however flawed, against excessive misuse by a ruler from a majority community. It is worth mentioning here that the well-known leaders of the anti-Emergency movement in India (particularly Jaya Prakash Narayan, George Fernandes and Chandra Sekhar) were highly appreciative of the leading role Akali Dal had played in mobilising mass opposition in Punjab against the Emergency and all of them remained life-long sympathisers of the Akali Dal due to this.[6]

We notice that in this phase the view was that to protect Sikhs as a minority in a Hindu-majority country from a long-term point of view required protection of democracy and democratic institutions. The impulse was protection of religious and cultural rights of Sikhs but the articulation of that impulse was as a struggle against undemocratic rule.

Agitating for federal devolution of powers (1977–1984): mass mobilisation without success

The Akali Dal came back to power in 1977 at the end of Emergency but the return of an Indira Gandhi-led Congress to power at the Centre in 1980 led to the dismissal of the Akali-led government. In opposition, the Akali Dal organised a movement in 1981 for Punjab's economic rights especially concerning river waters (Mali, 1989). This was the clearest demonstration of the Punjabi nationalist dimension in Akali Dal politics. The scope of that movement expanded to include political and religious demands but the most significant was the demand for implementation of the ASR asking for devolution of powers (A. Singh, 1992b; Jeffrey, 1994; P. Singh, 2008). Along with the

Akali-led peaceful movement there emerged an extremist tendency in Sikh politics that had roots in religious revivalism (Mukherji, 1984, 1985; P. Singh, 1987). Both the Akali and Sikh extremist tendencies competed against and, in some instances, complemented each other. The Akali-led movement was a massive success in terms of mass mobilisation (P. Singh, 1982) but its failure to get Punjab's demands accepted by the Centre (Bhambri, 1985) led to strengthening the extremist Sikh tendency. This eventually resulted in a bloody confrontation in 1984 between the Indian army and the armed Sikh militants hiding in the building complex in and around the Golden Temple, the holiest Sikh shrine (Brar, 1993; Govt of India, 1984; Kaur, 1990; Nayar & Singh, 1984; Tully & Jacob, 1985). This confrontation, known as Operation Blue Star, represented in its most tragic and violent form the clash between the perspectives of Punjabi/Sikh nationalism and Indian/Hindu nationalism (P. Singh, 2008, 2009). The events following Operation Blue Star opened up all the fault lines in the Indian/Hindu nationalism's relationship with Punjabi/ Sikh nationalism. It may be useful to elaborate briefly the hyphenated term Indian/Hindu nationalism used here. Indian nationalism even when claims are made to its secular character is heavily tinged by Hindu nationalism. Even more importantly in the present context, both the secular/semi-secular garb and the Hindutva garb of Indian nationalism are opposed to Punjabi and Sikh nationalism because of the feared potentiality of Punjabi and Sikh nationalism undermining unified Indian nationalism whether in secular or in Hindutva garb.

Confronting central authoritarianism and militant Sikh nationalism (1984–1997): competing nationalisms

All the dimensions of Akali Dal politics around nationalism and religion acquired the sharpest focus ever during this phase but the class dimension remained subdued and suppressed. The conflict over religion and nationalism was so sharp and overpowering that the tensions around class interests got hidden and buried.

The Akali Dal also faced being very isolated in Indian politics. One of the features of Akali Dal politics in the post-1966 period has been to seek non-Congress allies at an all India level as leverage against Congress, its main opponent in Punjab. Its attempts have varied between forming alliances with the Left, centre (Janata) and Hindu Right (Jan Sangh/BJP) all together (early United Front period) or with the Left (1980 Assembly elections) or with the BSP/ Dalits or with the Hindu Right. Akali Dal had an alliance with the Left, centre (Janata) and Jan Sangh in the first United Front Ministry it formed in 1967. It continued with a similar united front combination between 1969 and 1970 but with a move away from the Left and towards Jan Sangh. It moved decisively towards alliance with Janata and Jan Sangh between 1970–1971 and 1977–1980. It broke its alliance with the Jan Sangh and formed an alliance with the communist parties (CPI and CPM) for the 1980 Assembly Elections which the alliance narrowly lost.[7] It formed an alliance with the BSP for the 1996 parliamentary elections and the alliance won 11 seats out of 13. It snapped its alliance with the BSP shortly afterwards when the BSP joined hands with Congress in UP. Since 1997, it has been in a consistent, though not without tension, alliance with the BJP for all elections.[8]

Although anti-Congressism has been the driving force behind seeking the best partner at a particular point of time, the internal struggles within Akali Dal suggesting the relative strength of different class factions have also played a role, though a subordinate one, in explaining the shifting alliances. During the 1980 Assembly Elections, there was a clear polarisation between the Badal faction representing the agrarian and industrial bourgeoisie wanting an alliance with the trader-dominated Jan Sangh and the Talwandi-Tohra factions representing the small and middle peasantry wanting an alliance with the Left parties. The Talwandi-Tohra faction at that specific point of time was relatively stronger and the alliance was, therefore, eventually forged with the Left parties.[9] Subsequently, that faction became weaker and the Badal faction faced very little resistance in forging ties with Jan Sangh/later BJP. The pro-Congress tilt of the main Left parties, CPI/CPM, in the 1980s and the weakening of the Left in Punjab since the 1980s also facilitated the shift towards an alliance with the BJP. It is important to emphasise here that though competing class factions may be at play in advancing different alliance strategies, the deciding factor in choosing an electoral partner is the potential contribution of the partner in defeating the Congress party, the main rival of Akali Dal.

In the post-1984 period, Indian nationalism, whether in the semi-secular garb of the Congress or in the Hindutva garb of the BJP, has very decisively shaped the Indian political environment (Bose, 1998; Jaffrelot, 1996; P. Singh, 2005). In this environment, anti-separatist sentiments easily metamorphosed into anti-Akali Dal or even anti-Sikh sentiments. The Akali Dal came to be branded as a supporter, open or disguised, of separatism (P. Singh, 1984). No political party wanted to be branded as a supporter of separatism by associating with it and, therefore, all political parties shunned the Akali Dal. This experience of isolation had a very demoralising impact on the Akali leadership. The fear of being isolated terrified the leadership both from the viewpoint of its implications for Akali Dal as a party as well as for the Sikhs as a small minority in a heavily Hindu-majority country. It is this fear that has had a significant, perhaps even decisive, impact on the Akali Dal making an alliance with a clearly Hindu-oriented party BJP to allay even any lingering suspicion that Akalis or Sikhs harbour any anti-Hindu feelings or sentiments. Akali Dal believes that the alliance with the BJP has provided a sense of security to the beleaguered Sikh community in the post-1984 period that no other alliance could have provided.[10]

The emergence of a strong militant Sikh nationalist tendency (more commonly known as Khalistani tendency) in Sikh politics as a reaction against Operation Blue Star and its aftermath created a powerful rival to Akali Dal in Sikh and Punjab politics (A. Singh, 1992a, 2003, 2009; B.P. Singh 1998, 2002; G. Singh 1987, 1992; J. Singh 2006). The Akali Dal had to fight on two fronts simultaneously: one in mainstream Indian and Punjab politics with the purpose of avoiding being isolated and, two, in Punjab/Sikh politics to keep its support base in the Sikh community to avoid being sidelined by the militant separatist tendency. It was a politics of negotiating a path different from Indian nationalism and Sikh nationalism while simultaneously not opposed completely to either of these two competing nationalisms. The politics of Punjabiyat (Punjabi nationalism) was born out of this necessity to remain relevant in the Indian mainstream while attempting not to totally alienate the Sikh nationalist support base in the Sikh community.[11]

Seeking political domination in Punjab (1997–2013): promoting Punjabiyat[12] as an inclusive regional identity

With the collapse of the Khalistan movement that was brutally suppressed by the central Indian state (Dhillon, 1998, 2006; Kumar, 1998, 2008; Kumar, Singh, Agrwaal, & Kaur, 2003; P. Singh, 2001; Pettigrew, 1995; Sharma, 1996), gradual steps were taken by the Indian state to restart the democratic process of electing the regional Punjab state assembly that had remained suspended for over a decade. A flawed election was held in 1992 which was boycotted by all parties and organisations with electoral base amongst the Sikhs. The Congress government headed by Beant Singh came to power on the basis of a 20 per cent vote and that too from the mainly Hindu-majority urban constituencies (P. Singh, 2008). This government, therefore, lacked any credibility and legitimacy. The first proper democratic election after the long interlude of assembly suspension took place in 1997 and brought the Akali Dal back to power in Punjab (see Appendix). The massive electoral victory secured by Akali Dal reflected the success of Akali strategy of keeping the Sikh support base alive by occasional attacks against the Centre while expanding its base beyond its agrarian landowning classes and castes which had historically been its core social and political base. This attempt to expand its electoral base beyond its core support base was made by articulating an inclusive Punjabi nationalist perspective. This included attempts to appeal to lower castes amongst the Hindus, Sikhs and the small Christian community through social welfare measures, and to win over the rich Hindu bourgeoisie by offering to accommodate individuals from these strata by giving them posts of economic and political influence. The Akali Dal has persisted with this strategy, being returned to power in the 2007 and 2012 state assembly elections (Appendix, also see Kumar, 2007, 2012a, 2012b, M. Singh, 2012). There is certainly no doubt that the Akali Dal has become organisationally more representative of different segments of Punjabi society than it has ever been before. By giving greater prominence to the 'development' agenda than it has done before, it has sought to signal that its programme and politics are more inclusive than before.

In its self-perception as a party with a claim to power, the Akali Dal has made a huge transition. In the pre-1966 post-colonial Punjab, when the Sikhs were about 35 per cent of the multi-lingual Punjab's population (Brass, 1974, p. 301), the Akali Dal never visualised itself as a ruling party – its entire programme and politics were guided by its perception that it could only perform an oppositionist role, and its success as an organisation was viewed from the angle of how powerful and effective its opposition had been. In the post-1966 Punjab (with a nearly 60 per cent Sikh share in the population), Akali self-consciousness was of a party rightfully claiming to rule Punjab but only through alliances with other non-Congress parties. This self-consciousness was given a rude shock when successive Akali-led governments were dismissed by the Congress-led Centre (P. Singh, 2008). This paved the way for the framing of the ASR asking for curtailment of central powers. The post-1984 Akali Dal has increasingly come to view itself as a party with a claim to rule just on its own without any alliance. The formation of this view was given a big boost by the unprecedented victory of Akali Dal in the 1985 assembly elections when it won an absolute majority on its own (Appendix). The subsequent victories have cemented this self-perception, although it maintains an alliance with BJP with a view to have an all India party as an ally at the Centre (Kumar, 2007, 2012b; Kumar & Kumar, 2002). The retired civil servant I have referred to above was of the view that Akalis had entered a power-sharing arrangement with the BJP that is similar to what was offered to them by Mrs Gandhi during the Emergency except that there was one big difference. In Akali power sharing with the BJP in Punjab, the Akali Dal will be always a bigger party in the arrangement due to BJP's limited electoral base in a few Hindu-majority urban constituencies. This could not have been ensured with a power-sharing arrangement with a much bigger Congress party. In the course of its history in the post-1947 period, Akali Dal has come a long way from being an opposition party to a position of self-confidence as the natural ruling party in Punjab.

Although it remains wary of Congress-machinations at the Centre, it does not suffer any more from the fear of being arbitrarily dismissed by the Centre because the continued rule of the Congress at the Centre can no longer be assumed as it could be before the Emergency era in Indian politics. The change in the macro political environment in India with the emergence of coalition politics at the Centre where the regional parties have become key players has also made it difficult for any party ruling at the Centre to use arbitrarily article 356 of the Constitution to dismiss a state government (Chiriyankandath, 1997). This reassuring self-confidence is the main reason that Akali Dal no longer harks back to ASR although that resolution still remains the only document the party has produced through sustained inner party deliberations over a considerable period of time. The party may be forced to engage in a similar exercise to develop a long-term perspective that transcends some limitations of the resolution that has terminology suggesting a narrow Sikh-centred mode of thinking (P. Singh, 2013). The core of the resolution relating to demands for federal restructuring of India is robust but needs to be reframed in view of the changed new emphasis on Punjabi identity (see P. Singh 2010a, 2012a, 2012b, in press; Singh & Dhanda, 2014; Singh & Thandi, 1999). The Akali Dal being the only regional party in Punjab is bound to remain for a considerable period of time in the near future as the central driving force in shaping the contours of Punjab politics.

The 1997–2013 phase in Akali Dal's political history coincides with the launch of the neo-liberal economic policy regime by the Centre in 1991. In its modes of dealing with the pressures of globalisation associated with the neo-liberal policy regime, Akali Dal has defied simplistic characterisations of itself as either pro-neoliberal or anti-neoliberal. On one hand, it does appear to be a votary of neo-liberal economic paradigm in its support for privatisation initiatives in health, education, energy and infrastructural projects, and for entry of foreign direct investment but, on the other, it has disobeyed World Bank advice (World Bank, 2004) by continuing with its policy of providing subsidy supports of varying kinds to farmers and other low-income families.

Conclusions

Between the themes of class, nation and religion, the emphasis in Akali politics has been changing although this change has not been linear or unidirectional. Different moments of Punjab and Sikh history in the last 90 years have seen different aspects of Akali politics become dominant. In the light of the historical and analytical account we have provided of Akali Dal politics, it is clear that any one-dimensional view of Akali Dal is bound to be flawed. Let us look very briefly at three accounts of Akali Dal which are one dimensional in character and which we have touched upon very briefly in the introductory section.

One characterisation of Akali Dal is as a party of rich agrarian bourgeoisie (Purewal, 2000). This characterisation fails to explain Akali Dal government incurring the risk of running a deficit budget to fund social welfare programmes for the poor rural proletarian population. Through these social welfare pro-grammes, Akali Dal has been defying the World Bank dictates to reduce or even remove subsidies to the poor and curtail the role of state to create space for increased privatisation. Akali Dal has been so clearly committed to this pro-gramme that it risked a split by a faction in the party led by Manpreet Singh Badal who had been heading the finance ministry in the Akali government for a number of years and who had been strongly supporting the World Bank argument for reduction/removal of the subsidies.

Another characterisation of Akali Dal to challenge is that Akali Dal is just another regional party much like other regional parties in other states of India (Yadav & Palshikar, 2009). This characterisation fails to capture the important historical fact regarding regional parties in India that many of them, barring a few in Tamil Nadu, Kerala, Jammu and Kashmir and in India's North East, are the products of a faction of the Congress party in a state splitting away to float a new party. The ideological roots of such parties lie in the Congress party. Akali Dal, in contrast, is a party that evolved out of the logic of Sikh history. Akali politics has run parallel to the Congress politics since the beginning of the twentieth century. At times Akali Dal has collaborated with the Congress party but the logic of that collaboration has risen from the internal dynamic of Akali politics and not as a result of sharing the Congress vision. The fact that it is the oldest regional party in India highlights the independent and auton-omous character of its evolution in contrast with most other regional parties in India (our mention of Tamil parties highlights the independent character and long history of Tamil nationalism).[13] Undoubtedly, Akali Dal is a regional party and shares some of the features of other regional parties but without understanding the distinctive feature of Akali politics that is rooted in Sikh history, our understanding of Akali politics is bound to remain flawed.

A third characterisation of Akali Dal, following primarily from the work of historian Bipan Chandra, is that it is a party of Sikh communalism (Chandra 1987). Apart from several logical and structural flaws in Chandra's analysis of communalism that follow from his Indian nationalist perspective, the charac-terisation of the Akali Dal as a party of Sikh communalism is flawed because of the inability of this characterisation to explain Akali Dal's consistent demand for inclusion in Punjab of Chandigarh and other Punjabi-speaking areas left in Haryana and Himachal Pradesh. If these areas were to be included in Punjab, it would lead to a decline in the Sikh proportion of Punjab's total popu-lation and would potentially weaken Akali Dal's political base if it were to be merely considered as a Sikh communal party. These demands clearly reflect a Punjabi nationalist dimension in Akali Dal's mode of thinking and action.[14] Similarly, the Akali Dal's demands for riparian law-based distribution and allo-cation of river waters that will protect Punjab's control of its river water resources, and for the right of Punjab to control its energy resources generated from the Bhakra dam, represent aspirations and interests of all Punjabis and not only of Sikhs (Dhillon, 1983).

It is a party of Sikh nationalism but not only of Sikh nationalism. It is a party of Punjabi regional nationalism but not only of that. It has aspects that make it appear closer to Sikh nationalism especially when it deals with issues concerning religious rights of the Sikh community, and it has other aspects that make it appear closer to regional Punjabi nationalism when it defends the economic interests of Punjab. It is also a party that goes beyond Punjabi nationalism and seeks to defend and promote the interests of Sikh minorities in the other states of India and abroad. It does protect the interests of agrarian bourgeoisie but also those of the other segments of rural society in Punjab and in doing so, it even sacrifices sometimes the interests of the agrarian bourgeoisie. While responding to the pressures of rural bourgeoisie, it also attempts to include the representation of Punjab's urban Hindu and Sikh middle classes and bourgeoisie in its organisational structure and policy-making process. Akali Dal seeks hegemony in Punjab politics in a Gramscian sense by pursuing a politics of inclusive accommodation.[15]

One broad generalisation that can be made is that the changing character of Akali Dal reflects both its responsive mode to external factors such as British rule or Congress/BJP rule at the centre as well as the active role Akali Dal has played as an agency to force other political currents in Punjab and India to respond. Seen in this light, Akali Dal can be seen as an organisation that has responded to external pressures as well as pro-actively sought, as an agent, to change the external environment in which it has to operate.

Acknowlegements

The author is thankful to James Chiriyankandath, Prabhsharandeep Singh, Sumail Sidhu, Shinder Thandi and Andrew Wyatt for their very helpful comments and suggestions on an earlier version of the paper. The usual disclaimer applies.

Notes

1. In the history of Akali Dal, there have been several instances of small splinter groups breaking away from the main Akali Dal and then rejoining the main party later but at each moment, one Akali Dal faction that happens to have the largest mass support becomes the chief representative of the Akali tendency in Punjab politics. Our analysis here takes into account that mainstream Akali Dal. For the last over two decades, Akali Dal led by Parkash Singh Badal, the present Chief Minister of Punjab, is the mainstream Akali Dal and is recognised by the Election Commission of India as Shiromani Akali Dal. Its current President is Sukhbir Singh Badal, the Deputy Chief Minister of Punjab and son of Parkash Singh Badal. The only exception to the tradition of splintering groups rejoining the

mainstream Akali Dal is the Akali Dal (Amritsar) led by Simranjit Singh Mann which has marginal, though constant, support among the Sikhs in India and abroad who support the idea of secession from India through peaceful means. Other Akali Dal factions are named after famous Akali leaders such as Master Tara Singh and Sant Harchand Singh Longowal but they are insignificant in terms of political influence. For more detailed accounts of tendencies/factions in Akali politics, see P. Singh (1982, 1984, 2008) and Narang (2014).

2. The sources of these data are the websites of the regional political parties defined and recognised by the Election Commission of India.

3. For a greater elaboration of the importance of ASR in the context of Indian federalism, see P. Singh (2008). See also Govt of Punjab (1987), Govt of India (1987, 1988), G.A. Singh (1977) and A. Singh (1992b). For a political economy approach to federalism going beyond the specific constraints of ASR, see P. Singh (1993a, 1993b, 1994, 2007, 2014).

4. Mr Tarlochan Singh was kind enough to accept my request for quoting him. The retired civil servant also agreed to be quoted but wanted to remain anonymous.

5. He put it in Punjabi: *oh lokaan ton darde si* (they i.e. the Akali leaders were scared of people/masses being opposed to accommodation with the Congress). The reference to *lokaan*/people in this context meant the wider Sikh community mainly in Punjab but also beyond Punjab.

6. Both Tarlochan Singh and the retired civil servant I interviewed in Delhi spoke about this. I wish to add a personal experience on this. I was a student at India's Jawaharlal Nehru University when the Emergency was lifted and I attended one of the biggest rallies in the history of India that took place in Ram Lila grounds in Delhi in 1977 to celebrate the victory of the anti-Emergency movement. The leaders from all shades of the anti-Emergency movement spoke at the rally one by one. When Parkash Singh Badal's name was announced and he got up to speak, he got the second biggest applause (after JP Narayan) from the audience. I heard people sitting around me in the audience saying that they (Sikhs/Akalis) were brave people in having put up this resistance against the Emergency. It appears that the information had circulated that the Akalis had played the most critical role in mobilising opposition to the Emergency. However, there is little research on the subject and the Akalis themselves have not made much of this.

7. Congress won this election with 63 seats in a house of 117 giving it a very narrow margin of victory. Had the Akali-CPI-CPM alliance won the Punjab Assembly elections in 1980, it would not be an exaggeration to say that the history of Punjab in the last three decades would have been different.

8. The source of these data is a mixed one. I have relied upon Deol (1986, 2000), D. Singh (1981) and supplemented that information with discussions with a number of academics and political activists during a field trip to Delhi and Punjab in April 2013. See Appendix for the Akali share of seats and votes in the elections to the Punjab State Assembly from 1951 to 2012.

9. I first reported the class-based nature of competing factions in Akali Dal in P. Singh (1982).

10. This view was articulated by a senior Akali leader in London in 1997 with a small group of people who were friends of his friends. He said this with a sense of both anger and helplessness when a couple of his friends criticised Akali Dal for forging an alliance with the Hindu nationalist BJP. He said that it was easy for his friends sitting in the comfort of London to criticise Akali Dal for the alliance with BJP but they in India were acutely aware of the small weight they had in the

power structure of India with only a maximum of 13 MPs in a house of 543, and that they do need an ally at the Centre to protect the interests of both Punjab and the Sikhs.

11. As an instance of Akali Dal's attempt to negotiate a path between Indian nationalism and secessionist Sikh nationalism, I have analysed Akali Dal's politics of tight-rope dancing on human rights violations in Punjab as a result of the Indian state's attempt to militarily suppress Sikh nationalism. See P. Singh (2010b).

12. The idea and perspective of Punjabiyat has been explored in Singh and Thandi (1996, 1999), Singh and Talbot (1996), P. Singh (2010a), Punjab Research Group (2010), P. Singh (2012a, 2012b) and Singh and Dhanda (2014). See also Ayers (2008) for a focus on the perspective of Pakistani Punjabi identity.

13. For a good account of regional parties in India with a focus on South India, see Wyatt (2009).

14. On Punjabi nationalism, see P. Singh (1999a, 1999b, 2002).

15. For an early attempt at elaboration of my view of Gramsci's concept of hegemony and its application in the Indian context, see Gill (1974). I stopped writing my surname as Gill after this because of the awareness that surnames such as this are used to project caste identity.

References

Ahmed, I. (2012). *The Punjab bloodied, partitioned and cleansed: Unravelling the 1947 tragedy through secret British reports and first-person accounts*. Karachi: Oxford University Press.

Ayers, A. (2008). Language, the nation, and symbolic capital: The case of Punjab. *Journal of Asian Studies, 67*(3), 917–946.

Bhambri, C. P. (1985). The failure to accommodate. In Amrik Singh (Ed.), *Punjab in Indian politics: Issues and trends* (pp. 203–212). New Delhi: Ajanta.

Bose, S. (1998). Hindu nationalism and the crisis of the Indian state: A theoretical perspective. In S. Bose & A. Jalal (Eds.), *Nationalism, democracy and development* (pp. 104–164). Delhi: Oxford University Press.

Brar, K. S. (1993). *Operation Blue Star: The true story*. Delhi: UBS Publishers.

Brass, P. (1974). *Language, religion and politics in North India*. London: Cambridge University Press.

Chandra, B. (1987). *Communalism in modern India*. New Delhi: Vikas Publishers.

Chiriyankandath, J. (1997). 'Unity in diversity'? Coalition politics in India (with special reference to Kerala). *Democratization, 4*(4), 16–39.

Deol, H. (2000). *Religion and nationalism in India: The case of the Punjab*. London: Routledge.

Deol, J. S. (1986). *State politics in India (with special reference to Punjab)*. Jalandhar: New Academic Publishing.

Dhillon, K. S. (1998). A decade of violence. In J. S. Grewal & I. Banga (Eds.), *Punjab in prosperity and violence* (pp. 104–122). Delhi: K.K. Publishers and Chandigarh Institute of Punjab Studies.

Dhillon, K. S. (2006). *Identity and survival: Sikh militancy in India 1978–1993*. Delhi: Penguin Books.

Dhillon, P. S. (1983). *A tale of two rivers: Ravi–Beas water dispute*. Chandigarh: Dhillon Publications.

Fisher, M. H. (Ed.). (1999). *The politics of the British annexation of India 1757–1857*. Delhi: Oxford University Press.

Fox, R. G. (1987). *Lions of the Punjab: Culture in the making*. Berkeley/Delhi: University of California Press/Archives Publishers.

Gill, P. S. (1974). Gramsci's concept of hegemony. *Frontier*, annual no. 17 October, pp. 20–24

Gill, T. S. (1998). Nehru, Indira Gandhi and Punjab. In J. S. Grewal & I. Banga (Eds.), *Punjab in prosperity and violence*. (pp. 34–46). Delhi: K.K. Publishers and Chandigarh Institute of Punjab Studies.

Gill, T. S. (1999). Jawaharlal Nehru and the Punjab. In Pritam Singh & S. S. Thandi (Eds.), *Punjabi identity in a global context* (pp. 333–340). New Delhi: Oxford University Press.

Government of India. (1984). *White Paper on the Punjab agitation*. New Delhi: Government of India Press.

Government of India. (1987). *Commission on Centre–State Relations Report, part II*. Nasik: Government of India Press.

Government of India. (1988). *Commission on Centre–State Relations Report, part I*. Nasik: Government of India Press.

Government of Punjab. (1987). Memorandum (to the Sarkaria Commission). In *Government of India 1987*.

Grewal, J. S. (1996). *The Akalis: A short history*. Chandigarh: Punjab Studies Publications.

Grewal, J. S. (1998). *The Sikhs of the Punjab*. Cambridge: Cambridge University Press.

Jaffrelot, C. (1996). *The Hindu nationalist movement and Indian politics, 1925 to the 1990s*. London: Hurst.

Jeffrey, R. (1994). *What's happening to India? Punjab, ethnic conflict and the test for federalism* (2nd ed.) London: Macmillan.

Kapur, R. A. (1986). *Sikh separatism: The politics of faith*. London: Allen & Unwin.

Kaur, H. (1990). *Blue Star over Amritsar*. Delhi: Ajanta.

Kerr, I. J. (1988). Fox and the Lions: The Akali movement revisited. In J. T. O'Connell M. Israel, W. G. Oxtoby, W. H. McLeod, & J. S. Grewal (Eds.), *Sikh history and religion in the twentieth century* (pp. 211–225). Toronto: University of Toronto.

Kumar, A. (2007, June 2). Punjab elections: Exploring the verdict. *Economic and Political Weekly*, *42*, 2043–2047.

Kumar, A. (2012a, March). Just another election? *Seminar* Retrieved from http://www.lokniti.org/pdfs_dataunit/ashutosh-kumar-seminar.pdf.

Kumar, A. (2012b, April 7). Fourteenth assembly elections in Punjab. *Economic and Political Weekly, XLVII*(14), 71–75.

Kumar, A. & Kumar, S. (2002). The recent assembly elections in Punjab: Some reflections on results and changing voter preferences. *International Journal of Punjab Studies*, *9*(1), 113–135.

Kumar, P. (1998). Violence in retrospect. In J. S. Grewal & I. Banga (Eds.), *Punjab in prosperity and violence* (pp. 123–137). Delhi: K.K. Publishers and Chandigarh Institute of Punjab Studies.

Kumar, R. N. (2008). *Terror in Punjab: Narratives, knowledge and truth*. Delhi: Shipra Publications.

Kumar, R. N., Singh, A., Agrwaal, A., & Kaur, J. (2003). *Reduced to ashes: The Insurgency and Human Rights in Punjab Final Report: Volume One*. Kathmandu: South Asia Forum for Human Rights (for Committee for Coordination on Disappearances in Punjab).

Mali, M. S. (Ed.). (1989). *Punjab da Quami Masla: Khabe Pakhi Chintakan di Nazar Vich* [The national question in Punjab: Views of left wing intellectuals]. Sirhind: Lok Geet Parkashan.

Mukherji, P. N. (1984). Gandhi, Akalis and non-violence. *Man and Development, IV*(3), 58–77.

Mukherji, P. N. (1985). Akalis and non-violence: An inquiry into the theory and practice of non-violence. In A. Singh (Ed.), *Punjab in Indian politics: Issues and Trends* (pp. 71–118). Delhi: Ajanta.

Narang, A. S. (1983). *Storm over the Sutlej: The Akali politics*. New Delhi: Gitanjali Publishing House.

Narang, A. S. (2014). The Shiromani Akali Dal. In P. Singh & L. E. Fenech (Eds.), *The Oxford Handbook of Sikh Studies* (pp. 339–349). New Delhi: Oxford University Press.

Nayar, K. & Singh, K. (1984). *Tragedy of Punjab: Operation Blue Star and after*. New Delhi: Vision Books.

Pettigrew, J. (1995). *The Sikhs of the Punjab: Unheard voices of state and guerrilla violence*. London: Zed Books.

Punjab Research Group. (2010). *The idea of Punjabiyat*. Retrieved from http://theprg. co.uk/2010/06/03/the-idea-of-punjabiyat-by-pritam-singh/

Purewal, S. (2000). *Sikh ethnonationalism and the political economy of Punjab*. New Delhi: Oxford University Press.

Robinson, M. (1987). *Religion, class and faction: The politics of communalism in twentieth century Punjab* (DPhil Thesis). University of Sussex, East Sussex, UK.

Sarhadi, A. S. (1970). *Punjabi Suba: The story of the struggle*. Delhi: U.C. Kapur.

Sharma, D. P. (1996). *The Punjab Story: Decade of turmoil*. Delhi: APH Publishing.

Singh, A. (1992a). *Kharku Sikh Sangharash* [Militant Sikh struggle]. Sangrur: Vichar Prakashan.

Singh, A. (1992b). Anandpur Sahib Resolution. In H. Singh (Ed.), *The encyclopedia of Sikhism* (Vol. 1, pp. 133–141). Patiala: Punjabi University.

Singh, A. (2003). *Vihvin Sadi Di Sikh Rajniti: Iq Ghulami Ton Dooji Ghulami Tak* [Twentieth century Sikh politics: From one slavery to another]. Chandigarh: Narinder Singh.

Singh, A. (2009). *1984 Unchitviya kehar* (*1984: The unimagined catastrophe*). Amritsar: Singh Brothers.

Singh, B. P. (1998). The logic of Sikh militancy. In J. S. Grewal & I. Banga (Eds.), *Punjab in prosperity and violence* (pp. 138–155). Delhi: K.K. Publishers and Chandigarh Institute of Punjab Studies.

Singh, B. P. (2002). *Violence as political discourse: Sikh militancy confronts the Indian state*. Shimla: Indian Institute of Advanced Study.

Singh, D. (1981). *Dynamics of Punjab politics*. Delhi: Macmillan.

Singh, G. (1987). Politics of cultural assertion. In G. Singh (Ed.), *Punjab today* (pp. 180–186). Delhi: Intellectual Publishing House.

Singh, G. (1992, October). Paradigm behind the militancy. *Seminar*, no. 398.

Singh, G., & Talbot, I. (Eds.). (1996). *Punjabi identity: Continuity and change*. Delhi: Manohar.

Singh, G. A. (1977). *The draft of the new policy programme of the Shiromani Akali Dal*. Amritsar: Shiromani Akali Dal.

Singh, H. (1994). *The heritage of the Sikhs* (2nd ed.). Delhi: Manohar.

Singh, J. (2006). *Myth and reality of the Sikh militancy in Punjab*. New Delhi: Shree Publishers and Distributors.

Singh, K. (1997). Ranjit Singh. In H. Singh (Ed.), *The encyclopaedia of Sikhism* (Vol. 3, pp. 479–487). Patiala: Punjabi University.

Singh, M. (2012). A re-election in Punjab and the continuing crisis. *EPW, XLVIL*(13), 21–23.

Singh, M. (1978). *The Akali movement*. Delhi: Macmillan.

Singh, M. (1988). *The Akali struggle: A retrospect*. New Delhi: Atlantic Publishers.

Singh, P. (1982, October). Current Akali politics: Some trends. *Secular Democracy*, special Punjab issue, 46–52.

Singh, P. (1984, February 4). Akali agitation: Growing separatist trend. *Economic and Political Weekly, 19*(5), 195–196.

Singh, P. (1987). Two facets of revivalism. In G. Singh (Ed.), *Punjab today* (pp. 167–179). Delhi: Intellectual Publishing House.

Singh, P. (1993a). Federal fiscal arrangements in India. *Austrian Journal of Development Studies, Vienna, 9*(3), 261–278.

Singh, P. (1993b). Punjab's economic development and the current crisis. *Seminar Annual, 401*, 60–65.

Singh, P. (1994). Political economy of the British colonial state and the Indian nationalist state and the agrarian-oriental development pattern in Punjab. *Indo-British Review, XXI*(1), 97–110.

Singh, P. (1999a, September 23–24). *Punjabi nationalism: 'The third way' between Sikh secessionism and Indian nationalism*. Paper presented at the British Association for South Asian Studies annual conference, London School of Economics. Abstract Retrieved from http://www.staff.brad.ac.uk/akundu/basas/basasc99.html

Singh, P. (1999b). Capital, state & nation: Reflections with respect to Punjab. *International Journal of Punjab Studies, 6*(1), 85–99.

Singh, P. (2001, October 6). Punjab terrorism: Truth still uncovered. *Economic and Political Weekly*, pp. 3829–3831.

Singh, P. (2002). Political economy of nationalism: Minority left and minority nationalisms vs. mainstream left and majority nationalism in India. *International Journal of Punjab Studies, 9*(2), 287–298.

Singh, P. (2005). Hindu bias in India's 'secular' constitution: Probing flaws in the instruments of governance. *Third World Quarterly, 26*(6), 909–926.

Singh, P. (2007). Political economy of centralisation in India: Some critical notes from a decentralist perspective. In B. Nayak (Ed.), *Nationalizing crisis: The political economy of public policy in contemporary India* (pp. 17–45). Delhi: Atlantic Publishers.

Singh, P. (2008). *Federalism, nationalism and development: India and the Punjab economy*. London: Routledge (paperback edition 2009).

Singh, P. (2009, June). The third Sikh Ghallughara. Review of R.N. Kumar's 'Terror in Punjab'. *Himal Southasian*. Retrieved from http://www.himalmag.com/component/content/article/542-.html

Singh, P. (2010a, May). The idea of Punjabiyat. *Himal Southasian*. Retrieved from http://www.himalmag.com/component/content/article/173-the-idea-of-punjabiyat.html

Singh, P. (2010b). *Economy, culture and human rights: Turbulence in Punjab, India and beyond*. Delhi: Three Essays Collective.

Singh, P. (2012a, May). The diasporic dimension of Punjabiyat, *Asian Voice/Gujarat Samachar*.

Singh, P. (2012b). Globalisation and Punjabi identity: Resistance, relocation and reinvention (yet again!). *Journal of Punjab Studies, 19*(2), 153–172.

Singh, P. (2013, March 29–30). *Changing social values and political culture in Punjab: With special emphasis on the period since 1966.* Paper presented at the international conference on '(Re-) Building Punjab: Political Economy, Society and Values', University of California, Santa Cruz.

Singh, P. (in press). Capital, class and nation in Indian federalism with special emphasis on Punjab. In M. Mohanty & G. Sebestian (Eds.), *Class and its intersectionalities.* Delhi: Daanish Publishers.

Singh, P., & Dhanda, M. (2014). Sikh culture and Punjābiyat. In P. Singh & L. E. Fenech (Eds.), *The Oxford Handbook of Sikh Studies* (pp. 482–492). New Delhi: Oxford University Press.

Singh, P., & Rai, J. (2009). *Empire of the Sikhs: The life and times of Maharaja Ranjit Singh.* New Delhi: Penguin Books.

Singh, P., & Thandi, S. S. (Eds.). (1996). *Globalisation and the region: Explorations in Punjabi identity.* Coventry: Association of Punjab Studies (UK).

Singh, P., & Thandi, S. S. (Eds.). (1999). *Punjabi identity in a global context.* New Delhi: Oxford University Press.

Singh, S. (1980). Udasi establishment under Sikh rule. *Journal of Regional History, I,* 70–88.

Singh, S. (1983). Udasi beliefs and practices. *Journal of Regional History, IV,* 73–98.

Talbot, I. (1988). *Punjab and the Raj, 1849–1947.* Delhi: Manohar.

Talbot, I. (1994). Khizr, the unionist party and the struggle for a united Punjab: 1943–1947. *Indo-British Review, XXI*(1), 73–88.

Tiwana, N. (1999). Unionism in the British Punjab: A personal memoir. In P. Singh & S. S. Thandi (Eds.), *Punjabi identity in a global context* (pp. 253–256). New Delhi: Oxford University Press.

Tully, M. & Jacob, S. (1985). *Amritsar: Mrs Gandhi's last battle.* London: Pan Books.

World Bank. (2004). *Resuming Punjab's prosperity: The opportunities and challenges ahead.* Washington: Author.

Wyatt, A. (2009). *Party system change in South India: Political entrepreneurs, patterns and processes.* Abingdon: Routledge.

Yadav, Y. & Palshikar, S. (2009, February 7). Principal state level contests and derivative national choices: Electoral trends in 2004–2009. *Economic and Political Weekly, 44*(6), 55–62.

Yong, T. T. (1994). Prelude to partition: Sikh responses to the demand for Pakistan, 1940–1947. *International Journal of Punjab Studies, 1*(2), 167–195.

Appendix. Seats won and percentage of votes polled by Akali Dal in the Punjab State Assembly Elections (1951–2012)

Year 1	Seats won 2	Percentage of votes polled 3	Govt. formation 4
1951	13 out of total 126	12.44	Congress govt.
1957*	NA	NA	Congress govt.
1962	19 out of 154	11.87	Congress govt.
1967	26 out of 104 (includes 2 won by Master Tara Singh faction)	24.68 (includes 4.20% of Master Tara Singh faction)	Akali-led UF govt.
1969	43 out of 104	29.36	Akali-led UF govt.
1972	24 out of 104	28.52 (includes 0.88% of Gurnam Singh faction which did not win any seat)	Congress govt.
1977	58 out of 117	31.41	Akali-Janata govt.
1980	37 out of 117	26.92	Congress govt.
1985	73 out of 117	38.01	Akali govt.
1992	Akali Dal along with Sikh militant groups boycotted the elections	NA	Congress govt.
1997	75 out of 117 plus Mann Akali Dal wins one seat	37.64 plus Mann Akali Dal polls 3.10% votes	Akali-BJP govt
2002	41 out of 117	31.08 plus Mann Dal polls 4.65% but does not win any seat	Congress govt.
2007	48 out of 117	37.09 plus Mann Dal polls 0.52% votes without winning any seat	Akali-BJP govt

(Continued)

Appendix. Continued.

Year 1	Seats won 2	Percentage of votes polled 3	Govt. formation 4
2012*	56 out of 117	34.53 plus Mann Dal polls 0.28% votes without winning any seat	Akali-BJP govt.

*Notes: (1) The Akali Dal candidates had contested the 1957 election on Congress ticket under a deal worked out by the Akali leader Giani Kartar Singh but this 'merger' fell apart soon after the election due to opposition to it by the top Akali leader Master Tara Singh (Grewal, 1996, pp. 126–127; M. Singh, 1988, p. 164).

2. In 2013, there are 59 Akali MLAs. One Congress MLA (Jain from Moga) resigned from his party and got re-elected in the March 2013 bye-election on Akali Dal ticket. Two Akalis (Bains brothers from Ludhiana) contested as independents in the 2012 election due to a local-level inner-party conflict and rejoined Akali Dal after winning.

Source: Columns 1–3 adapted from data provided by Election Commission of India website (http://eci.nic.in/eci_main1/ElectionStatistics.aspx). Column 4 created by the author.

Incumbency, internal processes and renomination in Indian parties

A. Farooqui[a] and E. Sridharan[b]

[a]Department of Political Science, Jamia Millia Islamia, New Delhi, India;
[b]University of Pennsylvania Institute for the Advanced Study of India,
New Delhi, India

This paper analyses a critical aspect of the internal functioning of five
major Indian political parties, namely the nomination of candidates for
parliamentary elections, focusing on the pattern of renomination of
former candidates and incumbents. The data are analysed against the
literature on the structure and functioning of Indian parties, and
interview material on the process of nomination in the 2009 and 2004
elections. From the perspective of a six-fold typology of centralisation
of nomination processes drawn from the comparative literature, it is
found that all the parties analysed are in either the second-most
centralised, or even most centralised categories, and that for the three
major national parties, Congress, Bharatiya Janata Party and
Communist Party of India (Marxist), past performance plays a role in
nominations, the majority of incumbents being renominated in the post-
1989 period.

Introduction

This paper examines a particular aspect of the internal dynamics of major Indian
parties of varying types, namely the process of nominating candidates for the
parliamentary elections to the lower house (Lok Sabha), which is directly
elected from 543 single-member constituencies by the plurality rule (first-past-
the-post) system. The aim is to get a picture of the internal processes of
various parties and relate them to the nomination outcomes, and see if this is
related to party type, to whether there are institutionalised selection processes
within parties, and to whether early elections make a difference. We compare
the pattern of nominations in each election with the previous election over

time in the light of our knowledge of the nomination processes gleaned from post-2009 interviews about the nominations processes in 2009 and 2004 with key party functionaries involved. We select for our study, the two major national parties, the Indian National Congress (INC) and the Bharatiya Janata Party (BJP), and two other parties defined as national parties by the Election Commission of India (ECI), the Communist Party of India (Marxist) (CPI (M)) and the Bahujan Samaj Party (BSP), and the largest of what are defined as state parties by the ECI (and referred to in common parlance as regional parties, those that have significant vote shares in less than four states – in most cases effectively one state), the Samajwadi Party (SP). For the CPI (M), the BSP and the SP, we analyse their nomination processes only in their states of strength since they are marginal forces outside these states. Hence, we analyse the nominations of the CPI (M) in its three stronghold states of West Bengal, Kerala and Tripura only, and those of the BSP and the SP in the state of Uttar Pradesh (UP) only.

Our research is informed by the normative importance of the intra-party nomination process in national situations in which, as William Cross has argued, either or both of representational and policy outcomes are determined by who gets to be nominated by major parties because this substantially determines who gets to be elected, i.e. the composition of the legislature and cabinet (Cross, 2008). In the Indian case, nominations are very important for representational outcomes in a heterogeneous society and also, less definitively, for policy outcomes, the latter being more leadership-determined. This study has larger implications for predictable career paths for candidates within parties, entry barriers for new candidates, and in turn, whether there are incentives for working within existing parties as against moving to other parties or floating new parties.

Comparative candidate nomination processes and internal democracy

In this section, we review the comparative literature on internal democracy and candidate nomination processes in political parties in long-standing democracies. Broadly speaking, following Lars Bille, there are six types of nomination processes in political parties in Western European parliamentary democracies, ranging from completely top-down to completely bottom-up at the two extremes, with four intermediate levels of decentralisation or participation by the party rank-and-file, or in other words, by levels of inclusiveness of the selectorate for nominations. These fall, from the most to the least centralised, into the following six broad categories:[1]

(1) Candidate selection is completely controlled by the national party leadership.
(2) Subnational party organs propose names but national leadership makes the final decision.

(3) The national leadership provides a list of names from which the subnational party organs make the final selection.

(4) Subnational party organs make nomination decisions, but need the final approval of national leaderships, and the latter can add or delete names according to various criteria.

(5) Subnational party organs control the entire process and make the final decisions.

(6) Nomination decisions are based on membership ballots, which are not the same as an open primary, but nevertheless the closest to grassroots participation.

In the context of the present project, the USA represents the decentralised extreme, that of party primaries for presidential and Congressional elections. However, it needs to be noted that these party primaries are conducted by state and local officials, publicly funded and under public law, not by party officials under party rules and with party funds. This system came into effect for presidential primaries from 1912 to 1968, running in parallel to the party convention, and since then has become the determinant of candidacy for public office.[2]

India lies near the other extreme in that most of its major parties are at the completely or near-completely top-down of the six types of party nomination processes, with the national party leadership having the final say. From interview data pertaining to 2009 and 2004, and the literature on Indian parties, we can classify the Congress, BJP and CPI (M) as being in the second most centralised category and the BSP and SP as in the most centralised top-down category.

Most European parties fall in between these extremes. In Bille's broad survey of party nomination rules and how they changed from 1960 to 1990 (covering as many as 57 parties in 1960 and 71 in 1990) in Western Europe, he found that the

> predominant candidate selection procedure in force around 1960, as well as that at the beginning of the 1990s, is the one in which the subnational party organizations control the process completely. Around 1960, and also around 1990, nearly half of all the parties applied this approach. In 1960, only Austria, Belgium, Ireland and the United Kingdom did not have any parties granting subnational organs this influence. Around 1990, only Ireland and pre-1992 Italy were in this situation.[3]

Thus, he found that most the parties fell in category (5). Furthermore,

> The second most widely used candidate selection method is the one that gives the right to decide on the subnational party organs, subject to the approval of the

national party organization. Around one-third of the parties belonged to this category in both 1960 and 1989. In sum, then, more than three-quarters of the parties have rules that give the subnational party organizations the power either to control the process completely or, at least, to have a major and substantial influence. The parties in question cover the whole ideological spectrum and they are present in all countries. There is thus no pattern regarding either party families or countries.[4]

Thus, three-quarters of the parties fell in categories (5) or (4), that is, in the relatively decentralised part of the range of types of nomination procedures.

Lastly, a move towards party primaries based on membership postal ballots, somewhat akin to US-style primaries but distinct from the latter in that they are conducted by party officials under party rules and limited to party members, has been in evidence, increasing from under one-fifth of the parties in 1960 to about a quarter in 1990, representing an increase in the selectorate for candidate nomination. It should be noted that these classifications are based on formal party rules and that informal mechanisms for greater leadership influence over the process can and do exist in many countries. However, the general trend has been towards larger and more inclusive selectorates and more influential subnational party organs in this process.[5]

Party types and internal democracy

Here it is relevant to mention that the literature tends to relate internal democracy to party type, and party types are supposed to have evolved in a certain sequence. Thus, Richard S. Katz and Peter Mair argue for an evolutionary sequence of party types, based on their relationship to civil societies and states in different stages of economic and social development, each with its typical internal organisation and pattern of functioning (Katz & Mair, 1995). They argue that nineteenth-century clientelist parties of notables gave way to mass parties, of the industrial working class, based on trade unions. In turn, these gave way in the post-World War II period of the rapid growth of the welfare state, the white-collar middle class and the post-industrial service economy, to Otto Kirchheimer's catchall party or electoral–professional party, and eventually the cartel parties, both of the moderate left and right, in the post-1970s period, closely integrated with the bureaucracies of a managerial state deeply enmeshed in the economy, which Katz and Mair argue are adaptations of the mass parties to the rise of catchall parties.[6] They view the increase in internal decentralisation and democratisation of nominations processes over 1960–1990 (expansion of selectorates) in the context of pressures to so democratise felt by catchall parties that were pitted against mass parties, and then felt by cartel parties against these and each other. The moves to democratise and decentralise were made to combat the phenomena of political apathy, low turnout and shrinking party membership by incentivising people by participation in party nomination processes.

However, this West European sequence ignores two important types of parties in India (out of three important types – catchall or Congress parties, ideological parties and ethnic parties).[7] First, ideological parties of the Left and the Right, that is, the CPI (M) and its Left Front allies, and ideologically rightist parties like the Hindu nationalist BJP and the Shiv Sena in Maharashtra. Second, ethnic parties based on particular caste blocs like the BSP, based on the Scheduled Castes, and the SP, based on the Other Backward Classes (OBC), principally the Yadavs, the main OBC caste in the state of UP. Both SP and BSP are based in UP and enjoy a considerable degree of support from the Muslim minority due to the latter's fear of the BJP. While catchall parties like the Congress might have to depend more on nominating candidates representing various social or ethnic groups to retain their allegiance, ethnic parties might have more autonomous leaderships due to strong ascriptive allegiances, and might try to construct majorities by striking coalition deals with other parties, delivering an ethnic bloc vote in return, akin to the consociational politics of ethnic elites described by Lijphart (1977). However, they could also try to expand the social base of their parties to construct majorities by forming broader and more inclusive caste clusters. Likewise, ideological parties might also have more committed voter bases than catchall parties, somewhat akin to ethnic parties.

Election nomination processes in Indian parties

Early studies of the process of nomination of candidates in the then dominant umbrella party, the Congress, in the 1950s and 1960s revealed the following patterns and evolution. Roy (1966, 1967a, 1967b) found that the party was still groping for a mechanism to stabilise the relationship between the different organisational levels of the party in selecting candidates in the 1957, 1962 and 1967 elections. The process generally followed was that applications would be made at the local level although it is not clear if they were largely made to the District Congress Committees (DCCs) or the Pradesh Election Committee (PEC). The PECs were to make decisions on nomination based on consultation with the DCCs given that the latter bore the burden of local mobilisation and campaigning. A PEC representative would attend the meetings of the DCCs that covered the relevant parliamentary constituencies. Analogously, the All India Congress Committee (AICC) would depute a representative to participate in the meetings of the PECs. However, while the Central Election Committee (CEC) was normally supposed to approve the decisions of the PECs, it reserved for itself the right to have the final say.

Roy found two contradictory tendencies: the tendency of centralization of command and concentration of decision-making power into the hands of the higher level organs growing out of the necessity to inject order and rationality into a process which is highly vulnerable to the pushes and pulls of parochial claims. Opposed to this is the tendency towards fragmentation of authority which reflects pressures from below for autonomy and power.[8]

In the 1962 election the selection process gave relatively greater weight to the lower levels of the hierarchy, including to the Mandal Congress Committees and the Panchayat Samitis, levels below the DCCs. In the 1967 election, the process became somewhat more centralised since intense competition for nominations at the local level, including newly mobilised caste groups, necessitated mediatory interventions by the CEC to resolve conflicts due to casteism, communalism and localism. Candidates now applied directly to the PEC and while it was obligatory for them to consult the DCCs, the PEC became relatively more influential. The point to be noted here is that the tendency to centralisation of nominations is not just due to a unilateral centralising power drive by the top leadership but due to intense local-level factional rivalries rendering the DCCs and sometimes PECs dysfunctional and requiring and inviting mediation by the top.

Roy's account is supported by Palmer (1967) for the 1967 election. He found that:

> For the Congress and for most other parties, mandal, district, state and national committees were involved in the selection procedure .... In general, but by no means universally, the recommendations of the subordinate committees on the State level were endorsed. These committees ... in many cases (they) could not agree and therefore simply referred the selections to the national committees. (Palmer, 1967)

He noted that non-Congress parties wait to see who the Congress candidate is before nominating their own candidates, a point also noted by Narain and Lal (1969).[9] While the account of Narain and Lal is in general agreement with those of Roy and Palmer, the former are sceptical of finding a uniform pattern in the practice of nominations, the latter being situationally determined, the key interaction being between the character of the party and the nature of the constituency, which they elaborate as being the nature of factionalism and bossism in the party at the local and state levels on the one hand and the caste composition of the constituency on the other.[10]

Kochanek (1968) broadly agrees with the above authors but adds the important point that whatever the formal criteria, the criterion that carried greatest weight with the selection committee, whether DCC, PEC or CEC, was the candidate's ability to win, and that this depended considerably on the social – caste and religious community – composition of the constituency, which were always factored in to the selection process (Kochanek, 1968). He also adds that, in the context of the 1967 election which like the three earlier elections saw simultaneous parliamentary and state assembly elections, the state level selection process, formally managed by the PECs, was dominated by Chief Ministers, and the latter's main concern was that the majority of assembly candidates should be constituted of their followers and should enable them to form a government. This led to non-accommodation of dissident factions in several states and large-scale defections and independent candidatures by dissident Congressmen for the first time. Thus, the concern with victory prospects, factionalism in the selection process and the concern with caste and community were key factors in the selection process, going back to the 1950s and 1960s.

For the 2009 election and to some extent for 2004, we have the following detailed information from interviews with party functionaries, necessitated by the long gap in the literature after the 1970s.[11] In the case of the Congress, key functionaries were categorical that the elaborate bottom-up process described in the earlier literature became much more centralised after the Congress split of 1969 and the suspension of internal elections to the AICC from 1972, and that the restoration of the AICC elections since 1992 restored the balance only somewhat.[12]

The formal processes of candidate nomination in Indian parties in 2009 were as follows. In the Congress party, there was an elaborate system consisting of observers sent to each of 543 Lok Sabha constituencies who prepare reports on potential candidates in their constituency for the DCC and the Pradesh (State) Congress Committee (PCC). The DCCs and PCCs give inputs to the State Election Committee (SEC) in each state, which sends a panel of names listing the pros and cons and relevant details of each potential candidate to the AICC. The AICC appoints a Screening Committee for each state which consists of important party leaders, including a senior member of the Congress Working Committee, two senior leaders who do not belong to the state, the state PCC chief and the state Congress Legislature Party leader. The Screening Committees prepare a docket listing the pros and cons and relevant details of each potential candidate and send these to the CEC of the party, the highest organ in the process, which makes the final decision. Although the process is supposed to begin and be completed early, well ahead of the election campaign, which begins just after the last date for withdrawal of nominations, a few days after the last date for nomination of candidates by parties, in actual practice the screening and nomination process begins late and drags on to the last moment. This is deliberate because early nomination is feared to lead to disappointed nominees either leaving the party or sabotaging the nominee's prospects (see note 12). The process is one in which the central party organisation makes the final selection based on the dockets sent up by the

SECs and centrally appointed Screening Committees for each state, although even at that level there are senior leaders for each state who do not belong to that state and hence are supposed to play the role of neutral arbiters.

In the BJP, there are just two formal levels of decision, the SEC and the CEC. The SEC is the final authority for municipal and local government-level elections in each state, with there being no need for names of potential candidates to be sent to the CEC. For state assembly and parliamentary elections, SEC plays a recommendatory role, recommending names of candidates for each constituency but the CEC makes the final selection. Earlier, the CEC would usually accept the SEC's choices, with a few exceptions. However, in 2009 there was a significant change from 2004, part of an ongoing shift from the early 2000s, following the BJP's entrenchment in power nationally from its 1999 re-election. In 2009, unlike earlier, the SEC did not make a choice for each constituency and provide a list of preferences. It merely forwarded all the names to the CEC. And the CEC was itself sidelined by the formation of informal 'core groups' for each state by the central leadership, which included certain key central leaders (Arun Jaitley, Sushma Swaraj, Venkaiah Naidu, Ananth Kumar) and selected state leaders. Some individuals were on the 'core group' of two or more states and wielded enormous clout and functioned arbitrarily and with little knowledge of the grassroots realities in the states concerned.[13] Thus, the 'core groups' made the final selection, in effect, which was rubber-stamped by the CEC after perfunctory debate on only a few seats. In 2009, the process started nine months before the election and was chaotic and degenerated into a centralised process.

If the CEC cannot agree on nominees for certain constituencies, the BJP president is empowered to make the decision. This was so not only in the 2009 national election but also in some state assembly elections before that. Unpublished surveys for internal consumption were commissioned by the party president, hiring three different polling firms of allegedly doubtful integrity, whose results were used to justify preconceived notions and certain selections.[14] Additionally, the extra-party Hindutva ideological 'movement' organisation, the Rashtriya Swayamsevak Sangh (RSS) played an influential role in nominations in 2009 in some states (Madhya Pradesh (MP), Rajasthan, Chhattisgarh, and also in Delhi, Haryana, Assam and Orissa), exerting pressure towards rewarding ideological loyalty over constituency-level victory prospects. The RSS functionaries on loan to the BJP party organisation (*sangathan mantris*) no longer perform the function of constituency-level assessment of a candidate's strengths that they used to in the pre-2000 period, but rather, that of a lobby within the party for promoting ideological loyalists.

On the whole, there has been a shift within the BJP since 2000, and particularly since 2004, from field-oriented nomination and internal evaluation processes that assessed 'merit', that is, victory prospects, from constituency-level feedback from grassroots workers to central party organisation-oriented nomination processes which rewarded those who had cultivated connections at this level. This is further discussed in the second last paragraph of this section. There has been a greater emphasis on caste as a factor in nominations, particularly in the states of UP, Bihar, Rajasthan and MP, and in Delhi, Haryana, Assam and Orissa, according to confidential interviews with key functionaries.[15]

In the CPI (M), we focus on the nomination processes in its three strong-hold states, West Bengal, Kerala and Tripura.[16] In the CPI (M), the State Committee draws up the list of nominees for Lok Sabha candidates, which is cleared by the Politbureau of the Central Committee. However, this last step is basically a formality. It is the State Committee which essentially makes the nomination decision, particularly if some Central Committee members happen to be con-testing from the state for the Lok Sabha. The (State) Committee Secretariat, which is the executive body of the State Committee, prepares a list of candidates after going through lists prepared in consultation with the District Committees (of the Party). Since parliamentary constituencies overlap districts, two District Secretariats might be consulted in cases of overlapping constituencies. The State Committee consists of about 80 members, of which 7–8 might be MPs and another 25–30 MLAs. This is the pattern in West Bengal, the numbers being smaller in Kerala and much smaller in Tripura. As of 2012, a two-term limit for MPs is proposed, and has already been introduced in Kerala.

On what basis are candidates selected? The CPI (M) being a cadre-based party of about one million members, the key criterion is having been active in party work in their area. Potential candidates will need to have gained recognition in their area of work in the party's mass organisations and fronts, for example, among college teachers. There is some consideration given to caste/community, less so in West Bengal where caste politics is less important, more so in Kerala where caste and religion play a greater role in electoral politics. Also, in Kerala, the vote share difference between the rival coalitions, the CPI (M)-led Left Democratic Front and the Congress-led United Democratic Front being typically very narrow (1–2 per cent), there is a greater emphasis on wooing the floating vote, and hence, caste/community considerations are factored in to a greater extent. However, caste/community considerations play a much smaller role in the CPI (M), according to the party, compared to other parties, the track record of candidates in party activity being much more important. Linked to this is the pattern of relatively high repetition of winners and candidates, particularly in West Bengal, in 2009 and 2004. Repeating the candidates in the same constituencies, which is a strong pattern, is also linked to recognition in local party work, and to the fact of coalition politics, in which seats are shared with smaller partner parties which have sub-state local bases from which candidates are repeated.

In contrast to the above three national parties, in which there are institutionalised internal processes of selection in which proposed nomination start from below and move upwards although the final decision is made by the national leaderships, the nomination processes in the SP and BSP are very tightly controlled by the top.[17] The process in the SP is a top-down one in which party president Mulayam Singh Yadav takes the final decision on all MP and MLA candidate nominations, although he does this in informal, not institutionalised, consultation and bargaining with other major party leaders. While there is a formal process in which each constituency unit of the party sends up 8–9 possible names, the SP being effectively a single-state party this process is constantly intervened in by Yadav and those close to him since he knows a very large number of local leaders of his party personally and is in constant touch with them. In the SP, nominations are again ultimately about victory prospects. However, also pertinent are a combination of caste and religion (to make various caste groups and the Muslim minority feel represented), and, though to a lesser extent than the BSP, about candidates who can bring resources to the party and at least partly fund their campaign – the SP did give candidates some campaign funds (Rs. 5 million to a few tens of millions).[18] Caste matters not only in constituency-specific ways depending on the local demography but also has an effect on adjacent constituencies and on the state as a whole since party leadership resorts to 'caste balancing' in which no caste is seen to be 'over-represented' state-wise or in a region of the state to keep all segments of the social base of the party happy, while also trying to reach out to new social segments by offering nominations to candidates belonging to them. However, old loyalties and personal connections with Yadav, a veteran grass-roots political activist, also matter.[19]

In the BSP, the nomination process is centrally about money and candidates are expected to 'buy' their nominations by making contributions to the party, to be paid personally to the leader, Kumari Mayawati. The process begins with potential candidates approaching the district coordinators and mandal (covering 2–3 districts) coordinators, who are party functionaries, with initial payments for sending their names up to Mayawati. They then have to make direct payments to be considered for the nomination. In addition to money totalling anywhere between Rs. 5 million and tens of millions to be paid for a nomination in various ways including in purchase of campaign materials, as in the case of the SP caste balancing is a factor, and over and beyond this there was an attempt in 2009, beginning earlier in the UP assembly election of 2007 which the BSP won, at 'social engineering', that is, at constructing a majority by giving nominations to persons from a wide range of castes, principally, upper castes, outside the party's usual social base of the Scheduled Castes.

There were some attempts before 2007 to forge a broader caste base for the BSP. Kanchan Chandra is of the view that the BSP has always attempted to forge a broad social coalition and has attempted to reach out to the upper and backward castes since the early nineties. This was done at first by building an alliance with the SP, BJP and Congress, and later by appointing upper-caste office bearers and nominating a large number of upper-caste candidates. According to Chandra, though the groups included in the BSP's new social base might be same as the Congress, their terms of mobilisation are very different (Chandra, 2007). While the ticket distribution by the Congress party gave due consideration to caste identity, it did so quietly and kept it insulated from the identification of issues. Groups were targeted through patronage but rarely through the rhetoric of identity. In contrast, the BSP has done this through an open appeal to ethnic identity. While earlier, for the BSP, appeal to ethnic identity was restricted to Dalits, it now included its new social allies.[20]

Scholars like Sudha Pai have argued that failure of the BSP–SP alliance led to a change of strategy by the BSP in which it made a transition from a radical movement to a Dalit-based party with a primary aim of capturing state power (Pai, 2009). In order to realise this goal, the party followed a strategy of widening its social-base by giving tickets to non-Dalits and forming a coalition with the BJP. Though the party managed to broaden its base and increased its tally, by the latter 1990s, the BSP had hit a ceiling and was in need of a new strategy to fulfil its goal of forming a government on its own. Pai argues that the BSP did so by keeping its Dalit base intact and seeking support from twice-born castes – Thakurs, Vaishya and notably Brahmins. It also avoided bickering over ticket distribution by not contesting a number of by-elections and boycotting local elections in 2006.[21]

Sohini Guha argues that a committed Dalit poor in UP is willing to vote for a BSP candidate irrespective of caste as she has faith in the BSP's overall commitment to their long-term socio-economic empowerment (Guha, 2007). This is what makes them forgo patronage benefits in the short run and facilitates the BSP's nomination of candidates from Upper Castes, OBC's and Muslims, groups that only vote for the BSP when the party fields a candidate from their own community. For her the BSP has been able to attract multiple social groups within its fold by promising and delivering patronage based benefits to its non-'bahujan' voters while providing programmatic benefits to its core supporters.[22]

Christophe Jaffrelot carries forward the argument and states that the Dalits tend to vote for the BSP for both substantive and symbolic reasons. According to him, it will be wrong to classify the BSP as a Dalit party only on the basis of the social profile of its candidates. This is so because a large number of BSP candidates are from groups other than Dalits. Dalits vote for the BSP because its leader is a Dalit, but more so because, irrespective of the caste or social profile of its candidates, its agenda is 'Pro-Dalit' (Jaffrelot, 2012).

From the literature, we can conclude that while there have been earlier attempts at 'social engineering' by the BSP, the 2007 election was the first major electoral success of the strategy and it was based on a calculated nomination strategy that took caste into account. Overall, the BSP is the most centralised and top-down of all the parties we look at, with Mayawati tightly controlling the process and intervening at any stage (see note 19).

Is there any general principle discernible in candidate selection across parties? The general criterion is 'merit', a holistic judgement on current victory prospects taking all factors into consideration, and the general rule of thumb is 'sitting-getting', in Indian political parlance, that is, incumbents get the nomination unless they are perceived to be no longer likely to win, for example, if there are potentially damaging corruption or criminal charges against them, although this does not by itself rule them out. Caste and (religious) community considerations are very important factors and are taken into consideration in assessing current victory prospects but there is no mechanical formula based on caste/community. Past performance, and hence, 'sitting-getting' is also not an inviolable principle.

A further complication affecting renomination is the fact of coalition politics in which parties share seats in order to pool votes at the state level against the principal rival party or coalition. This entails not contesting in constituencies allotted by coalition agreement to one's coalition partner, and if such a seat happens to have been contested the last time by one's party, renomination of the candidate, even an incumbent, cannot happen. However, within both the major alliances, the Congress-led United Progressive Alliance (UPA) and the BJP-led National Democratic Alliance, both the number of seats allotted to each partner in a state and the particular seats allotted, tend to be fairly rigid and allow of adjustments only within a narrow band.[23] There is no smoothly adjusting electoral market mechanism whereby a party can claim greater support on the basis of intervening assembly elections, for example, which leads to surrender of seats by a partner party. The only way to be able to contest significantly more seats is to break the coalition deal and go it alone, for example, as the Congress did in UP and Bihar in 2009. Therefore, while coalitional seat-sharing has some effect on renomination, it has only a rather limited effect.

Three hypotheses on party type, internal processes and nominations

Before we present the Indian nomination data, we construct three hypotheses from our reviews of the comparative and Indian literature on party nominations, and from the interview material, against which we will later examine the nomination patterns.

We will examine the following three hypotheses:

(1) Early/snap elections, as in 1980, 1991, 1998 and 1999, or emergency/ crisis elections as after Indira Gandhi's assassination in 1984, will result in high rate of renomination of incumbents and nominees because the MPs will not have finished even the major part of their terms and it will be more difficult for party leaderships, particularly if relatively new, to deny them nominations.
(2) Ethnic (that is, caste- and/or religion-based) and ideological parties have a more loyal and committed, even if smaller, voter base, and therefore the leaderships of such parties have more leeway to drop incumbents without losing the support of their voters since such support is not for particular candidates representing particular interest groups. Catchall parties, on the other hand, depend on group represen- tation and patronage for retaining their support base and hence should find it more difficult to drop incumbents.
(3) Parties with institutionalised internal processes for nomination starting from below will find it more difficult to drop incumbents compared to parties with centralised, top-down selection processes. In the Indian context, parties that are most centralised by Bille's six-fold classification of centralised control of nominations, such as the BSP and SP, will find it easier to drop incumbents than more institutionalised parties which are at the second level of centralisation like the Congress, BJP and CPI (M).

The nomination data on five major Indian parties

We consider the nomination of candidates for five major parties, the BJP, CPI (M), BSP and SP, for the part of their existence that is relevant to such analysis, that is, when they are significant national parties or leading parties in their states. For the Congress, we consider the nomination data for the entire post- independence period, focusing on renominations in each election compared to the previous election from the second general elections of 1957 until 2009; for the BJP, from the time of its emergence as a significant party, that is renominations from 1991 to 2009, and likewise for the CPI (M) which emerged as a regionally significant party from 1967, that is renominations from 1971 onwards. We consider CPI (M) only in its three stronghold states of West Bengal, Kerala and Tripura. For the SP and the BSP, we focus on the 2004 and 2009 elections only for the state of UP, for the period of their emergence as the two leading parties in the largest state, UP, and with signifi- cance in national politics – their external support to the UPA I government was crucial in not making the Left Front's support pivotal for its survival.

A point to note is that there was a delimitation of constituencies before the 2009 election. We consider, for the purposes of this paper, the same constituency to mean constituencies which retained the same name. This is a proxy for the boundaries having changed only a little. In India, 101 constituencies (19 per cent of constituencies) changed from 2004 to 2009 according to our definition of name change, that is, 101 constituencies (19 per cent of constituencies) in 2009 were not matched by any constituency of the same name in 2004. For the state of UP, 11 out of 80 constituencies underwent a name change. As part of the delimitation process a small percentage of constituencies were unreserved or reserved for Scheduled Castes and Scheduled Tribes, which would have additionally affected renominations.

Congress

Taking the entire 1957–2009 period for the Congress (Table 1), the party has nominated 38 per cent (2611/6801) of its candidates of the preceding election. Looking at the data for the Congress from 1957–2009, we also conclude that the party has renominated a majority of its incumbents, hence largely adhering to the 'sitting-getting' thumb rule, the total percentage of winners getting renominated being 57 per cent (2079/3680). However, what needs to be explained is the substantial 43 per cent of incumbents who were not renominated. This is too high to be explained by the triple factors of death, defection to another party, or retirement from politics from one election to the next. It clearly shows that the party nomination process drops incumbents and brings in fresh blood to a considerable extent.

In 1989, Congress was faced with a united opposition and a house divided, Rajiv Gandhi being weakened by the Bofors arms imports payoffs allegations. Hence, the party repeated 68 per cent of its incumbents. From then on the party chose to repeat 65 per cent, 65 per cent, 70 per cent and 77 per cent of the winning candidates in 1991, 1996, 1998 and 1999, respectively, climbing to historical highs by the end of the 1990s. This could be because of the two elections taking place in quick succession (1991 after 1989, and 1999 and 1998 soon after 1996) and the party going ahead with the incumbents rather than scouting around for fresh faces and risking dissidence within its ranks in the wake of three lost elections (1989, 1996 and 1998) which saw the party plunge to historic lows. In 2004 and 2009, the party repeated 64 per cent (73/114) and 71 per cent (103/145) of incumbents, respectively.

Comparing the data for the Congress between the time period 1952–2009 and 1991–2009 (Table 2) we see no significant difference in the percentage of contestants of previous elections getting renominated. What is interesting is the rise in number of incumbents getting renominated. For the two time periods

Table 1. INC (1957–2009).

Indicators	1957	1962	1967	1971	1977	1980	1984	1989	1991	1996	1998	1999	2004	2009	Grand total
Renominated (by same party)/ nominated in previous election	174/ 479 (36%)	178/ 490 (36%?)	144/ 488 (30%)	149/ 516 (29%)	221/ 441 (50%)	155/ 492 (32%)	218/ 492 (44%)	302/ 517 (58%)	253/ 510 (50%)	189/ 500 (38%)	158/ 529 (30%)	184/ 477 (39%)	137/ 453 (30%)	149/ 417 (36%)	2611/ 6801 (38%)
Renominated (by same party) in same constituency/nominated in previous election	82/ 479 (17%)	108/ 490 (22%)	117/ 488 (24%)	142/ 516 (28%)	186/ 441 (42%)	139/ 492 (28%)	209/ 492 (42%)	297/ 517 (57%)	241/ 510 (47%)	181/ 500 (36%)	145/ 529 (27%)	164/ 477 (34%)	127/ 453 (28%)	112/ 417 (27%)	2250/ 6801 (33%)
Renominated (by same party) in different constituency/ nominated in previous election	92/ 479 (19%)	70/490 (14%)	27/ 488 (6%)	7/516 (1%)	35/ 441 (8%)	16/ 492 (3%)	9/492 (2%)	5/517 (1%)	12/ 510 (2%)	8/500 (2%)	13/ 529 (3%)	20/ 477 (4%)	10/ 453 (2%)	37/ 417 (9%)	361/ 6801 (5%)
Renominated by different party/ nominated in previous election	7/479 (2%)	10/490 (2%)	12/ 488 (3%)	33/ 516 (6%)	13/ 441 (3%)	57/ 492 (12%)	11/ 492 (2%)	10/ 517 (2%)	11/ 510 (2%)	34/ 500 (7%)	25/ 529 (5%)	19/ 477 (4%)	14/ 453 (3%)	5/417 (1%)	256/ 6801 (4%)
Incumbents renominated/winners in previous election	168/ 364 (46%)	163/ 371 (44%)	129/ 361 (36%)	137/ 283 (48%)	215/ 352 (61%)	76/ 154 (49%)	208/ 353 (59%)	282/ 414 (68%)	159/ 244 (65%)	159/ 244 (65%)	98/ 140 (70%)	109/ 141 (77%)	73/ 114 (64%)	103/ 145 (71%)	2079/ 3680 (57%)
Incumbents renominated in same constituency/winners in previous election	80/ 364 (22%)	102/ 371 (28%)	107/ 361 (30%)	132/ 283 (47%)	183/ 352 (53%)	68/ 154 (44%)	202/ 353 (58%)	278/ 414 (67%)	159/ 244 (65%)	156/ 244 (64%)	96/ 140 (69%)	102/ 141 (72%)	68/ 114 (60%)	81/ 145 (56%)	1814/ 3680 (49%)
Renominated (by same party)/ contestants in the current election	174/ 490 (36%)	178/ 488 (37%)	144/ 516 (28%)	149/ 441 (34%)	221/ 492 (45%)	155/ 492 (32%)	218/ 510 (42%)	302/ 510 (59%)	253/ 500 (51%)	189/ 529 (36%)	158/ 477 (33%)	184/ 453 (41%)	137/ 417 (33%)	149/ 440 (34%)	2611/ 6762 (39%)

Renominated (by same party) in same constituency/contestants in the current election	82/ 490 (17%)	108/ 488 (22%)	117/ 516 (23%)	142/ 441 (32%)	186/ 492 (38%)	139/ 492 (28%)	209/ 517 (40%)	297/ 510 (58%)	241/ 500 (48%)	181/ 529 (34%)	145/ 477 (30%)	164/ 453 (36%)	127/ 417 (31%)	112/ 440 (25%)	2250/ 6762 (33%)
Incumbents renominated/ contestants in the current election	168/ 490 (34%)	163/ 488 (33%)	129/ 516 (25%)	137/ 441 (31%)	215/ 492 (44%)	76/ 492 (15%)	208/ 517 (40%)	282/ 510 (55%)	159/ 500 (32%)	159/ 529 (30%)	98/ 477 (21%)	109/ 453 (24%)	73/ 417 (18%)	103/ 440 (23%)	2079/ 6762 (31%)
Incumbents renominated in same constituency/contestants in the current election	80/ 490 (17%)	102/ 488 (21%)	107/ 516 (21%)	132/ 441 (30%)	183/ 492 (37%)	68/ 492 (14%)	202/ 517 (39%)	278/ 510 (55%)	159/ 500 (32%)	156/ 529 (29%)	96/ 477 (20%)	102/ 453 (23%)	68/ 417 (16%)	81/ 440 (18%)	1814/ 6752 (27%)

Source: ECI Statistical Reports on General Elections 1952–2009.

Table 2.   INC aggregate 1952–2009 and 1991–2009.

Indicators	INC (1957–2009)	INC (1991–2009)
Renominated (by same party)/nominated in previous election	2611/6801 (38%)	1070/2886 (37%)
Renominated (by same party) in same constituency/nominated in previous election	2250/6801 (33%)	970/2886 (34%)
Renominated (by same party) in different constituency/nominated in previous election	361/6801 (5%)	100/2886 (4%)
Renominated by different party/nominated in previous election	256/6801 (4%)	108/2886 (4%)
Incumbents renominated/winners in previous election	2079/3680 (57%)	701/1028 (68%)
Incumbents renominated in same constituency/winners in previous election	1814/3680 (49%)	662/1028 (64%)
Renominated (by same party)/contestants in the current election	2611/6762 (39%)	1070/2816 (38%)
Renominated (by same party) in same constituency/contestants in the current election	2250/6762 (33%)	970/2816 (34%)
Incumbents renominated/contestants in the current election	2079/6762 (31%)	701/2816 (25%)
Incumbents renominated in same constituency/contestants in the current election	1814/6762 (27%)	662/2816 (24%)

Source: ECI Statistical Reports on General Elections 1952–2009.

1957–2009 and 1991–2009, the respective percentages are 57 per cent and 68 per cent. What perhaps explains this is the decline in Congress fortunes in the early 1990s and the party finding it increasingly difficult to win elections and therefore relying on the incumbents.

Bharatiya Janata Party

The BJP renominated a substantial minority (43 per cent) of its candidates and a great majority (76 per cent) of its incumbents in elections from 1991 to 2009. In the elections held in 1991, 1998 and 1999, in particular, the BJP renominated a large number of incumbents (Table 3). Elections in 1991, 1998 and 1999 were close elections with very little gap between the successive elections in 1989 and 1991, 1996 and 1998, 1998 and 1999. Hence, it would have made sense for the party to avoid new faces and internal dissidence and continue with the incumbents. Current victory prospects of candidates were important criteria here and the underlying principle was 'sitting-getting'. However, what needs to be

94

Table 3. BJP (1991–2009).

Indicators	1991	1996	1998	1999	2004	2009	Grand total
Renominated (by same party)/nominated in previous election	111/225 (49%)	144/468 (31%)	193/471 (41%)	223/388 (58%)	172/339 (47%)	125/364 (34%)	968/2255 (43%)
Renominated (by same party) in same constituency/nominated in previous election	96/225 (43%)	136/468 (28%)	188/471 (40%)	212/388 (55%)	168/339 (50%)	86/364 (24%)	886/2255 (39%)
Renominated (by same party) in different constituency/nominated in previous election	5/225 (2%)	8/468 (2%)	5/471 (1%)	11/388 (3%)	4/339 (1%)	39/364 (11%)	72/2255 (3%)
Renominated by different party/nominated in previous election	2/225 (1%)	3/468 (1%)	6/471 (1%)	4/388 (1%)	11/339 (3%)	13/364 (4%)	39/2255 (2%)
Renominated in the by same party (winning)/nominated in previous election	68/85 (80%)	76/120 (63%)	143/161 (89%)	160/182 (88%)	139/182 (76%)	69/138 (50%)	655/868 (76%)
Renominated by same party in same constituency (winning)/nominated in previous election	66/85 (78%)	75/120 (63%)	141/161 (88%)	153/182 (84%)	135/182 (74%)	52/138 (38%)	622/868 (72%)
Renominated (by same party)/contestants in the current election	111/468 (24%)	144/471 (31%)	193/388 (50%)	223/339 (66%)	172/364 (47%)	125/433 (29%)	968/2463 (39%)
Renominated (by same party) in same constituency/contestants in the current election	96/468 (21%)	136/471 (29%)	188/388 (49%)	212/339 (63%)	168/364 (46%)	86/433 (20%)	886//2463 (36%)
Renominated in the by same party (winning)/contestants in the current election	68/468 (15%)	76/471 (16%)	143/388 (37%)	160/339 (47%)	139/364 (38%)	69/433 (16%)	655/2463 (27%)
Renominated by same party in same constituency (winning)/contestants in the current election	66/468 (14%)	75/471 (16%)	141/388 (36%)	153/339 (45%)	135/364 (37%)	52/433 (12%)	622/2463 (25%)

Source: ECI Statistical Reports on General Elections 1991–2009.

explained is the 24 per cent of incumbents who were not renominated over 1991–2009. This figure is too high to be explained by death, defection or retirement from active politics from election to election. The BJP like the Congress drops incumbents and brings in fresh faces. A point to be kept in mind is that after 1996 the BJP was attempting to expand beyond its traditional upper-caste and urban voter base through what it called social engineering which implied bringing in nominees from newer segments of society.

Communist Party of India (Marxist)

Looking at the data for CPI (M) for the period 1971–2009 (Table 4), we discern that the CPI (M) is the only party which has consistently renominated a very high percentage of former candidates across parties, higher than the other parties. The party renominated a majority of its former candidates, 56 per cent (252/455), unlike the Congress and BJP, in the elections held from 1971. There has been only one instance, in 2004, where a former CPI (M) candidate has defected and contested on a different party ticket. The CPI (M) has renominated a large majority, 73 per cent (221/305), of its incumbents since 1971. These findings probably reflect the fact that the party has contested seats mostly from its three stronghold states of West Bengal, Kerala and Tripura, where it has either been in power for very long periods (West Bengal, 1977–2011, Tripura, 1993–2013) or alternated in power every term (Kerala since 1982). It would seem to make sense, in this context, to allow politicians the continuity to build political careers and also become the identifiable face of the party for the voters in the constituency.

Comparative picture for the Congress, BJP and CPI (M) in the post-Congress hegemony phase, 1991–2009

The 1989 election marked the end of Congress hegemony in that the Congress plurality of votes no longer converted to a majority of seats, and since then all elections have resulted in hung parliaments and minority governments or coalition governments. Hence, it is useful to compare the three major national parties, Congress, BJP and CPI (M) on renomination of candidates and incumbents since the 1991 election, the first after the 1989 watershed. We focus on the renomination of former candidates and of incumbents to see if any patterns are discernible and then try to explain those patterns. The patterns that emerge are as follows (from Table 5) for the Congress, BJP and CPI (M) for the period 1991–2009.

Of the candidates nominated between the years 1991–2009, only the CPI (M) renominated a majority (59 per cent or 154/262) of its former candidates;

Table 4. CPI (M) (1971–2009).

Indicators	1971	1977	1980	1984	1989	1991	1996	1998	1999	2004	2009	Grand total
Renominated (by same party)/nominated in previous election	16/27 (59%)	19/51 (37%)	16/31 (52%)	29/41 (71%)	18/43 (42%)	29/43 (67%)	24/41 (59%)	25/42 (60%)	28/43 (65%)	27/46 (59%)	21/47 (45%)	252/455 (56%)
Renominated (by same party) in same constituency/nominated in previous election	14/27 (52%)	16/51 (31%)	13/31 (42%)	26/41 (63%)	17/43 (40%)	28/43 (65%)	22/41 (54%)	25/42 (60%)	28/43 (65%)	27/46 (59%)	19/47 (40%)	235/455 (52%)
Renominated (by same party) in different constituency/nominated in previous election	2/27 (7%)	3/51 (6%)	1/31 (3%)	3/41 (7%)	1/43 (2%)	0/43 (0%)	0/41 (0%)	0/42 (0%)	0/43 (0%)	0/46 (0%)	2/47 (4%)	12/455 (3%)
Renominated by different Party/nominated in previous election	0/27 (0%)	0/51 (0%)	0/31 (0%)	0/41 (0%)	0/43 (0%)	0/43 (0%)	0/41 (0%)	0/42 (0%)	0/43 (0%)	1/46 (2%)	0/47 (0%)	1/455 (2%)
Incumbents renominated/winners in previous election	9/14 (64%)	16/24 (67%)	14/17 (82%)	27/37 (73%)	15/21 (71%)	24/29 (83%)	22/30 (73%)	23/30 (77%)	27/32 (84%)	25/31 (81%)	21/40 (53%)	221/305 (73%)
Incumbents renominated in same constituency/winners in previous election	7/14 (50%)	13/24 (54%)	12/17 (71%)	24/37 (65%)	0/21 (0)	24/29 (83%)	22/30 (73%)	23/30 (77%)	27/32 (84%)	25/31 (81%)	19/40 (48%)	196/305 (64%)
Renominated (by same party)/contestants in the current election	16/51 (31%)	19/31 (61%)	16/41 (39%)	29/43 (67%)	18/43 (42%)	29/41 (71%)	24/42 (57%)	25/43 (58%)	28/46 (61%)	27/47 (57%)	21/48 (44%)	252/476 (53%)

(Continued)

Table 4. Continued.

Indicators	1971	1977	1980	1984	1989	1991	1996	1998	1999	2004	2009	Grand total
Renominated (by same party) in same constituency/contestants in the current election	14/51 (28%)	16/31 (52%)	13/41 (32%)	26/43 (61%)	17/43 (40%)	28/41 (68%)	22/42 (52%)	25/43 (58%)	28/46 (61%)	27/47 (57%)	19/48 (40%)	235/ 476 (49%)
Incumbents renominated/ contestants in the current election	9/51 (18%)	16/31 (52%)	14/41 (34%)	27/43 (63%)	15/43 (35%)	24/41 (59%)	22/42 (52%)	23/43 (53%)	27/46 (59%)	25/47 (53%)	21/48 (44%)	221/ 476 (46%)
Incumbents renominated in same constituency/ contestants in the current election	7/51 (14%)	13/31 (42%)	12/41 (29%)	24/43 (56%)	0/43 (0%)	24/41 (59%)	22/42 (52%)	23/43 (53%)	27/46 (59%)	25/47 (53%)	19/48 (40%)	196/ 476 (41%)

Source: ECI Statistical Reports on General Elections 1967–2009.

Table 5.   Overall record for the Congress, BJP and CPI (M), 1991–2009.

Indicators	INC	BJP	CPM
Renominated (by same party)/ nominated in previous election	1070/2886 (37%)	968/2255 (43%)	154/262 (59%)
Renominated (by same party) in same constituency/ nominated in previous election	970/2886 (34%)	886/2255 (39%)	149/262 (57%)
Renominated (by same party) in different constituency/ nominated in previous election	100/2886 (4%)	72/2255 (3%)	2/262 (1%)
Renominated by different Party/nominated in previous election	108/2886 (4%)	39/2255 (3%)	1/262 (0.4%)
Incumbents renominated/ winners in previous election	701/1028 (68%)	655/868 (76%)	142/292 (74%)
Incumbents renominated in same constituency/winners in previous election	662/1028 (64%)	622/868 (72%)	140/192 (73%)
Renominated (by same party)/ contestants in the current election	1070/2816 (38%)	968/2463 (39%)	154/267 (58%)
Renominated (by same party) in same constituency/ contestants in the current election	970/2816 (34%)	886/2463 (36%)	149/267 (56%)
Incumbents Renominated/ contestants in the current election	701/2816 (25%)	655/2463 (27%)	142/267 (53%)
Incumbents renominated in same constituency/ contestants in the current election	662/2816 (24%)	62/2463 (25%)	140/267 (52%)

Source: ECI Statistical Reports on General Elections 1989–2009.

the BJP 43 per cent (968/2255) and the Congress 37 per cent (1070/2886). The difference between the BJP and the Congress is marginal, primarily due to the decline in BJP fortunes in 2004 and 2009.

Analysing the fate of the incumbents between 1991 and 2009, and hence, the prevalence of the 'sitting-getting' thumb rule or otherwise, we find that all three parties renominated a majority of their incumbents. The BJP renominated 76 per cent (655/868) of its incumbents, the CPI (M) 74 per cent (142/192) and the Congress 68 per cent (701/1028).

Viewing the renominations across parties from the perspective of the percentage of renominees in the total number of candidates nominated in a given election, we get the following picture. With the exception of the CPI (M) in several elections, and a few elections for other parties (Congress in 1989, BJP in 1999), only a minority of candidates in any election were candidates in the previous election, a result which holds even more strongly for incumbents (rows 7 and 9 for candidates and incumbents, respectively, in the tables).

Comparative picture of the five parties over the last two elections, 2004 and 2009

Comparing the five major parties that we analyse in the paper in the 2004 and 2009 elections can potentially yield useful insights into party behaviour on nominations. Comparing Congress, BJP, CPI (M), SP and BSP for the years 2004 and 2009 (Tables 6 and 7 for the BSP and SP specifically, and Table 8 comparing all five parties) we discover the following patterns.

Table 6. BSP (2004–2009).

Indicators	2004	2009	Grand total
Renominated (by same party)/nominated in previous election	14/85 (17%)	13/80 (16%)	27/165 (16%)
Renominated (by same party) in same constituency/nominated in previous election	13/85 (15%)	8/80 (10%)	21/165 (13%)
Renominated (by same party) in different constituency/nominated in previous election	1/85 (1%)	5/80 (6%)	6/165 (4%)
Renominated by different Party/ nominated in previous election	3/85 (4%)	3/80 (4%)	6/165 (4%)
Incumbents renominated/winners in previous election	6/14 (43%)	9/19 (47%)	15/33 (46%)
Incumbents renominated in same constituency/winners in previous election	6/14 (43%)	4/19 (21%)	10/33 (30%)
Renominated (by same party)/ contestants in the current election	14/80 (18%)	13/80 (16%)	27/160 (17%)
Renominated (by same party) in same constituency/contestants in the current election	13/80 (16%)	8/80 (10%)	21/160 (13%)
Incumbents renominated/contestants in the current election	6/80 (8%)	9/80 (11%)	15/160 (9%)
Incumbents renominated in same constituency/contestants in the current election	6/80 (8%)	4/80 (5%)	10/160 (6%)

Source: ECI Statistical Reports on General Elections 1999–2009.

Table 7.   SP (2004–2009).

Indicators	2004	2009	Grand total
Renominated (by same party)/nominated in previous election	28/84 (33%)	18/68 (27%)	46/152 (30%)
Renominated (by same party) in same constituency/nominated in previous election	28/84 (33%)	10/68 (15%)	38/152 (25%)
Renominated (by same party) in different constituency/nominated in previous election	0/84 (0)	8/68 (12%)	8/152 (5%)
Renominated by different Party/ nominated in previous election	6/84 (7%)	10/68 (15%)	16/152 (11%)
Incumbents renominated/winners in previous election	15/26 (58%)	15/35 (43%)	30/61 (5%)
Incumbents renominated in same constituency/winners in previous election	15/26 (58%)	8/35 (23%)	23/61 (38%)
Renominated (by same party)/ contestants in the current election	28/68 (41%)	18/75 (24%)	46/143 (32%)
Renominated (by same party) in same constituency/contestants in the current election	28/68 (41%)	10/75 (13%)	38/143 (27%)
Incumbents renominated/contestants in the current election	15/68 (22%)	15/75 (20%)	30/143 (21%)
Incumbents renominated in same constituency/contestants in the current election	15/68 (22%)	8/75 (11%)	23/143 (16%)

Source: ECI Statistical Reports on General Elections 1999–2009.

The Congress party renominated only 33 per cent (286/870) of its former candidates. For the BJP the figure was 42 per cent (297/703), for the CPI (M) 52 per cent (48/93) and for the SP and BSP, a relatively low 30 per cent (46/152) and very low 16 per cent (26/165), respectively. Clearly, with the exception of the CPI (M), the 'sitting-getting' rule does not apply to candidates, least of all to the BSP and SP, in the last two elections.

Defections and nominations by other parties were much higher in the case of the SP in particular. As an indicator of politicians defecting to other parties before elections in search of nomination, 11 per cent (16/152) of SP candidates were nominated by some other party, and likewise, 4 per cent (6/165) BSP candidates, 2 per cent Congress (19/870), 3 per cent (24/703) BJP candidates and 1 per cent CPM (1/93). The SP's and BSP's former candidates for the years 2004 and 2009 nominated by other parties were in the SP's case, the BSP (11) and Congress (3), BJP (1), National Labour Party (1) and the BSP's case, the SP (2), Shiromani Akali Dal (1) and BJP (3).

Table 8. Aggregate for Congress, BJP, CPI (M), SP and BSP 2004–2009.

Indicators	INC	BJP	CPM	SP	BSP
Renominated (by same party)/nominated in previous election	286/870 (33%)	297/703 (42%)	48/93 (52%)	46/152 (30%)	27/165 (16%)
Renominated (by same party) in same constituency/ nominated in previous election	239/870 (28%)	254/703 (36%)	46/93 (50%)	38/152 (25%)	21/165 (13%)
Renominated (by same party) in different constituency/ nominated in previous election	47/870 (5%)	43/703 (6%)	2/93 (2%)	8/152 (5%)	6/165 (4%)
Renominated by different Party/nominated in previous election	19/870 (2%)	24/703 (3%)	1/93 (1%)	16/152 (11%)	6/165 (4%)
Incumbents renominated/winners in previous election	180/259 (70%)	208/320 (65%)	46/71 (65%)	30/61 (49%)	15/33 (46%)
Incumbents renominated in same constituency/winners in previous election	149/259 (58%)	187/320 (58%)	44/71 (62%)	23/61 (38%)	10/33 (30%)
Renominated (by same party)/contestants in the current election	286/857 (33%)	297/797 (37%)	48/95 (51%)	46/143 (32%)	27/160 (17%)
Renominated (by same party) in same constituency/ contestants in the current election	239/857 (28%)	254/797 (32%)	46/95 (48%)	38/143 (27%)	21/160 (13%)
Incumbents Renominated/contestants in the current election	180/857 (21%)	208/797 (26%)	46/95 (48%)	30/143 (21%)	15/160 (9%)
Incumbents renominated in same constituency/ contestants in the current election	149/857 (17%)	187/797 (24%)	4/95 (46%)	23/143 (16%)	10/160 (6%)

Renominations from the same constituencies and by the same parties?

Two other important findings from the all the tables above, taken together, are as follows.

All parties, when they renominate either candidates or incumbents, tend to renominate them overwhelmingly from the same constituency (rows 2, 3 and 5 of the tables contain information on this). The only exception seems to be 2009 because the delimitation of constituencies, mentioned earlier, necessitated a certain degree of renomination from new constituencies, that is, those whose names were changed. Likewise, only a small percentage of politicians defected to and obtained nominations from other parties (row 4 of tables).

Renomination of former candidates and incumbents

In conclusion, does the 'sitting-getting' rule of thumb for candidate and incumbent renomination apply in general?

For candidates, the pattern is as follows. Overall, with the exception of the CPI (M) which renominated 56 per cent of candidates since 1971, the 'sitting-getting' rule of thumb does not apply to any party except for occasional years when over 50 per cent were renominated (only 1989 for the Congress since 1957, and 1999 for the BJP since 1991). For the BSP the renomination rate was as low as 17 per cent. However, a substantial minority of candidates, on average, were renominated for the Congress (38 per cent), BJP (43 per cent) and SP (30 per cent) for the relevant periods, indicating that while the rule of thumb might be a starting point in the internal process, particularly for parties with institutionalised internal processes that start from the bottom, the actual criteria are the candidate's current victory prospects, and that applying this criterion the majority of losing former candidates tend to get eliminated at some stage in the internal processes described in the literature review.

For incumbents, the pattern is as follows. Overall, the Congress renominated 57 per cent of its incumbents over the 1957–2009 period, the post-Congress hegemony period of 1991–2009 seeing a rise to 68 per cent. In contrast, it renominated only a minority of incumbents in the first four elections in our dataset, 1957–1971, falling to a low of 36 per cent in 1967. After 1977, it fell below 50 per cent only in 1980 (49 per cent). The BJP renominated a high overall 76 per cent of incumbents in the 1991–2009 period, the CPI (M) 73 per cent over 1971–2009, the SP 49 per cent and the BSP 46 per cent over 2004–2009. Clearly, the 'sitting-getting' rule of thumb applies to nomination of incumbents, or at the very least is the starting point for the internal processes of parties, particularly for those that have relatively institutionalised selection processes that start from the bottom. However, since the percentage of incumbents dropped is also very considerable, and for the BSP and SP a majority, as was the case for the Congress up to 1971, the internal processes of parties also weed out incumbents for varying reasons including most probably, from interview material, because of incumbent's current victory prospects look poor, and to accommodate new faces sometimes representing new sections of the electorate the parties want to woo.

How do the three hypotheses fare?

How do these patterns relate to our three hypotheses on party type, early/snap elections, institutionalisation of selection processes, and nominations?

The hypothesis about early/snap elections tending towards higher repetition of incumbents finds the following degree of support. There were five early elections, 1971, 1980, 1991, 1998 and 1999. The hypothesis gets support as far as the BJP is concerned in that its renomination of incumbents in the last three early elections (80 per cent, 89 per cent and 88 per cent) is higher than its overall for the period (76 per cent). The hypothesis also gets support, although less strongly, for the CPI (M), whose renomination of incumbents in the last four early elections (82 per cent, 83 per cent, 77 per cent, 84 per cent) was above its overall for the period (73 per cent). The picture for the Congress is more mixed. The first two early elections were after the 1969 and 1978 splits in the Congress, which were also reflected in the lower than overall rate of renominations of candidates, as a significant number of former candidates and incumbents went to the breakaway factions or the Janata party, respectively, after 1969 and 1977 and 1978. The rates of renomination in 1991, 1998 and 1999 (65 per cent, 70 per cent and 77 per cent) were higher, however, than the overall 57 per cent for the entire period, and in the last two early elections higher than the 68 per cent overall figure for the post-1989 period. The postassassination election of 1984 also saw a higher renomination percentage than all but one election until then, perhaps a new leader (Rajiv Gandhi) coming to power less than two months before the election not having the time or inclination to make changes in what was to an extent a plebiscitary election. Conversely, we might add, a weakened leadership in 1989, due to the Bofors allegations, also might have been constrained to renominate a large percentage of incumbents.

The hypothesis of ethnic or ideological parties that can take their voter base more or less for granted and hence being more autonomous in dropping candidates, finds support in the relatively low renomination rates for both incumbents and candidates by the caste- and community-based BSP and SP compared to the Congress, BJP and CPI (M). However, if one looks at the ideological parties like the CPI (M) and BJP we find a relatively high rate of renomination of incumbents. For both, the relative stability of their core voter base has to be balanced against the more institutionalised process of selection that both parties have. Also, party leaderships, even if more autonomous due to assured core voters based on ideology and not on interest group representation and patronage, might not be inclined to drop their incumbents if they calculate that they are likely winners. For the BJP, we have to factor in the fact that of the six elections since 1991, three were early elections. Also, for the BJP we need to factor in the fact that in the post-1989 period, particularly after 1996, it was in the process of becoming a more catchall party that was consciously expanding beyond its traditional core voter base of the urban, upper castes and middle classes.

Constituency instability in nominations, and other-party acceptance of defectors, are fairly low, indicated by nominations by the same party from another constituency, and other-party nominations of a particular party's candidate, both being under 5 per cent for the overall period of most parties. However, the ideological parties, BJP and CPI (M), show the least degree of defection or shuffling of constituencies. The larger point that emerges about relationship of incumbents to constituents is that there is a fairly strong relationship that is reflected in the low rate of reshuffling of constituencies in renominations.

The hypothesis of parties with more institutionalised and bottom-up internal processes for candidate selection finding it more difficult to drop incumbents finds support. The Congress, BJP and especially CPI (M), have a significantly higher rate of renomination of incumbents, majorities in each case, compared to the BSP and SP which have dropped the majority of their incumbents in each of the two elections since they emerged as significant parties. However, this has also to be viewed against the background of party strategy in each of these elections. The BSP and SP have both attempted to broaden their base and incorporate new segments of the electorate in their stronghold state of UP over this period. This implies including members of such segments as candidates in at least some constituencies. In practice, this means reaching out to caste groups that would normally be outside the party's fold or making a catchall pitch that would attract votes. Outreach to new caste groups has been termed 'social engineering' by the BJP and has been attempted by the BSP and SP. Such outreach dictates accommodative politics to newly mobilised groups or groups traditionally with other parties, which means giving them representation in nominations, which could also imply dropping incumbents in a large percentage of constituencies to include candidates who represent groups that are being wooed. The leadership of ideological or ethnic parties could, if they were so inclined, deny nomination to incumbents and former candidates without losing the support of their core voters. The larger point that comes out from the data and interviews about the relationship of candidates to party hierarchies (leaderships) is that the major Indian parties are leadership-dominated and find it possible to drop the majority of candidates of the past election.

Conclusion

This paper is a first cut at the relationship between incumbency, renomination and internal processes in some major Indian parties. It is based on trying to relate the renomination data to three hypotheses related to election timing, party type and internal processes, based on the existing comparative and Indian party nomination literature and interview material. We have demonstrated support for the 'sitting-getting' rule for incumbent renomination, though not for candidate renomination, and predominant support for the two hypotheses on early elections, and on institutionalised internal selection processes, tending to result in higher rates of repetition of incumbents, while yielding mixed support for the hypothesis that ethnic and ideological parties with assured voter bases can more easily drop incumbents. More definitive conclusions will require detailed interview material on nomination strategy for each election, something that is not possible given that some of the key players are no more, and even those that are still with us will not be able to recall the precise details of much earlier elections, even of the 1990s. However, a potentially fruitful direction for additional work is state-level patterns of renomination for both Lok Sabha and assembly elections, particularly for the past decade for which key actors might remember procedural details.

Acknowledgements
The anonymous referees and Carole Spary are thanked by the authors for their comments. The anonymous interviewees, who include two Central ministers and a former Central minister and chief minister, and leading party functionaries of the different parties, involved in the nomination process are also thanked. The support of the Center for the Advanced Study of India, University of Pennsylvania, at whose conference in Philadelphia in February 2011 an earlier version of this paper was presented is acknowledged.

Notes
1. The categorisation below paraphrases Bille (2001).
2. See Aldrich (1995) and Epstein (1986) for the evolution of party organisation and primaries.
3. Ibid, pp. 367–368.
4. Ibid, p. 368.
5. For such trends across a range of countries, see Bille (2001), LeDuc (2001), Hopkin (2001) and Rahat and Hazan (2001).
6. See Kirchheimer (1966) for the catch-all party; Panebianco (1988) for the electoral–professional party; Katz and Mair, 'Changing Models . . . .', for the cartel party.
7. For a detailed typology of political parties, see Gunther and Diamond (2001); for a typology applied to India, see Sridharan and Varshney (2001).
8. Ibid, p. 835.
9. Palmer, ibid, p. 280, and Narain and Lal (1969).

10. Narain and Lal, ibid, 210–211.
11. There is very little work focusing on candidate renomination from 1970s onwards. Hence the jump from the candidate nomination process from the 1970s to the 2009 election.
12. Confidential interviews, 31 August 2009, and 25 December 2010, respectively, with two Central ministers involved in the Congress nomination process, and likewise, 14 June 2012, with a former Central minister and chief minister involved in the process.
13. Confidential interview, 4 January 2011, and follow-up telephonic interaction with key BJP party functionary dealing with assessment of potential candidates, evaluation of party electoral prospects and observer for the election nomination process in some states.
14. Interview, see note 20; this opinion of the polling firms was this functionary's opinion, which was critical of the party president.
15. Confidential interview, 4 January 2011, and follow-up telephonic interaction with key BJP party functionary dealing with assessment of potential candidates, evaluation of party electoral prospects and observer for the election nomination process in some states.
16. The account below is based on a detailed interview with Prakash Karat, General Secretary of the CPI (M), 29 October 2012.
17. When we speak of institutionalised processes, these need not necessarily be democratic. They can be controlled or guided processes. However, they are processes with stages nevertheless, and not arbitrary decisions or interventions by the top leadership.
18. Interview with an editor and newspaper proprietor who was a BSP candidate in 2009 and who was earlier an SP member of parliament and knows both parties very well from the inside as a long-time associate of their top leaders, 15 February 2011; he is now again with the SP.
19. Interview with an editor and newspaper proprietor who was a BSP candidate in 2009 and who was earlier an SP member of parliament and knows both parties very well from the inside as a long-time associate of their top leaders, 15 February 2011.
20. Ibid.
21. Ibid.
22. Ibid.
23. Interviews with party insiders in the Congress, BJP, SP and BSP involved in the nomination process including two current and two former Central ministers in both the Congress and the BJP, and with Prakash Karat, General Secretary of the CPI (M), 29 October 2012.

References

Aldrich, J. W. (1995). *Why parties? The origin and transformation of political parties in America*. Chicago: University of Chicago Press.
Bille, L. (2001). Democratizing a democratic procedure: Myth of reality? *Party Politics*, 7(3), 363–380, p. 367.
Chandra, K. (2007). *A benign rupture in UP politics*. Retrieved September 10, 2013, from http://www.indianexpress.com/news/a-benign-rupture-in-uttar-pradesh/30668/0

Cross, W. (2008). Democratic norms and party candidate selection: Taking contextual factors into account. *Party Politics*, *14*(5), 596–619.

Epstein, L. D. (1986). *Political parties in the American mold*. Madison: University of Wisconsin Press.

Guha, S. (2007). *Asymmetric representation' and the BSP in UP.* Retrieved September 10, 2013, from http://www.india-seminar.com/2007/571/571_sohini_guha.htm

Gunther, R., and Diamond, L. (2001). Types and functions of parties. In L. Diamond & R. Gunther (Eds.), *Political parties and democracy* (pp. 3–39). Baltimore: Johns Hopkins University Press.

Hopkin, J. (2001). Bringing the members back in? Democratizing candidate selection in Britain and Spain. *Party Politics*, *7*(3), 343–361.

Jaffrelot, C. (2012). *The caste based mosaic of Indian politics*. Retrieved September 10, 2013, from http://www.india-seminar.com/2012/633/633_christophe_jaffrelot.htm

Katz, R. S., & Mair, P. (1995). Changing models of party organization and party democracy. *Party Politics*, *1*(1), 5–28.

Kirchheimer, O. (1966). The transformation of Western European party systems. In J. La Palombara & M. Weiner (Eds.), *Political parties and political development* (pp. 177–200). Princeton: Princeton University Press.

Kochanek, S. A. (1968). *The Congress Party of India: The dynamics of one-party democracy* (pp. 267–298). Princeton: Princeton University Press.

Lijphart, A. (1977). *Democracy in plural societies: A comparative exploration*. New Haven: Yale University Press.

LeDuc, L. (2001). Democratizing party leadership selection. *Party Politics*, *7*(3), 323–341.

Narain, I., & Lal, M. (1969, March). Election politics in India: Notes toward an empirical theory. *Asian Survey*, *9*(3), 202–220, p. 209.

Pai, S. (2009). New social engineering agenda of the Bahujan Samaj party: Implications for state and national politics. *South Asia: Journal of South Asian Studies*, *32*(3), 338–353.

Palmer, N. D. (1967, May). India's fourth general election. *Asian Survey*, *7*(5), 275–291, p. 280.

Panebianco, A. (1988). *Political parties: Organization and power*. Cambridge: Cambridge University Press.

Rahat, G., & Hazan, R. Y. (2001). Candidate selection methods: An analytical framework. *Party Politics*, *7*(3), 297–322.

Roy, R. (1966, December 31). Selection of Congress candidates – I: The formal criteria. *Economic and Political Weekly*, *1*(20), 833–840.

Roy, R. (1967a, January 7). Selection of Congress candidates II: Pressures and counter-pressures. *Economic and Political Weekly*, *2*(1), 17–24.

Roy, R. (1967b, January 14). Selection of Congress candidates – III: Claims and counter-claims. *Economic and Political Weekly*, *2*(2), 61–76.

Sridharan, E., & Varshney, A. (2001). Toward moderate pluralism: Political parties in India. In L. Diamond & R. Gunther (Eds.), *Political parties and democracy* (pp. 206–237). Baltimore: Johns Hopkins University Press.

Women candidates and party nomination trends in India – evidence from the 2009 general election

Carole Spary

Department of Politics, University of York, Heslington, York, UK

More women MPs than ever before were elected to the lower house of the national parliament of India in the 2009 general election. Yet, the increase in women's presence in the Lok Sabha cannot necessarily be attributed to the increased willingness of political parties to field more women candidates, despite rhetorical party political support for increasing women's participation in political institutions. This article analyses party political nomination of women as candidates in the 2009 election, and finds significant variations in levels of nomination across parties and across India's states. The article also examines in detail the nomination of female candidates by the two largest political parties, the Indian National Congress party and the Bharatiya Janata Party, both of which support proposals for introducing reserved seats for women in national and state legislatures. The findings reject the proposition that parties only nominate women in unwinnable seats, but finds support for the proposition that parties are risk averse when it comes to nominating women, and that this can restrict the number of women nominated for election. The article concludes with some further questions for future research on gender and political recruitment in India.

Introduction

As a result of the 2009 general election in India, more women MPs than ever before were elected to the lower house of the Indian national parliament, the Lok Sabha (House of the People). The proportion of women MPs in the Lok Sabha surpassed a significant threshold of 10 per cent, with 58 women MPs elected out of a total of 543 elected MPs. In the two previous elections of 2004 and 1999, women MPs made up only 8 and 9 per cent, respectively. Thus, the 2009 outcome represented some modest, incremental gains for women's political participation in the national legislature. A consolidation followed shortly after with the election of the first female Speaker of the Lok Sabha, Meira Kumar. Despite these achievements, this article argues that there is still reason to be cautious about what the 2009 general election in India signified for women's political recruitment and their participation as candidates and elected MPs.[1] Women's political participation in India since the first general election in 1951 has increased only very gradually, in part due to a reluctance of political parties to nominate higher numbers of women to contest elections. Contrary to the rhetoric of political parties supporting efforts to increase women's political participation, in 2009 the proportion of women candidates nominated to contest the election did not increase from the previous general election in 2004. Furthermore, the nomination of women candidates continued to be significantly uneven across parties and across states. This article argues that the increase in women's presence in the Lok Sabha cannot necessarily be attributed to the increased willingness of political parties to field more women candidates.

The unwillingness of political parties to increase their nomination of women candidates is particularly significant given party support for legislative proposals to reserve a third of seats in national and sub-national legislatures for women. Since 1996, a third of all seats in local level councils (panchayats) have been reserved for women as a result of the 73rd and 74th Constitutional Amendments. Legislative attempts to reserve seats for women in the national parliament and sub-national assemblies have been controversial and ongoing for at least 17 years. At the time of writing, the legislation had been approved by the Rajya Sabha on 9 March 2010 and is due to be introduced in the Lok Sabha but so far has been stalled due to a lack of consensus among parties. The enduring resistance to nominating women as candidates in elections poses important questions for electoral politics in India, whether instrumental in terms of the electoral challenges likely to be faced by political parties in the event that the reservation bill is passed, or normative, concerning democratic legitimacy and justice as long as women's participation remains low.

This article explores the party political nomination of women candidates in the 2009 Indian general election. At the outset it is acknowledged that (i) women in electoral politics are not a homogeneous group; (ii) that there are different reasons for why women are nominated which may be unrelated to issues of gender-inclusiveness, including very experienced female politicians who have served their constituencies over long periods of time, and (iii) that the low presence of women in electoral politics in India, as elsewhere, is a product of various factors not all of which relate to party nomination practices. However, the analysis here focuses on *women* candidates, recognising that women are still a minority in electoral politics, while still recognising that *some* women, such as Dalit women, working class women and Muslim

110

women, are even less likely to be part of this minority. It also acknowledges the important role of political parties in acting as gatekeepers to participation in democratically elected representative institutions.

The article begins by outlining pertinent questions on gender and political recruitment, and highlights the lacunae of research on the Indian case (first section). It presents analysis of more aggregate-level data on women's candidacy in the 2009 general election (second section), before discussing aspects of women's nomination by the two largest political parties in India, the Bharatiya Janata Party (BJP) and the Indian National Congress (INC) party (third section). This includes a disaggregated analysis across India's states relative to their strength in each state, investigating whether these two parties nominate women primarily in safe seats or unwinnable (marginal) seats. The article concludes by discussing these findings and identifies further questions for research on gender, political recruitment, and elections in India.

Gender, representation, and party nominations

Since the 1990s, efforts to increase the political participation and presence of women within legislatures have gathered momentum with an increasing number of electoral systems employing legally mandated or voluntarily constituted affirmative action measures (Krook, 2009). Rationales offered for increasing the numbers of women in electoral politics vary but might include the following: (i) female representatives will represent 'women's interests' better than male representatives (e.g. 'substantive representation'); (ii) women will change the substance and style of politics, making it more cooperative and less corrupt; (iii) that women have a right to participate in democratic politics and should not be prevented from doing so as a result of discrimination (justice argument); (iv) that women's presence in political institutions will increase the democratic legitimacy of these institutions as a result of their increased representativeness of the population; and (v) that higher numbers of women in politics will have a symbolic, role model effect on potential aspirants, altering the notion that electoral politics is a male-dominated domain (Bacchi, 2006; Mansbridge, 1999; Phillips, 1991, 1993; Sawer, 2000).

Despite recent gains, it is well established in the literature on political recruitment that (a) political parties serve as gatekeepers to elected office via the distribution of candidate nominations for election, and (b) gender-based discrimination by party elites during the recruitment process is one among many factors that explains the low proportion of women among candidates contesting elections for political office (Caul, 1999; Norris & Lovenduski, 1995). The United Nation's Beijing Platform for Action in 1995 called on governments to 'encourage political parties to integrate women in elective and non-elective public positions in the same proportion and at the same levels as men'

(Beijing PfA Action 190 (b), cited in UN Women (n.d.)). It mandated political parties to 'consider examining party structures and procedures to remove all barriers that directly or indirectly discriminate against the participation of women'; 'consider developing initiatives that allow women to participate fully in all internal policy-making structures and appointive and electoral nominating processes'; and to take 'measures to ensure that women can participate in the leadership of political parties on an equal basis with men' (Beijing PfA Actions 191 (a), (b), and (c), respectively, in UN Women (n.d)).

Party political nomination practices in India, and their relationship to low levels of women's participation in electoral politics, remain an under-explored area of research. Most political science analyses of general elections in India which include a focus on gender tend to remain at the aggregate level of how many women contested and were elected, and the proportion of women candidates nominated by each party (Roy & Wallace, 2007; Singh Rana, 2006). Many of these studies focus on either party nomination trends at the all-India level only, or in one or two states, and rarely do any attempt to compare nomination trends across India's states. Analyses of the National Election Study which do discuss women and electoral politics often focus on the gaps between men and women's voting behaviour such as in party political support and attitudes towards party policies (Deshpande, 2004). Dagar's analysis of women candidates in the 2009 election provides some disaggregated analysis of women candidates in the 2009 election and is one of a few important exceptions (Dagar, 2011).

Few studies of political recruitment in India exist and even fewer explicitly focus on the recruitment of women.[2] Notable among these are Kochanek's study of political recruitment processes within the Congress party prior to the 1967 general election (Kochanek, 1967), Palmer's study of Congress recruitment practices for the 1972 state assembly elections, and a series of articles by Ramashray Roy, again on the Congress, in relation to recruitment practices for the 1957 and 1962 general elections (Roy, 1966, 1967a, 1967b, 1967c, 1967d). Katzenstein's (1978) study of the political prominence of women in India also acknowledges the role of the Congress party in selecting women for election. However, these are restricted to the Congress party, understandably given its dominance in the early post-Independence years, and are also somewhat dated. More recent studies of political recruitment in India are few and far between. One focus has been caste-based parties in north India and their shifting recruitment practices in the Bahujan Samaj Party (BSP) in relation to expanding their recruitment pool from among their traditional representational base, the Dalit community, to include the recruitment of higher caste candidates (Pai, 1999, cited in Jaffrelot, 2011). Perhaps understandably, political recruitment and selection is notoriously difficult to research, because it concerns the inner workings of parties behind closed doors

(Niven, 1998), although occasionally, disputes over nominations are made public, especially when unsuccessful applicants or party workers disagree with nomination decisions; for example, if parties select new entrants to contest elections instead of loyal party workers seeking their party's nomination.

Several studies exist on the profile of women in electoral politics in India, but not necessarily how they are recruited by parties and nominated to contest elections, and many of these studies are dated (Agnew, 1979; Kumari & Dubey, 1994; Kumari & Kidwai, 1998; Rai & Hoskyns, 1998; Wolkowitz, 1987). Mishra's more recent study of women legislators in Odisha is an exception, but he devotes only one chapter to the issue of political recruitment and focuses on the pre-legislative experience of women and their profiles as candidates, but does not pay much attention to party attitudes towards the nomination of women (Mishra, 2000). Manikandan and Wyatt's recent analysis of the Dravida Munnetra Kazhagham (DMK) considers *inter alia* the difficulties for women in developing political careers within the DMK, with a lack of access to important party posts (district secretaries) being one of several key impediments (Manikandan & Wyatt, 2013). Rai's recent analysis of the politics of access also contributes an insightful analysis of how female politicians negotiate access to political candidacy (Rai, 2012).

Women's limited participation in Indian democratic politics is well known, but what is missing among studies of India's elections is a meso-level analysis of party political nomination of women, within and across parties and states and in particular constituencies. This is the focus of this article. After a brief macrolevel analysis of parties' nomination of women in the Indian General Election of 2009, it focuses on the particular nomination patterns of India's two largest parties, the incumbent Indian National Congress party (hereafter Congress, or INC), and the largest party of opposition, the right-wing Hindu nationalist party, the BJP. These two parties are selected on the basis that as the two parties returning the largest number of women candidates to the Lok Sabha – two-thirds of all women MPs in 2009 – they play an important role in determining the total number of women members in parliament. Key questions include: (i) are parties consistent in their nomination of women across India's states?; (ii) is there a relationship between a party's anticipated likelihood of success and the nomination of women in a particular state?; and (iii) can one observe consistent differences in the nomination strategies of the two parties across states, or similarities between parties in particular states? In other words, does the political culture, history of women's nomination, and party competition present in any one state have a bearing on the nomination and election of women to the Lok Sabha from that state? The analysis draws on official quantitative data on the 2009 election and previous general elections and state Assembly elections in India, which is publicly available from the

Election Commission of India, as well as qualitative data on the profile of women politicians as candidates and elected MPs, available from parliamentary and party profile pages, and to a limited extent, press reports.

India's electoral system and the 2009 general election

The Lok Sabha, or lower house of the national parliament of India, is currently made up of 543 parliamentary constituencies, as well as two seats for members from the Anglo-Indian community, the latter being nominated by the President of India. The lower house is elected by simple plurality vote with single member constituencies. Parliamentary terms run for a maximum of five years and there is no limit on how many terms MPs can be re-elected. In accordance with Article 330 of the Constitution of India, a number of constituencies are reserved for members of Scheduled Caste (currently 84 seats) and Scheduled Tribe (currently 47 seats) communities in constituencies where these communities are relatively numerous, and only candidates from these communities can contest these seats. Thus, affirmative action in the shape of reservations either in electoral politics or in state employment and educational institutions is a familiar and established mechanism for ensuring the representation of (some but not all) marginalised communities in India (Randall, 2006).[3]

Prior to the 2009 general election, the incumbent government was headed by Congress along with a number of parties in coalition. In the last two decades, coalitions between political parties have become an important feature of electoral politics in India. Despite a long period of single party dominance by the INC party after Independence, India's party system has become increasingly fragmented since the 1980s with a number of regional and identity-based parties competing or collaborating with national parties, making electoral politics in India increasingly competitive and complex. The two most powerful coalitions in recent years have been the United Progressive Alliance (UPA), headed by the Congress and in government from 2004, and the National Democratic Alliance (NDA), headed by the BJP and in government from 1999 to 2004. Smaller parties, some of which are electorally dominant at the sub-national level, have become important coalition partners at the national level and play a significant role in deciding electoral strategies, in the post-election distribution of ministerial portfolios, and in maintaining coalition stability and legislative support for, or opposition to, government policy throughout the parliamentary term. Coalition politics have also been an enduring factor in the opposition to increasing legal quotas for women in the national parliament, with the anti-quota stance of some smaller state-based parties preventing the passage of national legislation.

The Indian general election of 2009 took place in five phases across the country, in which more than 8000 candidates contested, representing 368 parties in 543 constituencies, with more than 700 million Indian citizens eligible to vote, and more than 400 million votes recorded (ECI, n.d.).[4] In three states, assembly elections were also held alongside the general election. Key alliances included the incumbent Congress-led UPA (with some changes as a result of shifting relations between the government and their allies towards the end of the last parliament). The NDA, led by the BJP, also continued their alliance, albeit it in a slightly modified form. The final phase of voting ended on 13 May and having won a comfortable majority, the Congress party and its allies formed the new government.

Fifty-eight women were elected in 2009, making up nearly 11 per cent of all MPs in the lower house. Consistent with overall results, the highest number of women elected was from the Congress party, with 23 women elected in total, making up 11 per cent of all Congress MPs, and 40 per cent of all women MPs. Among the female Congress MPs elected were party chairperson Sonia Gandhi and a number of former ministers from the previous government. The proportion of women elected from the BJP party was the same (11 per cent), but totalled only 13, although this did include a few high-profile politicians such as Sushma Swaraj, Deputy Leader of the Opposition, and Sumitra Mahajan, elected for her 7th term in the Lok Sabha. Together, women MPs from the BJP and the INC made up nearly two-thirds of all female MPs in the new parliament. Notably, female members were proportionally more numerous in seats reserved for Scheduled Caste communities (12 out of 84 seats or more than 14 per cent, compared to 11 per cent overall), whereas women's election to constituencies reserved for Scheduled Tribe communities was more reflective of their strength in the house overall (5 out of 47 seats or 11 per cent). According to the constitutional provision for ensuring the representation of the minority Anglo-Indian community in parliament, the President nominated two MPs, one of whom was a woman, bringing the total number of women to 59 out of 545 MPs.

Party nominations and women's electoral success in 2009

Despite the celebratory mood surrounding the highest ever proportion of women MPs elected to parliament, and the reasonably high profile of a few women in parliament, the proportion of women candidates in the 2009 general election *did not substantially increase* from the previous general election in 2004. This runs contrary to the rhetorical commitment to increasing opportunities for women's political participation from a significant number of parties. Female candidates constituted only 6.9 per cent of all candidates, or 556 women out of a total of 8070 candidates. Compared to the general election in 2004, this represented a *large increase in numbers* (57 per cent increase from 355 women contesting in 2004), but actually a very *small decline in the proportion* of women candidates relative to the total number of candidates (from 7.0 to 6.9 per cent). In other words, while more women contested in 2009 compared to 2004, the total number of candidates was also larger, meaning *the proportion of women candidates stayed relatively the same*. Furthermore, the proportion of women running as independent candidates also increased in 2009 to 37 per cent of all women candidates, compared to 33 per cent in 2004. Therefore, the *proportion of women candidates who were nominated by political parties in 2009 actually declined* from 67 per cent in 2004 to 63 per cent in 2009 (the importance of party nominations is discussed further below).

For the national parties, the nomination of women candidates did not exceed much beyond 10 per cent (see Table 1). The BJP nominated 44 women, making up 10.2 per cent of all BJP candidates. Similarly the Congress party nominated 43 women, a slightly lower proportion of all Congress party candidates at 9.8 per cent. Parties of the Left did not achieve the same level – for the Communist Party of India (CPI) and Communist Party of India (Marxist) (CPM), women made up 7.1 and 7.3 per cent of their parties' total candidates, respectively. This is consistent with the unimpressive record of the Left parties in India on issues relating to women's inclusion in electoral politics, despite having a high-profile feminist advocate such as Brinda Karat of the CPM among the senior party leadership and a prominent party affiliated women's organisation, All-India Democratic Women's Association (Randall, 2006). The BSP, a party that champions the cause of India's most oppressed group in the caste hierarchy, the Dalits or Scheduled Castes, and is headed by a woman, Kumari Mayawati, nominated a lower proportion of women, 5 per cent of total candidates or 23 women. Both the performance of the Left parties and the BSP is significant as it contests the notion that parties which are built upon claims to social justice and equality will be more likely to nominate women candidates (Caul, 1999). It also raises interesting questions regarding inter-sectional identities and multi-layered processes of marginalisation, resulting in complex dynamics of political inclusion and exclusion. Compared with the previous general election in 2004, there was no clear pattern of improvement or decline across the national parties. The BJP and the CPI both put forward a slightly higher proportion of women candidates in 2009 (compared to 8 and 6 per cent, respectively, in 2004), whereas the Congress party, the CPM and the Nationalist Congress party, a UPA constituent, fielded proportionally fewer women candidates this time (11, 12 and 16 per cent in 2004). The BSP showed very little movement in its nomination of women candidates from 2004, which was also 5 per cent.

Most regional parties nominated a lower proportion of women than the two major national parties of the BJP and Congress, though this was not true for all parties, and varied across states. Even where the relative proportion of women

Table 1. Women as Lok Sabha candidates and Lok Sabha MPs state-wise in 2009.

State/UT	Seats	No. of women candidates	Women as % of candidates in state	No. of women elected	% women MPs
States					
Andhra Pradesh	42	39	6.9	5	12
Arunachal Pradesh	2	0	0.0	0	0
Assam	14	11	7.0	2	14
Bihar	40	46	6.8	4	10
Chhattisgarh	11	15	8.4	2	18
Goa	2	2	11.1	0	0
Gujarat	26	26	7.2	4	15
Haryana	10	14	6.7	2	20
Himachal Pradesh	4	1	3.2	0	0
J&K	6	6	7.4	0	0
Jharkhand	14	14	5.6	0	0
Karnataka	28	19	4.4	1	4
Kerala	20	15	6.9	0	0
Madhya Pradesh	29	29	6.8	6	21
Maharashtra	48	55	6.7	3	6
Manipur	2	3	18.8	0	0
Meghalaya	2	3	27.3	1	50
Mizoram	1	0	0.0	0	0
Nagaland	1	0	0.0	0	0
Odisha	21	9	5.7	0	0
Punjab	13	13	6.0	4	31
Rajasthan	25	31	9.0	3	12
Sikkim	1	0	0.0	0	0
Tamil Nadu	39	48	5.8	1	3
Tripura	2	1	5.3	0	0
Uttar Pradesh	80	100	7.3	12	15
Uttarakhand	5	7	9.2	0	0
West Bengal	42	29	7.9	7	17
UTs					
A&NI	1	1	9.1	0	0
Chandigarh	1	1	7.1	0	0
D&D	1	0	0.0	0	0
D&NH	1	0	0.0	0	0
Lakshadweep	1	0	0.0	0	0
NCT Delhi	7	18	11.3	1	14
Puducherry	1	0	0.0	0	0
Total	543	556	6.9	58	10.7

Source: Compiled by the author from data on *Election Commission of India* website (ECI, n.d.).

candidates was higher, the small total number of candidates of many of these parties meant that the number of women nominated was even smaller, for example, the Rashtriya Lok Dal, the Maharashtra Navnirman Sena, the Punjab-based Shiromani Akali Dal, and the Trinamul Congress in West Bengal. Some smaller parties had similar levels of support for women candidates despite different positions on women's reservation. Some parties nominated no women candidates, including the Biju Janata Dal in Odisha, and the Janata Dal (Secular). In contrast, a fledgling party called the United Women's Front nominated four female candidates and two male candidates in Delhi, Haryana, Bihar, and Andhra Pradesh. Suman Krishan Kant, the wife of the former Vice President of India, had established the party in 2007 with the aim of increasing the space for women in the political process (*The Hindu*, 2007).

Evidently, levels of party political nomination of women varied significantly among parties. Yet, women were more likely to run as party-nominated candidates than as independents compared to men, often due to financial and other resource-based obstacles to effective campaigning. While more than a third (37 per cent) of female candidates ran as independents in 2009, nearly half of all male candidates ran as independents (48 per cent). Very few independents are ever elected to parliament and more often than not they are forced to forfeit their security deposits due to the low number of votes they attain. As was the case in 2004, none of the 207 women independent candidates were elected in 2009 and only 9 of the 3623 men independents were elected compared to 5 in 2004 (although in terms of seats the latter represented 9 out of 543 or about 1.6 per cent). All women independent candidates and 99.3 per cent of men independent candidates forfeited their deposit in the 2004 Lok Sabha election.[5] The non-existent success rate among female independents (and low success rate among male independents) serves to re-emphasise the importance of party nomination for electoral success in the Indian context, and typically more so for women than men.

Party nominations of women candidates: across states and within parties

So far, data on women candidate nomination have been presented at the aggregate all-India level, and have focused on variations *across* parties but not *within* parties. However, a party's national average of nomination of women may be unrepresentative of substantial variations across states. For example, a national party nomination average of 10 per cent for the Congress party obscures the fact that in the states of Odisha or Jharkhand the Congress party did not nominate any women at all, yet in another state, Rajasthan, women made up 20 per cent of Congress party candidates. Here, I test the proposition that parties see women as high-risk candidates and, because parties are risk averse towards their strong-holds, parties will only nominate women to contest in unwinnable seats. This is explored at state and parliamentary constituency levels to determine the relation-ship between women candidate nominations and (i) the party's chance of success in a particular state (based on previous election success, notwithstanding an anti-incumbency effect) and (ii) the party's chance of success in particular constitu-encies (marginal seats, incumbency, and strongholds).

With regard to the first proposition, the party as a gatekeeper is a strong determining factor as to the number of women nominated to contest elections (discussed earlier). Parties are risk averse when it comes to distributing nomi-nations and see (most) women candidates as high risk. They will therefore be reluctant to nominate women, where political contests are tight or where they do not have a strong electoral presence.[6] This implies that 'winnability' has a specifically gendered component – women, by virtue of their sex, are seen as less likely to win elections, and as a result they are less likely to be nominated. Thus, parties will select women only where the party is popular and where they expect to do well, and at the same time, where they are contesting a large number of seats and so have a larger number of nominations to distribute.

With regard to the second proposition, either internal party pressure from the national leadership, internal advocacy for including more women, or exter-nal public pressure to nominate more women candidates might compel parties to nominate a larger proportion of women candidates. If women are deemed less likely to win, parties will not risk winnable seats by nominating women candidates, and so parties are inclined to nominate women only in hard-to-win or unwinnable constituencies. Any seats women do win will be a bonus to the party but will not jeopardise the party's success in more winnable seats. Unless attention is paid to *where* women are nominated, focusing just on levels of women's nomination may be misleading in terms of the probability of electoral success. Furthermore, election data show that often women rep-resent a larger proportion of elected MPs than their proportion as candidates, demonstrating that their success rate is higher than that of male candidates. This statistic has been employed to argue that not only can women win elec-tions, but that they often do better than male candidates. While there is some validity in this argument, it understates the extent to which risk-averse parties may only nominate the *strongest or most experienced* female candi-dates, and that they take more risks in nominating male candidates. This may explain why the smaller number of strong women candidates tends to do better than the larger pool of male candidates who are more varied in the like-lihood of their success. Therefore it is inaccurate – and potentially damaging to arguments advocating for increasing women's participation in electoral politics – to suggest that women are typically more capable than men at contesting elec-tions. It should be anticipated that if parties took the same risks with female candidates that they do with male candidates, that success rates would even out between men and women (assuming the absence of voter discrimination against male or female candidates).

Candidate nomination in two national parties: the Congress and the BJP

The analysis focuses on the two largest national parties, the Congress party (the largest party of the UPA and incumbent government prior to 2009) and the BJP (largest party of opposition and of the previously ruling NDA from 1999 to 2004). While this presents its own limitations in terms of representativeness across all parties, the advantage of comparing these two national parties is that they contest elections in a larger range of constituencies: all (Congress) or nearly all (BJP) of India's 35 states and Union Territories (UTs). Another significant advantage is that, as by far the largest two parties in parliament, one may reasonably assume that their nomination of women candidates will have an important bearing on the total number of women elected to parliament.

Another reason to focus on these two parties is to test claims regarding their self-declared support for increasing women's political participation in electoral politics. The 2009 election manifestoes of the Congress and the BJP were both explicit in their pledges towards female voters. The Congress party's manifesto pledged that if elected they would pass legislation reserving a third of seats in the national parliament and state assemblies during the next parliament effective for the following general election (INC, 2009, pp. 7, 14).[7] The BJP's 2009 election manifesto similarly promised to implement a 33 per cent reservation for women. Both manifestoes contained an array of special incentives and programmes targeted at women and girls' health, education, employment and training, and more effective implementation of existing legislation. Commitment to the women's reservation bill from the leadership of both parties was evidenced by its passage in the Rajya Sabha in March 2010, yet the Congress and BJP have different histories with regard to nominating women for election. In the last 30 years, the proportion of women nominated by the Congress for Lok Sabha elections has fluctuated between 6 and 11 per cent, peaking in 1999 (see Figure 1). In contrast, the BJP started low in the early 1980s and has risen fairly steadily to match Congress in the 2009 election.

Both parties have made efforts to increase the presence of women in internal organisational structures. Historically, in the 1950s and 1960s the Congress party operated a 15 per cent party quota for nominating women candidates in elections, although as research shows, this quota was never achieved due to internal party resistance and subsequently, at the level of party strategy (Katzenstein, 1978; Kochanek, 1967; Palmer, 1972; Roy, 1966). As Singer (2007, p. 22) argues, 'the growing realisation that women did not necessarily vote for women contributed to the cessation of that Congress policy'.

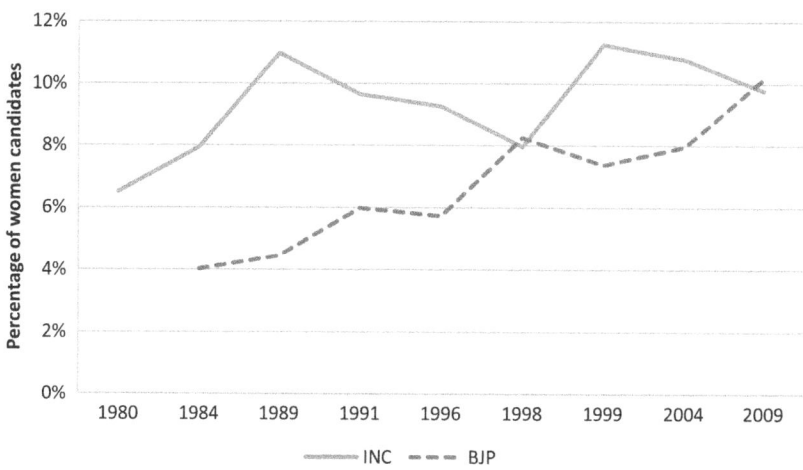

Figure 1. Women candidates in Lok Sabha elections as a percentage of total candidates, by party, 1980–2009.
Source: Data compiled by the author from various election reports of the Election Commission of India, available at www.eci.nic.in

However, the Congress party leadership's nomination and election of the first female President in 2007, their nomination and election of the first female Speaker in 2009, and their apparent efforts to pass the Reservation Bill demonstrate that Congress are again consciously seeking to demonstrate their commitment to women's political empowerment, even if only symbolically in the cases of these two high-profile posts.

Similar efforts have been made by the BJP to increase the presence of women within party structures. The National Election Study in 2004 showed that on average fewer women than men vote for the BJP (Deshpande, 2004). In June 2007, the BJP president Rajnath Singh announced that 33 per cent of party positions at all levels of the party would be allocated to women (*The Hindu*, 2007). Reportedly, this was to signal their commitment to women's political empowerment and to counter competitive pressures from the Congress in attracting women voters. Rajnath Singh was also reported to have said that the BJP was specifically trying to recruit women as new members into the party (*The Hindu*, 2007).

Pressure has also come from BJP female party members to increase the nomination of women candidates for elections. With the approaching assembly elections in the southern state of Karnataka in 2008, the president of the Karnataka branch of the BJP Mahila Morcha (women's wing), insisted that the party leadership allocate to women candidates at least one 'winnable' constituency in each district (*The Hindu*, 2008a). It was also reported that the party's women's wing president in each state would sit on the State Election Committee which selects candidates for the elections. While the BJP have professed support for the women's reservation bill, they have also expressed support for party quotas as an alternative to mandated legal quotas (*The Hindu*, 2008b). This would allow the party leadership to determine in which constituencies to nominate women, similar to the current system, except that, if consistent with similar party quota models outside India, parties would be penalised if they fail to achieve a mandated proportion of female candidates to total candidates. This format ostensibly provides increased opportunities but does not guarantee their election.

Nominating women: the Congress and BJP state-wise in 2009

Have efforts to increase women's presence in party structures had an effect on the nomination of women for contesting elections? Both parties fluctuated in their nomination of female candidates across states in 2009.[8] This section draws on election data prior to 2009 to assess whether nomination levels in 2009 are related to previous electoral success of the two parties across India's states in both national and sub-national level elections. It employs data from the 2004 General Election and the most recent Assembly election held in each state prior to the 2009 General Election.

The INC party

The Congress party contested the 2009 election in every State and UT of India, but nominated women in only 17 of 35 States and UTs (see Table 2). The Congress party average for nominating women in 2009 was 10 per cent, but varied across major states, reaching 21.4 per cent in West Bengal (3 out of 14 candidates) and 20 per cent each in Haryana (2 out of 10 candidates) and Rajasthan (5 out of 25 candidates). In most of the 18 states and UTs where Congress did not field any women, numbers of male Congress candidates were also small, but Congress also fielded no women candidates in the eastern states of Jharkhand and Odisha, where they put forward 9 and 21 male candidates, respectively.

Above average party nomination of women by Congress was recorded in the states of Andhra Pradesh, Bihar, Chhattisgarh, Haryana, Punjab, Rajasthan, and West Bengal. Women candidates contesting in the four large states of Andhra Pradesh, Bihar, Rajasthan, and Uttar Pradesh made up half of all women Congress candidates. While women's candidacy was rarer in small states and UTs, where there are often only one or two seats available to contest, in the two-seat state of Meghalaya, the daughter of a former Speaker of the Lok Sabha and incumbent MP Agatha Sangma was one of two Congress

Table 2. Nomination of women candidates in 2009 by INC, across states and UTs.

State/UT	No. of seats available	Seats contested by INC	Women (no.)	Men (no.)	Women as % of total candidates	2004, women candidates (%)	1999, women candidates (%)
Andhra Pradesh	42	42	5	37	11.9	14.7	9.5
Assam	14	13	1	12	7.7	7.1	7.1
Bihar	40	37	6	31	16.2	50.0 (2/4)	12.5
Chhattisgarh	11	11	2	9	18.2	9.1	n/a
Gujarat	26	26	2	24	7.7	4	7.7
Haryana	10	10	2	8	20	10	–
Karnataka	28	28	2	26	7.1	7.1	10.7
Kerala	20	17	1	16	5.9	17.6	5.9
Madhya Pradesh	29	28	2	26	7.1	13.8	10
Maharashtra	48	25	1	24	4	7.7	4.8
Meghalaya	2	2	1	1	50	–	–
Punjab	13	13	2	11	15.4	36.4	27.3
Rajasthan	25	25	5	20	20	4	16
Tamil Nadu	39	15	1	14	6.7	10	9.1
Uttar Pradesh	80	69	6	63	8.7	8.2	18.4
West Bengal	42	14	3	11	21.4	10.8	12.2
NCT of Delhi	7	7	1	6	14.3	14.3	14.3
Sub-total	476	382	43	339	11.3	–	–
Other states/UTs where no female candidates nominated by INC	67	58[a]	0	58	0	–	–
Total	543	440	43	397	9.8	10.8	11.3

[a]The INC did not nominate any women in the following states and UTs (no. of men nominated by INC/no. of seats available): Arunachal Pradesh (2/2), Goa (1/2), Himachal Pradesh (4/4), Jammu & Kashmir (3/6), Jharkhand (9/14), Manipur (2/2), Mizoram (1/1), Nagaland (1/1), Odisha (21/21), Sikkim (1/1), Tripura (2/2), Uttarakhand (5/5), Andaman & Nicobar Islands (1/1), Chandigarh (1/1), Dadra & Nagar Haveli (1/1), Daman & Diu (1/1), Lakshadweep (1/1), and Puducherry (1/1).
Source: Compiled by the author from data on *Election Commission of India* website (ECI, n.d.).

candidates in the state. A female Congress candidate was also nominated in one of Delhi's seven constituencies.

No clear trend can be observed when comparing Congress' nominations of women in 2009 based on their performance in the previous Lok Sabha election of 2004 and in the most recent Assembly election in each state (including both seats won and vote share). It appears that *Congress mostly nominated higher percentages of women in states where they were more likely to do well*, based on recent electoral performance, but there are some notable exceptions. The party's higher than average nomination of women in the major states of Andhra Pradesh (12 per cent), Haryana (20 per cent), and Rajasthan (20 per cent) was where the Congress party won the most recent Assembly elections in these states. Congress also recorded higher than average nomination of women in Chhattisgarh (18 per cent) and Punjab (15 per cent) where they did not win the last Assembly elections, even though they achieved a respectable 39 and 41 per cent of vote share in Chhattisgarh and Punjab, respectively, coming a close second to the BJP in the former and the Shiromani Akali Dal-BJP alliance in the latter. The Congress party also recorded a lower than average nomination in the western state of Gujarat where the BJP is electorally dominant, the latter winning nearly two-thirds of all seats in the last Assembly election in 2007 and achieving a 10 per cent vote share margin over the Congress. Similarly, the Congress party's nomination of women was lower in Madhya Pradesh, another stronghold of the BJP where the latter had won twice as many seats as Congress in the 2008 Assembly election. Finally, Congress nominated a lower than average proportion of women in the large northern state of Uttar Pradesh, where in 2007 it won only 22 of 393 seats contested and registered only 9 per cent vote share in the state, coming fourth in the state behind the BSP, the BJP, and the SP.

Contradictory to the more general picture was the party's higher than average nomination of women in Bihar (16 per cent) and West Bengal (21 per cent) where Congress had low vote shares in 2004 and where other political parties have been dominant in state-level government at least in recent years. Congress also recorded lower than average nomination of women in Assam, where the party won the last Assembly election in 2006 and was elected in 9 out of 14 Lok Sabha seats in 2004. The Congress also chose not to nominate any women in the state of Odisha, despite having gained a 40 per cent vote share in 2004.

It is not clear whether electoral alliances at the state level impact negatively on the proportion of women nominated by reducing the number of seats available to contest. The Congress registered lower than average nomination in Maharashtra (4 per cent) and Tamil Nadu (7 per cent) where state-based alliances were in operation with Congress as the minority partner. It is also not clear whether a conventionally lower presence of female candidates in any given state creates less of an obligation across all parties to nominate women. In the southern state of Kerala, numbers of women in state politics and representing the state in the national parliament have remained low (only 5 per cent of state legislators elected in 2006 were women), despite the state's reputation as having some of the highest levels of female achievement in literacy and health-related indicators in the country, which suggests forms of institutional exclusion specific to electoral politics. Yet Congress did badly in the 2004 Lok Sabha election, winning no seats despite achieving a 32 per cent share of the vote, and won only 24 of 140 seats in the 2006 Assembly election. This might also explain Congress reluctance to field women candidates – only 6 per cent in 2009.

The BJP

The national party average for the BJP in terms of nominating women was around 10 per cent. While the BJP contested in 32 of 35 states and UTs, it chose to nominate female candidates in around half of these (see Table 3). There was no contest for BJP women in 16 states and UTs, including mostly small states and UTs but, like Congress, in Jharkhand where the BJP fielded 12 male candidates. Percentages of female candidates also varied significantly across major states reaching 27.3 per cent in Chhattisgarh (3 out of 11 candidates) and 23.8 per cent in Odisha (5 out of 21 candidates).

As with the Congress party, trends across states in terms of women's nomination and recent electoral performance also suggests that the BJP *mostly nominated higher number of women in states where they were likely to do well* but again there is contradictory evidence which prevents generalisation. The BJP recorded higher than average nomination of women in Chhattisgarh, Gujarat, Madhya Pradesh, and Odisha where BJP won last Assembly elections (including some with coalition allies such as in Odisha) and had high vote shares in 2004. Also, there was a higher than average nomination of female candidates in Delhi, where they recorded a high-vote share in 2004, even though they only won one seat, and in Rajasthan where the party had won 21 out of 25 seats contested with 49 per cent of the votes, even though Congress won the subsequent Assembly election in 2008. The BJP registered a lower than average nomination in Andhra Pradesh where the Congress party is dominant (and the main rival is a regional party), in Maharashtra where Congress and an allied party are dominant, and in West Bengal which is a Left stronghold.

However, again the results are contradictory given that the BJP also registered a higher than average nomination of women in the southern state of Tamil Nadu, where the party typically has a low presence; in Assam, where, as noted above, the Congress are strong; and in Kerala where the party's presence is low. The BJP also nominated few women in Karnataka despite winning the last

Table 3. Nomination of women candidates in 2009 by BJP, across states and UTs.

State/UT	No. of seats	Seats contested by BJP	Women (no.)	Men (no.)	Women as % of total candidates	2004, women candidates (%)	1999, women candidates (%)
Andhra Pradesh	42	41	2	39	4.9	–	–
Assam	14	7	1	6	14.3	8.3	8.3
Bihar	40	15	1	14	6.7	–	6.9
Chhattisgarh	11	11	3	8	27.3	9.1	n/a
Gujarat	26	26	3	23	11.5	15.4	11.5
Haryana	10	5	1	4	20	10	20
Karnataka	28	28	1	27	3.6	4.2	10.5
Kerala	20	19	2	17	10.5	5.3	7.1
Madhya Pradesh	29	29	4	25	13.8	10.3	7.5
Maharashtra	48	25	1	24	4	7.7	7.7
Odisha	21	21	5	16	23.8	11.1	11.1
Rajasthan	25	25	3	22	12	16	8.3
Tamil Nadu	39	18	3	15	16.7	–	–
Uttar Pradesh	80	71	10	61	14.1	6.5	6.5
West Bengal	42	42	3	39	7.1	–	7.7
NCT of Delhi	7	7	1	6	14.3	28.6	14.3
Sub-total	452	380	44	346	11.6	–	–
Other states/UTs where no female candidates nominated by BJP	91	53[a]	0	43	0	–	–
Total	543	433	44	389	10.2	8	7.4

[a]The BJP did not nominate any women in the following states and UTs (no. of men nominated by BJP/no. of seats available): Arunachal Pradesh (2/2), Goa (2/2), Himachal Pradesh (4/4), Jammu & Kashmir (4/6), Jharkhand (12/14), Manipur (2/2), Punjab (3/13), Sikkim (1/1), Tripura (2/2), Uttarakhand (5/5), Andaman & Nicobar Islands (1/1), Chandigarh (1/1), Dadra & Nagar Haveli (1/1), Daman & Diu (1/1), Lakshadweep (1/1), and Puducherry (1/1).
Source: Compiled by the author from data on Election Commission of India website (ECI, n.d.).

Table 4. Summary of state nomination of women candidates relative to party's overall proportion of women candidates nominated.

Party		Higher than average	Average (approx.)	Lower than average[a]
		States and UTs	States and UTs	States and UTs
INC	States	Andhra Pradesh, Bihar, Chhattisgarh, Haryana, Meghalaya, Punjab, Rajasthan, West Bengal, NCT Delhi	Uttar Pradesh	**Arunachal Pradesh**, Assam, **Goa**, Gujarat, **Himachal Pradesh, Jammu & Kashmir, Jharkhand**, Karnataka, Kerala, Madhya Pradesh, Maharashtra, Manipur, **Mizoram, Nagaland, Odisha, Sikkim,** Tamil Nadu, **Tripura, Uttarakhand**
	UTs			**Andaman & Nicobar Islands, Chandigarh, Dadra & Nagar Haveli, Daman & Diu, Lakshadweep, Puducherry**
BJP	States	Assam, Chhattisgarh, Gujarat, Haryana, Madhya Pradesh, Odisha, Rajasthan, Tamil Nadu, Uttar Pradesh, NCT Delhi	Kerala	Andhra Pradesh, **Arunachal Pradesh,** Bihar, **Goa, Himachal Pradesh, Jammu & Kashmir, Jharkhand,** Karnataka, Maharashtra, **Manipur, Punjab, Sikkim, Tripura, Uttarakhand,** West Bengal
	UTs			**Andaman & Nicobar Islands, Chandigarh, Dadra & Nagar Haveli, Daman & Diu**

[a]States/UTs listed in bold indicates no women candidates nominated.
Source: Compiled by the author from Tables 2 and 3 and ECI data (ECI, n.d.).

Assembly election in 2008, although the proportion of women nominated in Karnataka was low across most of the major parties. In sum, the analysis suggests there is no clear evidence of a relationship between party nomination of women candidates in 2009 and previous electoral success in any given state (see Table 4). This is not to rule out previous electoral success as a factor which influences parties' decisions around nomination, but to suggest instead that there are a number of complex factors which may also play a part and which need further investigation.

Marginal and safe seats: where women candidates are nominated

While the state-level analysis showed no clear relationship between the proportion of women candidates nominated by either the BJP or Congress and the likelihood of success in any given state, a clearer picture is revealed at the constituency level as to whether parties nominate women in winnable or unwinnable seats. Studies of gender and political recruitment suggest that it is not sufficient for the party to nominate higher numbers of women to contest elections if the constituencies for which they are nominated are unwinnable. Two measures – (i) the margin of victory during the previous general election in 2004, and (ii) the candidate's relative standing in the constituency – are used to test whether the Congress and BJP nominate women in winnable seats. A marginal seat is defined here as one where in the previous election, the margin of victory was 5 per cent of votes or less. Due to the relatively larger victory margin, a non-marginal seat may either be a safe seat if the sitting MP is from the same party or an unwinnable seat if the incumbent is from a rival party. In the latter case, challengers may be less likely to win the seat. The combination of marginality and incumbency and its effect on the 'winnability' of the seats is shown in Figure 2.

Due to the frequently large number of parties in electoral contests, as well as the large number of marginal constituencies,[9] another measure of analysis is employed – the relative standing of both the individual candidate and the

	Incumbent	
	Same party	Rival party
Marginal	Potentially winnable	Potentially winnable
Non-marginal	Winnable	Unwinnable

Figure 2. 'Winnability' of seats relative to previous margins of victory and status of incumbency of candidates and parties.

party in a particular constituency. Candidates are divided into three categories: A, B, and C, and are defined as follows: whether the same individual candidate contesting in 2009 (category A) or the party via another candidate (category B) either won or placed second in the constituency in either of the last two general elections in 1999 and 2004.[10] If neither the candidate nor the party won or came second in 1999 or 2004, this was classified as category C. Candidates in categories A and B are deemed to have a higher chance of success because they are a known quantity with established links in the constituency.[11] Candidates and parties classified in category C are determined as relative outsiders for the purpose of comparison and assumed to be less likely to win (see Figure 3). While total numbers are small, it is possible to make some tentative observations as to party nomination trends for the two parties (see Table 5).

For the Congress party around half (21 of 39) of female candidates were nominated to contest potentially winnable seats (marginal seats of rival incumbents and non-marginal seats of own party incumbents). A further four candidates were nominated to contest potentially vulnerable seats in which their own party was incumbent. In terms of constituency familiarity (categories A–C), in 34 out of 39 seats the Congress party nominated women in seats where either the party or the individual candidate had achieved electoral success or had come second in the last two elections. Only five women were nominated in seats where the candidate or party was a relative outsider. This is equivalent to nearly 90 per cent of seats where Congress nominated women in 2009. Findings were confirmed in the election of 23 out of 43 women candidates, or 53 per cent, including successes in 7 out of the 12 marginal (swing) seats and 5 of the 14 safer seats held by non-Congress incumbents. One candidate in Uttar Pradesh also won in a Category C seat, defeating both of the main party contenders, the BSP and the SP, as well as the BJP who had polled third in the constituency in 2004 and 1999. These findings suggest that Congress nominated more women in seats which were potentially winnable than unwinnable. However, due to the low numbers of women overall, it also suggests that Congress took fewer chances on nominating women in a greater number of contests including those that were higher risk in terms of marginality.

Category	Status of 2009 candidate relative to first place and second place candidates in 2004
A	Same candidate
B	Different candidate but same party
C	Different individual and different party

Figure 3. Categories of 2009 candidates based on relative standing of candidates and parties in any given constituency.

Table 5.   Marginal seats, candidate familiarity, and party nomination of female candidates.

	Party INC	BJP
Total no. of women nominated	43	44
No. of constituencies included[a]	39	39
Marginal seats		
Party incumbents	4	1
Rival incumbents	12	10
Total	16	11
Non-marginal seats		
Party incumbents	9	9
Rival incumbents	14	19
Total	23	28
Relative familiarity		
A	14	4
B	20	21
C	4	14
Total	38	39

[a]Some constituencies were excluded from the analysis due to the lack of comparable data as a result of delimitation of constituencies since 2004 (see endnote 3).
Source: Calculated from 2004 and 2009 General Election data compiled from the Election Commission of India's website (ECI, n.d.).

For the BJP the proportion of women nominated to potentially winnable seats was lower but not considerably so. Again around half (19 out of 39) of all nominated female candidates were contesting in potentially winnable seats. Eleven out of 39 seats were classified as marginal but most of these were occupied by non-BJP incumbents and therefore were potentially winnable. Another eight seats were non-marginal and occupied by BJP incumbents. Yet, nearly half of the 39 constituencies (compared to one-third of seats for Congress) were non-marginal seats occupied by non-BJP incumbents, meaning that candidates were outsiders or challengers. Nearly two-thirds of seats (64 per cent) were classified as category A or B, compared to 90 per cent for Congress, with one-third positioning the candidate as a relative outsider (category C). In other words, the BJP fielded fewer women candidates than Congress in seats where they had a reasonable chance of winning the election contest.

Women candidates and political experience

The finding that, in the 2009 general election, the Congress party and the BJP nominated women in winnable seats contradicts observations that political parties in India mostly nominate women in unwinnable seats. However, this should not be understood as confirmation that these two parties have made significant efforts to increase the probability of election for their women candidates. The fact still remains that the proportion of women candidates to total candidates in either party does not extend much beyond 10 per cent. Furthermore, if we examine the individual profiles of these candidates, we see that the majority of women have significant political experience. For example, of the 43 women candidates nominated by the Congress party, nearly half (20) had already served at least one term in the Lok Sabha, and a further six had served at least one term at the state level in the state assemblies. Of the remaining 17, several had previously contested (unsuccessfully) either Lok Sabha or State Assembly elections (as in the cases of Killi Krupa Rani, Vinita Vijay, and Sudha Rai), had political experience at the sub-state level (e.g. as city mayors, as in the cases of Sarubala R. Thondaiman (Trichy) and Rita Bahuguna Joshi (Allahabad)), or had occupied party organisational posts (such as State or District Congress Committee President, or national general secretary of the Mahila Congress, as in the case of Shahida Kamal in Kerala).

Data for the BJP show similar results. Of the 44 women candidates nominated, around a third (13) had served a term in the Lok Sabha and a further six had served at least one term in the state assemblies. Of the remaining 25 candidates, several had contested previous Lok Sabha or state assembly elections (e.g. Radhrani Panda in Odisha, and Tamilisai Soundararajan and Lalitha Kumaramangalam in Tamil Nadu), had political experience at the sub-state level (e.g. Saroj Pandey as former Mayor of Durg, Meera Kanwaria as former Mayor of Delhi, and M. Bindu Teacher as a municipal councillor in Kerala), and/or had held important party posts (e.g. as BJP State Mahila Morcha Presidents, such as Rema Raghunandan in Kerala and Yadlapati Swarupa Rani in Andhra Pradesh).

This evidence of women candidates' political experience suggests that *while these two parties have nominated women in mostly winnable seats, they have nominated mostly women who are strong candidates based on previous political experience.* This explains why the success rate of female candidates is generally higher than that of male candidates; it is reasonable to expect that the disparity in success rate between male and female candidates would diminish as the proportion of male and female candidates equalises. But it also suggests that these two parties are highly risk averse when selecting female candidates. This prevents the extension of opportunities to contest elections to women with a wider range of political experience and restricts the potential pool of women as elected representatives, especially given that these two national parties have a substantial impact on the total number of women elected to parliament.

Conclusions

Women candidates are often nominated to contest elections for a variety of reasons unrelated to concerns of gender inclusivity. However, women's participation in electoral politics *as women* at the national and state level continues to be low. Trends in the nomination of women candidates in the 2009 general election in India were not consistent with rhetorical party support for increasing the political participation of women in electoral politics. Overall, the nomination of women candidates had not increased from the previous general election in 2004. The small increase in the proportion of women elected to the Lok Sabha cannot be attributed to an increase in the nomination of women by political parties. As such, election nomination data continue to strongly contest the 'incremental track' assumption that women's political participation will gradually increase with each election over time. It is clear that, in the absence of legislative quotas, women's participation in electoral politics will only increase if parties make efforts to nominate a higher proportion of women candidates.

However, to understand the dynamics of the low nomination of women, a more disaggregated analysis is needed. The analysis presented here showed significant variation in nomination levels across parties and across states which warrants further explanation. For example, the BJP in 2009 nominated its highest ever proportion of women candidates, but this varied widely across states. Perhaps unsurprisingly, given the complexity of different intervening factors, no clear relationship could be determined between the proportion of women nominated as candidates and the likelihood of success for two main national parties, the BJP and the Congress, in any given state. Thus a more state-focused analysis or party-focused analysis, or both, may be able to better explain why the nomination of women candidates within parties is much lower (or non-existent) in some states compared to others. Potential directions for future research include analyses of party political practices of recruitment and selection, such as party norms, criteria, and decision-making structures influencing the nomination of women candidates. Salient questions might include, but are not limited to, the following:

- What are the internal party debates, if any, over increasing the proportion of women candidates nominated in elections?
- What are the obstacles to increased levels of recruitment and nomination of women candidates within parties and within states?
- To what extent do party attitudes to nominating women vary across state units of a particular party?

132

- How is the nomination of women candidates related to women's political participation and accumulation of experience within party organisational structures?

From the analysis presented here, we can conclude that in 2009 the two main national parties took few risks on women candidates, nominating mostly strong female candidates and mostly in winnable seats (including in constituencies the candidates have themselves cultivated). While this varied slightly between the two major national parties studied, this general risk-averseness towards women candidates limits the total number of women nominated to contest elections. Of course, even if numbers of women candidates increase, this does not necessarily mean their chances of winning elections will rise simultaneously. Expanding the pool of strong female candidates requires parties to enable opportunities for women to build political experience in party organisational structures and to show leadership in nomination processes which matches their rhetorical commitment to women's political empowerment (and to subsequently support less experienced women candidates particularly when they face hostility from rival aspirants within their own party). Further investigation into the low levels of women's nomination and election, particularly in states such as Kerala and Karnataka which have relatively better profiles in terms of women's empowerment than states which recorded a higher proportion of women's nomination such as Rajasthan, would also yield insights into the gender-inflected exclusionary practices operating in the specific institutional context of electoral politics as opposed to wider society.

Finally, given that legislation for the Women's Reservation Bill is currently pending in the Lok Sabha at the time of writing, it would be politically expedient for political parties to pay greater attention to supporting women's inclusion in electoral politics. With substantial variations between states in the participation of women in electoral politics, addressing the exclusion of women from electoral politics may take on more urgency in some states compared to others. Yet, rather than continuously deferring to the introduction of gender quotas, which may or may not materialise, as a time when political parties will make efforts to include women in electoral politics, a more *immediate* research enquiry into party-based and state-based obstacles to women's inclusion in electoral politics is required, as part of a broader concern with making institutions of representative democracy in India more inclusive at all levels.

Acknowledgements

Some of the research for this article was conducted during a postdoctoral fellowship funded by the Leverhulme Trust at the University of Warwick. The author is very grateful to Andrew Wyatt, James Chiriyankandath, and an anonymous reviewer for their very helpful comments on an earlier draft of this article.

Notes

1. At nearly 11%, the proportion of women in India's lower house is below Asia's regional average of 19.1% and the world average of 21.7%, although exceeds Japan (8.1%), Malaysia (10.4%), and Sri Lanka (5.8%) (IPU, 2013). These figures represent the situation as at 1 September 2013 from the Inter-Parliamentary Union database on women in national parliaments (IPU, 2013) and include countries without and with quotas for women in the *lower* houses of parliaments.
2. This lack of attention to gender and political recruitment contrasts with a more substantial literature on women's reservation in panchayats (local councils) since 1996 (see, for example, Hust, 2004; Jayal, 2006; Kudva, 2003), debates and disagreements over the various incarnations of the women's reservation bill (Dhanda, 2008; Kishwar, 1996, 2006; Narasimhan, 2002; Rai, 1999; Randall, 2006; Sharma, 1998; Singer, 2007), as well as excellent micro-level studies of intra-party activism and male-dominated intra-party social networks (Bedi, 2007; Ciotti, 2006; Govinda, 2008; Rogers, 2009; Sarkar & Butalia, 1995; Sen, 2007). Others focus on senior female politicians in India and analyse gendered narratives of political leadership, including and beyond dynastic paths to political office (Banerjee, 2004, 2007; Basu, 1993; Spary, 2007; Sunder Rajan, 1993). However, focusing on the participation of a few elite women provides only partial explanations for the low level of women's participation in electoral politics generally (Fleschenberg, 2008; Goetz, 2007).
3. The 2009 general election was significant as it involved the first delimitation exercise in 30 years. The total number of seats in the lower house remained fixed (to be revisited after 2026), but the number and location of reserved seats for Scheduled Castes and Scheduled Tribes were updated to reflect the 2001 census figures. Some constituencies were converted to reserved status and some lost their reserved status. This affected the (re)nomination of party candidates and party electoral strategies. It also made the constituency-wise results of the 2009 election less directly comparable to previous elections.
4. At the time of writing, the Election Commission of India had yet to release their official report on the election results.
5. Data on forfeiture of deposits in the 2009 election were not yet publicly available from the Election Commission of India at the time of writing.
6. Many nominated women candidates have strong bases of support for a variety of reasons – their political experience, their seniority and proximity to the party leadership, historical links with their constituency, community affiliations, and family links. But the majority of *aspiring* women candidates may have limited support in the absence of such resources and links.
7. The Congress 2009 election manifesto included, as achievements of their previous term, the passage of domestic violence legislation in 2005, equal rights for women to inherit property, and large-scale training of women to deliver primary health care in villages (INC, 2009, p. 7). They proposed to reserve a third of all central government jobs for women and expand the enrolment of rural women in self-help group schemes, promote business development schemes for women, and ensure 'comprehensive social security' to single-woman headed households (INC, 2009, pp. 11,

14). They proposed measures to improve education for, and reduce discrimination against, girl children, particularly in areas with an adverse sex ratio (INC, 2009, p. 15). The BJP's pledges included income tax exemptions for women, emphasis on girls' education at secondary level including financial incentives, bicycles for girls from poor families to facilitate school attendance, improvements in women's participation in local governance institutions, elimination of gender disparities in pay and legal property rights, special investment in training schemes for conflict-affected regions, pro-enterprise policies for women-run businesses or those employing large numbers of women, strict implementation of anti-violence legislation for women, increasing wages of female government workers in child care schemes, and a non-coercive and gender sensitive approach to 'population stabilisation', among other policies (BJP, 2009).

8. Disaggregating nomination data across India's states is important as party strength, party competition, coalition alliances, outcomes of sub-national elections, the salience of regional or caste identity, for example, varies significantly across states. Electoral strategies are often calculated on a state by state basis with the central party leadership of national parties drawing upon party representatives from internal state units to recommend prospective candidates, though some state units of large national parties may have considerable autonomy from the national level leadership, as Guichard (2013) discusses in the case of the BJP in Gujarat. A party's likelihood of success will vary by state, impacting on the extent to which parties take 'risks' in nominating female candidates.

9. The average vote margin in 2004 was 12.2 percentage points. This ranged from 0.06 (lowest) to 61.41 (highest) percentage points. Yet, more than a quarter of contests (28% or 152 constituencies out of 543) registered less than 5 percentage points vote margin in 2004 (figures calculated from ECI, n.d.). The 2009 election was an even closer contest overall than 2004, with a mean vote margin of 9.71 percentage points, a median vote margin of 7.01 percentage points, with more than a third of contests (36.3% or 197 constituencies) recording a vote margin of under 5 percentage points (figures calculated from ECI 2009 election data).

10. Data from both 1999 and 2004 were used to avoid undue bias towards Congress party nominations as the incumbent government prior to the 2009 election, and because the BJP were in government from 1999. Both winners and those placing second in 1999 and 2004 are included for similar reasons. Due to the delimitation exercise that altered some constituency boundaries prior to the 2009 election, a small number of constituencies are excluded from the analysis due to incomparability with the 2004 and 1999 results.

11. This could prove to work against them if voters are displeased with their performance, but this is also true of category B in terms of an anti-incumbency effect.

Notes on contributor

Carole Spary is a Lecturer in Politics at the University of York. Her research interests include the politics of development and democracy in India, particularly gender and development; gender and political representation; party politics and elections; and parliamentary norms and practices. Her work has appeared in Democratization, Commonwealth and Comparative Politics, Journal of Legislative Studies, Nationalism and Ethnic Politics, and Feminist Theory. Her monograph, 'Gender, Development and the State in India', is under contract with Routledge.

References

Agnew, V. (1979). *Elite women in Indian politics*. New Delhi: Vikas.

Bacchi, C. L. (2006). Arguing for and against quotas: Theoretical issues. In D. Dahlerup (Ed.), *Women, quotas and politics* (pp. 32–51). London: Routledge.

Banerjee, M. (2004). Populist leadership in West Bengal and Tamil Nadu: Mamata and Jayalalitha compared. In Rob Jenkins (Ed.), *Regional reflections: Comparing politics across India's states* (pp. 285–308). New Delhi: Oxford University Press.

Banerjee, S. (2007). Chaste like Sita, fierce like Durga: Indian women in politics. In Ramashray Roy & Paul Wallace (Eds.), *India's 2004 elections: Grass roots and national perspectives* (pp. 34–57). New Delhi: Sage.

Basu, A. (1993). Feminism inverted: The real women and gendered imagery of Hindu nationalism. *Bulletin of Concerned Asian Scholars*, *25*(4), 25–36.

Bedi, T. (2007). The dashing ladies of the Shiv Sena. *Economic and Political Weekly*, *42*(17), 1534–1541.

BJP. (2009). Manifesto: Lok Sabha election 2009: To build a prosperous powerful nation, recall India's past. Retrieved March 10, 2011, from http://www.bjp.org/index.php?option=com_content&view=article&id=137:manifesto-lok-sabha-election-2009&catid=50:election-manifestos&Itemid=549

Caul, M. (1999). Women's representation in parliament: The role of political parties. *Party Politics*, *5*(1), 79–98.

Ciotti, M. (2006). At the margins of feminist politics? A comparative analysis of women in Dalit politics and Hindu right organisations in north India. *Contemporary South Asia*, *15*(4), 437–452.

Dagar, R. (2011). Gender discourse in elections: Constructing a constituency? In P. Wallace & R. Roy (Eds.), *India's 2009 elections: Coalition politics, party competition and congress continuity* (pp. 110–139). New Delhi: Sage.

Deshpande, R. (2004). How gendered was women's participation in election 2004? *Economic and Political Weekly*, *39*(51), 5431–5436.

Dhanda, M. (Ed.). (2008). *Reservations for women*. New Delhi: Women Unlimited.

ECI. (n.d.). Electoral Commission of India – Archive of General Elections 2009. Retrieved March 11, 2011, from http://eci.nic.in/eci_main/archiveofge2009/archive_ge2009.asp

Fleschenberg, A. (2008). Asia's women politicians at the top: Roaring Tigresses or Tame Kittens? In K. Iwanaga (Ed.), *Women's political participation and representation in Asia: Obstacles and challenges* (pp. 23–54). Copenhagen: Nordic Institute of Asian Studies Press.

Goetz, A. M. (2007). Political cleaners: Women as the new anti-corruption force?. *Development and Change*, 38(1), 87–105.

Govinda, R. (2008). Re-inventing Dalit women's identity? Dynamics of social activism and electoral politics in rural north India. *Contemporary South Asia*, *16*(4), 427–440.

Guichard, S. (2013). How autonomous are the branches? A study of Narendra Modi's BJP. *Economic and Political Weekly*, *48*(9), 40–46.

The Hindu. (2007, June 26). 33% BJP posts for women. *The Hindu*. Retrieved February 16, 2011, from http://www.hindu.com/2007/06/26/stories/2007062651070100.htm

The Hindu. (2008a, February 5). BJP's Mahila Morcha to seek ticket for women candidates. *The Hindu*. Retrieved February 16, 2011, from http://hindu.com/2008/02/05/stories/2008020556510300.htm

The Hindu. (2008b, January 19). Ready to back EC proposal on quota for women: BJP. *The Hindu*. Retrieved March 11, 2011, from http://www.thehindu.com/2008/01/19/stories/2008011960050100.htm

Hust, E. (2004). *Women's political representation and empowerment: A million Indiras now?* New Delhi: Manohar.

INC. (2009). Lok Sabha elections 2009: Manifesto of the Indian National Congress. Retrieved February 22, 2011, from http://www.aicc.org.in/new/manifesto09-eng.pdf

IPU. (2013). 'Women in National Parliaments', data compiled by the Inter-Parliamentary Union, situation as of 1 September 2013. Retrieved October 5, 2013, from http://www.ipu.org/wmn-e/world.htm

Jaffrelot, C. (2011). The BSP in 2009: Still making progress, but only as a Dalit party. In P. Wallace & R. Roy (Eds.), *India's 2009 elections: Coalition politics, party competition and congress continuity* (pp. 140–162). New Delhi: Sage.

Jayal, N. G. (2006). Engendering local democracy: The impact of quotas for women in India's *panchayats*. *Democratization, 13*(1), 15–35.

Katzenstein, M. Fainsod. (1978). Towards equality? Cause and consequence of the political prominence of women in India. *Asian Survey, 18*(5), 473–486.

Kishwar, M. (1996). Women and politics: Beyond quotas. *Economic and Political Weekly, 31*(43), 2867–2874.

Kishwar, M. (2006). 'No' to Zenana Dabbas: Deghettoizing women's politics and enhancing their representation in legislatures'. In Peter Ronald de Souza & E. Sridharan (Eds.), *India's political parties* (pp. 356–383). London: Sage.

Kochanek, S. (1967). Political recruitment in the Indian National Congress: The fourth general election. *Economic and Political Weekly, 7*(5), 292–304.

Krook, M. L. (2009). *Quotas for women in politics: Gender and candidate selection reform worldwide*. New York: Oxford University Press.

Kudva, N. (2003). Engineering elections: The experiences of women in Panchayati Raj in Karnataka, India. *International Journal of Politics, Culture and Society, 16*(3), 445–463.

Kumari, A., & Kidwai, S. (1998). *Crossing the sacred line: Women's search for political power*. Delhi: Orient Blackswan.

Kumari, R., & Dubey, A. (1994). *Women parliamentarians: A study in the Indian context*. Delhi: South Asia Books.

Manikandan, C., & Wyatt, A. K. J. (2013, September 18–19). *Elite formation within a political party: The case of the DMK*. Paper presented at the ESRC-UKIERI workshop on 'Institutionalising Marginal Actors', University of Edinburgh, Edinburgh.

Mansbridge, J. (1999). Should blacks represent blacks and women represent women? A contingent "yes". *The Journal of Politics, 61*(3), 628–657.

Mishra, Ramesh Chandra. (2000). *Role of women in legislatures in India: A study*. New Delhi: Anmol.

Narasimhan, S. (2002). Gender, class, and caste schisms in affirmative action policies: The curious case of India's women's reservation bill. *Feminist Economics, 8*(2), 183–190.

Niven, D. (1998). Party elites and women candidates. *Women & Politics, 19*(2), 57–80.

Norris, P., & Lovenduski, J. (1995). *Political recruitment: Gender, race, and class in the British parliament*. Cambridge: Cambridge University Press.

Pai, S. (1999). BSP's new electoral strategy pays off. *Economic and Political Weekly, 34*(44), 3099–3101.

Palmer, N. (1972). Elections and the political system in India: The 1972 state assembly elections and after. *Pacific Affairs*, *45*(4), 535–555.

Phillips, A. (1991). *Engendering democracy*. Cambridge: Polity Press.

Phillips, A. (1993). *Democracy and difference*. Cambridge: Polity Press.

Rai, S. M. (1999). Democratic institutions, political representation and women's empowerment: The quota debate in India. *Democratization*, *6*(3), 84–99.

Rai, S. M. (2012). The politics of access: Narratives of women MPs in the Indian parliament. *Political Studies*, *60*(1), 195–212.

Rai, S. M., & Hoskyns, C. (1998). Gender, class and representation: India and the European Union. *European Journal of Women's Studies*, *5*, 345–365.

Randall, V. (2006). Legislative gender quotas and Indian exceptionalism: The travails of the women's reservation bill. *Comparative Politics*, *39*(1), 63–82.

Rogers, M. (2009). Between fantasy and 'reality': Tamil film star fan club networks and the political economy of film fandom. *South Asia: Journal of South Asian Studies*, *32*(1), 63–85.

Roy, R. (1966). Selection of Congress candidates I: The formal criteria. *Economic and Political Weekly*, *1*(20), 833+835–840.

Roy, R. (1967a). Selection of Congress candidates II: Pressures and counter-pressures. *Economic and Political Weekly*, *2*(1), 17–24.

Roy, R. (1967b). Selection of Congress candidates III: Claims and counter-claims. *Economic and Political Weekly*, *2*(2), 61–63+65.

Roy, R. (1967c). Selection of Congress candidates IV: Socio-demographic characteristics of applicants. *Economic and Political Weekly*, *2*(6), 371–376.

Roy, R. (1967d). Selection of Congress candidates V: Structures of authority in the congress. *Economic and Political Weekly*, *2*(7), 407+409+411+413–416.

Roy, R., & Wallace, P. (2007). *India's 2004 elections: Grass roots and national perspectives*. New Delhi: Sage.

Sarkar, T., & Butalia, U. (Eds.). (1995). *Women and right-wing movements*. London: Zed Books.

Sawer, M. (2000). Parliamentary representation of women: From discourses of justice to strategies of accountability. *International Political Science Review*, *21*(4), 361–380.

Sen, A. (2007). *Shiv Sena women: Violence and communalism in a Bombay slum*. London: C. Hurst.

Sharma, K. (1998). *Power vs. representation: Feminist dilemmas, ambivalent state and the debate on reservation for women in India* (Occasional Paper No. 28). New Delhi: Centre for Women's Development Studies

Singer, W. (2007). *A constituency suitable for ladies' and other social histories of Indian elections*. New Delhi: Oxford University Press.

Singh Rana, M. (2006). *India votes: Lok Sabha and Vidhan Sabha elections, 2001–2005*. New Delhi: Sarup and Sons.

Spary, C. (2007). Female political leadership in India. *Journal of Commonwealth and Comparative Politics*, *45*(3), 253–277.

Sunder Rajan, R. (1993). *Real and imagined women: Gender, culture and postcolonialism*. London: Routledge.

UN Women. (n.d.). The United Nations fourth world conference on women: Platform for action: Women in power and decision-making. Retrieved March 15, 2011, from http://www.un.org/womenwatch/daw/beijing/platform/decision.htm

Wolkowitz, C. (1987). Controlling women's access to political power: A case study in Andhra Pradesh, India. In H. Afshar (Ed.), *Women, state and ideology: Studies from Africa and Asia* (pp. 205–225). Albany, NY: State University of New York Press.

Parties, political decay, and democratic regression in Sri Lanka

Neil DeVotta

Department of Politics and International Affairs, Wake Forest University, Winston-Salem, USA

Among states that gained independence following World War II, Sri Lanka was widely considered to have a good chance of succeeding democratically. This promise was sundered when successive leaders embraced ethnocentric policies that were geared towards empowering the majority Sinhalese Buddhists at the expense of minorities. This ethnocentrism contributed to civil war and adversely affected the country's institutions – including the island's political parties. The attendant political decay has not only led to malgovernance and democratic regression, it has pushed the country in an authoritarian direction. Sri Lanka thus represents a classic case of how ethnocentrism can undermine democratic institutions and of the long-term negative consequences.

Sri Lanka (called Ceylon until 1972) gained independence from the British in 1948, and it did so minus the tumultuous nationalist movement that neighbouring India experienced. Indeed, the country was considered a model colony, so much so that the British instituted universal suffrage in 1931 – merely three years after doing so in Britain! Independence itself was achieved in the most peaceful fashion – especially when compared with the decolonisation process elsewhere in Asia and in Africa – with Sri Lankan Tamil elites casting aside concerns about their place in a predominantly Sinhalese polity and instead placing faith in their fellow Sinhalese elites. The transfer of power to Sri Lanka's mainly pro-western leaders was so placid that people in the countryside hardly realised how momentous the event was: the end of nearly 450 years of colonial rule that stretched from the Portuguese and Dutch to the British.

The two main political parties in the period leading up to independence were the Trotskyite Lanka Sama Samaja Party (Lanka Equal Society Party – LSSP), which was formed in December 1935, and the pro-Moscow United Socialist Party, which became the Communist Party (CP) in 1943. While trade union politicking galvanised both and hence local and British entrepreneurs (especially in the estate sector) considered them a threat to the free-market system, the parties hardly challenged British rule in Sri Lanka. The island's mostly conservative electorate was leery of communism, and this was one reason the LSSP and CP failed to gain strong political traction especially in the post-independence era. The other main reason had to do with the institutional set up the Donoughmore Constitution, which was in operation from 1931 to 1947, created. Under the Donoughmore Constitution legislators were divided among seven executive committees in the State Council and the committee chairmen formed the board of ministers that superintended local government. The structure promoted individualism and nullified the need for political parties (Kumarasingham, 2013).

The promise of independence and British style parliamentary governance, however, saw the Tamil Congress, Federal Party, Viplavakari Lanka Samaja Party, United National Party (UNP), and Sri Lanka Freedom Party (SLFP) being formed between 1944 and 1951 (Kearney, 1983, p. 18). While all went on to play important and controversial roles in post-independence Sri Lanka's political affairs, the UNP and SLFP stand out for having become the island's main parties under which all successive governments have since been formed (albeit sometimes in coalition with smaller parties).

It is impossible to discuss party politics in Sri Lanka without seriously considering the nationalist movements among the majority Sinhalese and minority Tamils. For instance, while the UNP was formed in 1946 and the SLFP was created in 1951, when its founder S.W.R.D. Bandaranaike left the UNP and crossed over to the opposition, the SLFP first came to power in 1956 as part of an election that capitalised on Sinhalese-Tamil animus. At a time when the country was engulfed in a debate on whether to replace English with Sinhala and Tamil as national languages, Bandaranaike and especially the Sinhalese Buddhist nationalists who supported him embraced a Sinhala only platform to catapult themselves to power. The SLFP's rise led to a two party system in the island, even as the basis for the party's rise also led to communal politicking and a politics rooted in ethnic outbidding that saw the UNP and SLFP compete with each other on who could best accommodate the majority Sinhalese demands – often at the expense of the Tamil minority (DeVotta, 2004; Horowitz, 1985; Rabushka & Shepsle, 1972).

Sri Lanka's main political parties headed by the UNP and SLFP, notwithstanding some leaders' secular and liberal proclivities, embraced a pernicious Sinhalese Buddhist nationalism that has over the last five decades compromised democracy and good governance. This is best evidenced by how the Sinhalese Buddhist nationalism that the Sinhala only movement (and the subsequent ethic outbidding) unleashed led to laws and policies that consolidated the majority community's standing at the expense of good governance. This is an association that many Sinhalese Buddhists have failed to grasp or acknowledge.[1] Sinhalese Buddhist nationalists and apologists for successive governments have argued that the separatist, terrorist movement that the Libration Tigers of Tamil Eelam (LTTE) waged was Sri Lanka's biggest impediment to development and ethnic harmony – thereby conveniently absolving the majority community and the island's major parties from the communalism they embraced. As has been amply documented, the Tamil quest for separatism, which the LTTE hijacked, was a desperate reaction – indeed, a reactive nationalism – to the majority community's rabid nationalism that was rooted in exclusivist and racist notions of Sinhalese Buddhist superordination and Tamil subordination (DeVotta, 2007; Seneviratne, 1999; Tambiah, 1986, 1992; Wilson, 2000). As Nigel Harris (1990) aptly observed,

> if the Tamils had not existed, Colombo would have had to invent them. And, in an important sense, it did. It was [Sinhalese elites in] Colombo that forced the inhabitants of the north to become different, to cease to be Sri Lankan and become exclusively Tamil. (p. 221)

The communal politics that Sinhalese leaders and their parties embraced were so divisive and destabilising, 'if the gods had wished to destroy, the madness of Sri Lanka's rulers gave them every opportunity' (Harris, 1990, p. 222). This is a far cry from the assessment Howard W. Wriggins had made three decades earlier, when he thought Sri Lanka, among the countries undergoing decolonisation, had 'the best chance of making a successful transition to modern statehood' (1961, p. 316).

Sri Lanka's political parties embraced ethnocentrism and illiberal governance because they wanted to win elections and stay on in power. With the Sinhalese population at nearly 70 per cent (and now at nearly 75 per cent), the island's leaders could afford to, in the main, disregard the minorities' legitimate demands – especially if accommodating such demands upset the majority community's preferences. What these parties and their leaders failed – or refused – to acknowledge is that illiberalism cannot be compartmentalised (so as to affect merely one community or just minorities), since over time the democratic regression associated with it spreads to all.

The civil war that Sinhalese Buddhist nationalism and Tamil reactive nationalism unleashed lasted nearly 30 years. It ended in May 2009 when the country's military decisively defeated the LTTE. The victory over the LTTE has also been a victory for Sinhalese Buddhist nationalists. It is certainly being celebrated as such, with nationalist elements more emboldened than ever in their determination to ensure that Sri Lanka remains a country of the Sinhalese Buddhists, ruled by Sinhalese Buddhists, for the betterment of Sinhalese Buddhists. This is consistent with Sinhalese Buddhist nationalist ideology, which claims Sri Lanka is the island of the Sinhalese who have been ennobled to preserve it as the designated sanctuary of Buddhism (DeVotta, 2007; Seneviratne, 1999; Tambiah, 1992). The irony is that in getting to this point Sri Lanka has regressed democratically, so much so that the island may be categorised as a semi- or soft-authoritarian state (DeVotta, 2011). The ethnocentrism that Sinhalese Buddhist nationalism facilitated – and continues to facilitate – is thus a major reason for Sri Lanka's democratic regression.

In the island's case the illiberalism rooted in ethnocentrism undermined the state's ability to deal with Tamils dispassionately even as it weakened independent institutions. Thus the country's two autochthonous constitutions that were put in place by the SLFP and UNP in 1972 and 1978, respectively, were partly influenced by ethnocentrism and majoritarianism and played a major role in deinstitutionalisation and the trajectory towards authoritarianism. This link between ethnocentrism and institutional or political decay[2] is crucial to understanding how the island's political parties manipulated the opportunities Sinhalese Buddhist nationalism afforded them to undermine democratic governance.

This paper, consequently, looks at how political parties, specifically the UNP and SLFP, have contributed to democratic regression in Sri Lanka, and it does so within the context of political decay. The paper's first section briefly evaluates the phenomenon of political decay while the second section discusses how the UNP and SLFP advertently and inadvertently facilitated deinstitutionalisation and political decay as they, at varied levels, pandered to majoritarianism and Sinhalese Buddhist nationalism. The final section looks at how the current government headed by the Sinhalese Buddhist nationalist Mahinda Rajapaksa and his family have continued to undermine institutions so that the island today operates less like a multiparty democracy and more like a single party, authoritarian state. The essay concludes by arguing that the country's extant authoritarian dispensation is likely to continue into the foreseeable future and that the island is unlikely to revert to a liberal democratic set up without severe rupture.

Theorising political decay

The late Samuel Huntington defined institutions as 'stable, valued, recurring patterns of behavior' (1968, p. 12). Francis Fukuyama builds on Huntington's definition to suggest that 'institutions are rules or repeated patterns of behavior that survive the particular individuals who operate them at any one time' (2011, p. 451). Another common definition is that offered by Douglass North, who said 'institutions are rules of the game in a society or, more formally, humanly devised constraints that shape human interaction' (1990, p. 3). These rules typically make clear what

> individuals *must* or *must not* do (compulsion or duty), what they *may* do without interference from other individuals (permission or liberty), what they *can* do with the aid of the collective power (capacity or right), and what they *cannot* expect the collective power to do in their behalf (incapacity or exposure). (Commons, 1968, p. 6)

In short, the rules that determine acceptable and proscribed behaviour constitute a country's institutions. The more willingly a country's population adheres to these rules the more robust the institutionalisation of such rules. Suppressing, discarding, or negating such rules without introducing acceptable and equivalent alternatives in place are what cause deinstitutionalisation and political decay.

Institutional change takes place when the rules enforcing and procedures governing institutions shift so as to encourage alternate behaviours. While such transformations take place gradually (Levy, 1990, p. 407; North, 1990, p. 89), change can be radical especially during or after 'wars, revolutions, conquests, and natural disasters' (North, 1990, p. 89). The consequences from institutional change can be both positive and negative. The latter, which results in political decay, is 'a process marked by the erosion and breakdown of previously accepted and observed rules and norms governing organisational behavior' (Barany, 2008, p. 585). Institutions, once formed, tend to operate in a rigid fashion partly due to bureaucratic and societal resistance to change and partly due to vested interests and patron–client ties the extant institutions have facilitated (Fukuyama, 2011, pp. 452–453). Political decay is thus directly related to deinstitutionalisation, or the inability of institutions to operate in predictable ways for whatever reasons.

Fukuyama likewise says 'political decay occurs when political systems fail to adjust to changing circumstances' (2011, p. 7).[3] However, in the case of soft-authoritarian states the malady may have just as much to do with the deliberate undermining of institutions. Therefore, while political decay can happen due to insufficient adoptability, it can also be foisted by opportunistic, venal, and predatory elites who seek to monopolise power and arrogate wealth.

Thus political decay can ensue when the rules governing political and economic interactions lose legitimacy because they deteriorate or are fashioned/refashioned in non-inclusive ways so as to marginalise a particular group or enable monopolistic and predatory practices among privileged groups (Acemoglu & Robinson, 2012; Bromley, 2008, p. 541). Examples include high transaction costs due to extractive policies; parties disregarding contractual obligations due to political patronage; the rule of law ceasing to apply dispassionately due to ethnic, political, or nepotistic considerations or because law-enforcing authorities are easily cowed and bribed; and the judicial process being compromised due to graft, intimidation, violence, and political affiliation.

Political systems and the institutions that legitimate them undergird what we commonly call the state. The more these institutions representing the state ensure predictable and secure expectations, the more effective they get at minimising rents, enhancing transparency, and promoting advantages to society. This in turn makes them more relevant and embedded and inspires others to aspire to similar institutions. On the other hand, malgovernance ensues when institutions are deliberately weakened and the attendant political decay causes entities representing the state to function in a corrupt, partial, and violent manner whereby they jettison the norms, values, and practices that ensure liberal democracy, operate with impunity, engender anomie, and undermine citizen's confidence in the state.

Liberal democracy requires both a strong state and strong society: an inclusive state that has a monopoly over the use of force and can effectively enforce laws within its territory; and a cohesive polity with a strong civil society that can 'impose accountability on the state' (Fukuyama, 2011, p. 479). Both aspects mandate constraining behaviour and hence the importance of institutions. The post-Cold War world, however, has seen various leaders promoting strong states with weak societies so as to propagate authoritarianism. The annual country rankings tabulated by Freedom House over the past decade testify to this trend, as do the vast scholarship dealing with such hybrid regimes.

What is novel about hybrid regimes is how their leaders have blended aspects of electoral democracy with authoritarianism, thereby differentiating themselves from previous ruthless autocrats and also claiming some legitimacy for their rule. Many such regimes embrace populist measures and encourage electoral competition while seeking to concentrate power within the executive.[4] Today's authoritarian rulers clamor for legitimacy from their people and the international community (Dobson, 2012), and the competition is therefore craftily designed to suggest opposition forces can come to power (Levitsky & Way, 2010) even as the electoral process is rigged by: ensuring weak opposition parties or creating malleable opposition parties; tarnishing the legitimate opposition's credentials by linking it to allegedly hostile foreign governments; controlling the main media outlets while permitting some critical coverage with limited reach; vilifying local and western election monitors as puppets who are part of foreign-funded conspiracies while hosting sympathetic monitors from fellow authoritarian states; introducing onerous registration requirements among those communities that are most likely to vote against the government; manipulating electoral rules to disqualify opponents; using the bureaucracy and other state machinery to promote the governing party; making voting grueling and cumbersome in areas supporting the opposition; and gerrymandering (*Economist*, 2012, p. 23). Conducting multiple investigations against opposition members for real and manufactured infractions so as to keep them off balance and slapping fines against them and their parties are other ways to harass challengers and ensure conformity and loyalty. A nationalist narrative and strong support within the military can also go a long way in consolidating authoritarian rule. All such practices weaken democracy and the rule of law and can contribute to political decay over time.

Sri Lanka represents one such case. The island's civil war most certainly contributed to democratic regression, but the country's political decay began in the mid 1950s when successive leaders embraced ethnocentric policies. While the presidential set up that came into being in 1978 assisted this process of deinstitutionalisation, the current government's authoritarian proclivities and determination to manipulate Sinhalese Buddhist nationalism and the military victory over the LTTE to create a political dynasty have exacerbated political decay like never before.

Party politics and political decay

The institution of universal suffrage 17 years prior to independence and inter-ethnic camaraderie between especially Sinhalese and Tamil elites placed Sri Lanka in a favourable position to consolidate its nascent democracy. Yet within eight years Sinhalese elites especially within the SLFP and UNP disregarded the flimsy constitutional guarantees for minorities and began outbidding each other on who could better empower the majority community.[5] This ethnic outbidding laid the foundation for the ethnic animus that unleashed the civil war (DeVotta, 2004; Horowitz, 1985; Rabushka & Shepsle, 1972).

The genesis of Sri Lanka's political decay can be located in the insidious Sinhala Only Act and the subsequent ethnocentric 1972 constitution. The literature on path dependence makes clear how 'political development is often punctuated by critical moments and junctures that shape the basic contours of social life' (Pierson, 2000, p. 25), and this is certainly the case when one retrospectively analyses how the Sinhala Only Act and the 1972 constitution affected the country's ethnic and political trajectories. Indeed, the Sinhala Only Act, besides marginalising Tamils, inadvertently laid the groundwork for the mediocrity, nepotism, favouritism, and anomie that followed. The so-called 'ape anduwa' (our government) mentality that pervaded Sri Lankan politics following the Act made one being Sinhalese Buddhist, not superior qualifications or aptitude, the most important criterion. It was a slippery slope towards institutional degeneration. It also influenced events that led to the civil war.

Tamils had, for various reasons, been overrepresented within the state bureaucracy and universities and beginning in the early 1960s the governments headed by Sirimavo Bandaranaike (1960–1965 and 1970–1977) went about instituting affirmative action policies for the majority community – i.e. recruiting and promoting personnel who were mainly Sinhalese Buddhists.[6] This was accompanied by a number of other discriminatory policies: Tamil civil servants were forced to learn Sinhala to be promoted; Sinhalese civil servants were stationed in Tamil areas and Tamils forced to interact with them in Sinhala; Sinhala only was instituted into the courts system; development of the predominantly Tamil northeast was neglected even as the government sponsored Sinhalese colonisation in these areas; and Tamil students were required to score higher on university entrance examinations. The Sinhala Only Act, which was designed to Sinhalise the state, was in turn used as the basis for such discrimination.

The 1972 constitution was also a major turning point in the process of deinstitutionalisation partly because of the sectarianism it propounded and partly due to the way in which it vitiated impartial bureaucracies. It incorporated Sinhala as the country's only official language, gave Buddhism the foremost place, and branded the island a unitary state. It built on the deinstitutionalisation the Sinhala Only Act facilitated by drastically altering the standard operating procedures of state institutions, thereby furthering political decay and democratic regression.

For instance, in 1963 the elite Ceylon Civil Service (CCS) was disbanded and replaced with the Ceylon Administrative Service (CAS) since Mrs. Bandaranaike's government felt CCS personnel were not sufficiently sensitive 'to the spirit of the new times' (Weerakoon, 2004, p. 127). While the government claimed the CCS obstructed cabinet decisions from being implemented, what actually offended it were the administrative officials' independence, impartiality, and sense of rectitude. The government preferred 'more obedient, less intellectually inclined, and less argumentative people to take ... orders and carry them out' (Weerakoon, 2004, p. 127). The forced retirements that followed conveniently allowed the government to replace many Tamils in the CCS with Sinhalese CAS officials.[7]

This professionally retrograde and ethnocentric move was advanced further when the 1972 constitution disbanded the impartial Public Service Commission with the State Services Advisory Board (SSAB) and the State Services Disciplinary Board (SSDB). The president appointed members to both bodies, which were thereafter placed under the Cabinet of Ministers who were empowered to determine officials' 'appointment, transfer, dismissal, and disciplinary control'.[8] The ministers were also permitted to operate outside the purview of the judiciary as the courts too were considered a threat to the 'popular will' (Edirisinha & Selvakkumaran, 2000, p. 103). The hitherto vaunted public service was thus instantly transformed into 'a more political and pliant public service' (Edirisinha & Selvakkumaran, 2000, p. 104). Overnight the dictates of politicians superseded professional norms, ministerial rules and regulations, and standard operating procedures that had been institutionalised since colonial times. What is important to recognise is that such deinstitutionalisation was superimposed, often against the will of high-ranking bureaucrats; it did not stem from institutional incapacity or ineffectiveness. While the 1978 constitution did away with the SSAB and SSDB, it continued Cabinet dominance over public servants. Indeed, given the extent to which the 1978 constitution concentrated power within the executive branch, the president and his advisors were able to continue interfering in the public services and undermine their independence.[9]

While many among those who were appointed to the upper echelons of the public service were connected to the country's elite, these persons were not without qualifications: they were typically university educated and had to sit for the competitive civil service exams. The changes that were made led over time to top administrators (the so-called Permanent Secretaries) being instead recruited from private industry, the universities, and well connected political families – with the goal being to recruit personnel who were cooperative (Devendra, 2012). Whereas previously administrators were alerted to their promotions and transfers by mail, soon government ministers arrogated to themselves the right to personally deliver letters of appointments using choreographed functions – thereby making clear their power over the bureaucracy.

The new milieu also quickly led to lower ranking public servants being appointed using the so-called 'chit system', whereby constituents and relatives with notes from ministers were granted jobs in various ministries.[10] The appointments were part of a government job bank programme that allowed members of parliament to recommend up to 1000 individuals for employment within the lower echelons of the public sector. With the state at the time being the biggest employer, such patronage ensured political support even though it came at the expense of standards, professionalism, etiquette, and respect for line of authority within the government sector.[11] Indeed, the administrative service was soon so politicised that one president thought nothing of ordering the supposedly independent administrative servants to attend his party's gatherings (Devendra, 2012). As many of the old guard professionals retired or left the island in disgust, the new guard that was recruited mostly due to political and ethnic considerations became the vanguard. This 'chit system' more or less continues and has led to Sri Lanka having approximately 1.4 million state employees (including military personnel), leading to one of the largest ratios of public servants to citizens in the world. If the ethnocentric nature of this recruitment is obvious given that nearly 96 per cent of government servants today are Sinhalese, the degree of democratic regression is also evident given how governments now think nothing about using government employees for campaigning purposes. For instance, today not only does the Mahinda Rajapaksa government use government servants to paste and distribute posters and attend SLFP political rallies, it also uses these so-called civil servants to mobilise counter-protests against unions, civil society organisations, and opposition political parties protesting government policies.[12]

With parliament passing legislation that explicitly discriminated against minorities and bureaucracies changing procedures and policies so as to humiliate them, the new milieu that the Sinhala Only Act and the 1972 constitution created contributed to a superior and arrogant mindset among especially new Sinhalese recruits in the universities, military, and bureaucracy when interacting with Tamil colleagues and the Tamil-speaking public.[13]

True democracy promotes inclusion, not exclusion; and undemocratic reactions are bound to occur whenever democratic processes get manipulated to promote ethnic exclusion (Horowitz, 1993, p. 28). In short, an ethnocentric state disqualifies itself from being considered a true democracy and Sri Lanka had officially retrogressed to such a state by the time the 1972 constitution got passed. Consequently, Sri Lanka's democratic regression and civil war are rooted in Sinhalese Buddhist nationalism (De Silva, 1998; Tambiah, 1986). It is now fashionable for Sinhalese Buddhist nationalists and their apologists to try and argue that Sri Lanka never had an ethnic problem; it merely had a terrorist problem in the form of the LTTE. Such blame displacement and revisionism seek to confuse cause and effect and are easily countered by a reading of the events that led to the civil war. For it was the Sinhala Only Act that led to the first ever anti-Tamil riots (in 1956 and 1958), influenced the above-noted anti-minority policies, and motivated humiliated Tamil youth to cast aside their community's moderate politicians and resort to separatism. It also led to political decay and laid the foundation for the authoritarian politics now playing out in the island.

The above-noted deinstitutionalisation and burgeoning Tamil grievances could have been reversed had the UNP's J.R. Jayewardene used his five-sixth majority in parliament to transform politics for the better. He instead allowed racists within his government to whip up anti-Tamil sentiment, and this led to ethnic riots in 1977 and an island-wide anti-Tamil pogrom in July 1983. The latter marginalised Tamil moderates, legitimated extremist youth hijacking the Tamil cause, and led to the disastrous quest to create Eelam (a Tamil state).

Jayewardene also introduced a new constitution in 1978 that was designed to ensure the UNP stayed perpetually dominant. He refused to hold parliamentary elections that would most certainly have led to a loss of seats for the UNP and instead held a severely compromised referendum that extended the party's five-sixth majority for another term. He even forced all UNP ministers to turn in signed but undated resignation letters, which ensured that they followed his dictates. His attitude towards the democratic process was best captured when he boasted:

> We are contesting the election to win and at a time most favorable to us. We intend ... to demolish and completely destroy the opposition politically. After that I say to you, roll up the electoral map of Sri Lanka. You will not need it for another ten years. (Samarakone, 1984, p. 86)

Jayewardene's penchant for a more authoritarian politics was partly influenced by his determination to propel Sri Lanka towards an open market system, which he introduced soon after the UNP came to power in 1977. This quest to see Sri Lanka succeed economically was being undermined by the Tamil rebellion, and meeting this threat in turn led to drastic counter-terror laws that disregarded human rights and democratic practices. For instance, the Prevention of Terrorism Act of 1979 allowed the police to arrest, detain, and leave incommunicado without trial for 18 months anyone suspected of furthering terrorism, and hundreds of innocent Tamils were caught in its dragnet. The Act continues to be in operation, and it has been put to good use by the Mahinda Rajapaksa government – this time against Tamils and everyone else.

Jayewardene's successors, Ranasinghe Premadasa of the UNP and Chandrika Kumaratunga of the SLFP, continued to wage war against the LTTE (which by the late 1980s had become the dominant rebel group) even while failing to come up with a solution to the conflict (mainly due to the government's inability to convince Tamils of its sincerity and the LTTE's intransigence).

If the nearly 30 year civil war had led to human rights and civil liberties being compromised, defeating the LTTE led to practices that blatantly undermined democracy. In doing so, President Rajapaksa, a Sinhalese Buddhist nationalist, was ably assisted by his brother, Defense Secretary Gotabhaya Rajapaksa, and the Army Commander, Sarath Fonseka. While the government and military resorted to a no-holds barred strategy when countering the LTTE, they also adopted extraconstitutional and extrajudicial methods to control opinion and stymie dissent throughout the country. The state, consequently, weakened and marginalised the opposition, muzzled the media, attacked civil society, resorted to abductions and disappearances, and popularised the notion that those who spoke ill of the government and military were traitors. It also disregarded differentiating between rebel combatants and civilians. The LTTE had unleashed carnage using suicide bombings and other methods of sabotage, and a war weary population tolerated the Rajapaksa administration's draconian practices especially since they came with military successes. The final stage of the conflict may have caused between 40,000 and 70,000 Tamil civilian deaths and has led the United Nations and western governments to claim that the Sri Lankan government and military committed war crimes.

The decimation of the LTTE in May 2009 and the euphoria it caused especially among Sinhalese ensured the government's popularity in the near future, but none fully anticipated the manner in which the government would use its victory over the LTTE to consolidate its position at the expense of party politics and good governance.

Indeed, many expected the Mahinda Rajapaksa government to address certain Tamil grievances following its defeat of the LTTE. The government, however, has not merely neglected Tamils' needs; it has wallowed further in Sinhalese Buddhist nationalism, through which it seeks to consolidate Rajapaksa control over the state and create a political dynasty. This has led to a politics by executive diktat even in the most mundane matters. The next section details how Sri Lanka's increasingly authoritarian post-civil war politics is exacerbating deinstitutionalisation, undermining competitive politics, and hurtling the island towards authoritarianism.

The politics of authoritarianism

The first and most important post-war development that has contributed to an authoritarian dispensation in Sri Lanka is the 18th Amendment to the constitution, which was incorporated in September 2010. The amendment abolished the 17th Amendment and terminated the two term limit for presidents.

Sri Lanka's parliament passed the 17th Amendment unanimously in 2001; and while it failed to achieve full enforcement, the amendment mandated the creation of a Constitutional Council with sole powers to appoint and dismiss commissioners overseeing elections, public service, police, finance, human rights, and bribery and corruption. The Constitutional Council was further empowered to appoint the chief justice and other justices on the Supreme Court, president and judges of the Court of Appeal, members of the Judicial Services Commission (excepting its chairman), attorney general, inspector general of police, auditor general, parliamentary commissioner for administration (or ombudsman), and secretary general of Parliament. This was a belated attempt to halt political interference and promote independent, impartial, and professional operations among and within these institutions.

The 18th Amendment did away with the Constitutional Council and now empowers the president to appoint personnel to lead the institutions that were under its purview. The president merely has to take into consideration the 'observations' of the prime minister, speaker, and leader of the opposition when doing so. The 18th Amendment also permits the president to contest more than two terms, allowing President Rajapaksa to run for a third term on or before 2016 and additional terms thereafter. The president engineered cross-overs from the opposition to ensure he commanded the requisite two-thirds majority to pass the amendment, and by some accounts some of these politicians were paid over half a million dollars to abandon the parties under whose banner they got elected. While the government justified the change by claiming it was inherently democratic, as the people would need to vote to reelect any president, the amendment promotes democratic regression by making a powerful executive branch even more powerful.

A second post-war development that highlighted the government's authoritarianism was the impeachment of the country's first ever female Chief Justice in January 2013. President Rajapaksa appointed Shirani Bandaranayake Chief Justice in May 2011; and she, like her predecessors and fellow justices, initially contributed to court rulings that strengthened the executive presidency. Yet when Chief Justice Bandaranaike ruled that the government's desire to create a *Divinegume* (Improving Lives) Department – which amalgamated the operations of three extant entities under the current Minister of Economic Development and presidential sibling Basil Rajapaksa and provided him with an additional $600 million (under the guise of development) to expand the First Family's patronage system – violated aspects of the constitution, the president set up a Parliamentary Select Committee (PSC) comprising politicians from the ruling coalition that found her guilty of financial and official misconduct, leading to her impeachment. This was done despite the Supreme Court ruling that the PSC had no right to investigate a senior judge and the Appeals Court ordering parliament to abandon the impeachment process. Civil society organisations, clergy members, foreign governments, and various international bodies likewise objected strenuously. The president disregarded their entreaties and summarily signed the order removing the Chief Justice, even as pro-government henchmen brandishing poles gathered outside her official residence to make sure she relinquished her post. In the lead up to this, parliamentarians among the governing coalition affirmed their willingness to defenestrate the Chief Justice by signing a blank sheet of paper devoid of the impeachment motion. Parliamentarians who are part of a governing party are expected to support that party's policies within the legislature, but this action highlighted the degree to which parliament has abdicated its role as a potential counter to the executive overreach.

While Sri Lanka's judiciary has grappled with corruption and 'telephone justice', whereby someone in the president's office or Attorney General's office calls judges and tells them how to rule on particular cases, is said to be a common occurrence, a president that could so blatantly impeach a Chief Justice can even more easily throw out any justice. And this was partly the message being communicated to the country's already compromised judiciary. The manner in which the chief justice's impeachment unfolded and the way United People's Freedom Alliance (UPFA) parliamentarians supinely supported the 18th amendment evidenced the real absence of checks and balances in the island's governance structure. This is made all the more clear when one realises the control the Rajapaksa family, now branded the First Family, exerts on the Sri Lankan state and the extents to which its patronage and highly personalised politics have contributed to a weak party structure and deinstitutionalisation.

The first family and the demise of checks and balances

Mahinda Rajapaksa, besides being president, is also the minister for defense and urban development, finance and planning, ports and highways, and law and order. These combined portfolios place 78 government institutions directly under his control. While charming and politically savvy, the president brooks little dissent. This has led to a supine cabinet of ministers who dare not cross the president lest they lose their positions and perks. This was most obvious in how no minister or parliamentarian opposed the 18th Amendment being passed through parliament as an Urgent Bill – which precluded Gazette noti-fication and public debate and also minimised parliamentary debate. An Urgent Bill cannot be challenged in court and merely requires the Supreme Court to determine its constitutionality within 24 hours. The court meekly went along as well, which collectively highlighted the lack of checks and bal-ances among the island's major governing institutions.

The president's younger brother, Basil, is the Minister of Economic Devel-opment, which includes the Board of Investment and the Tourist Promotion Bureau. Basil Rajapaksa also chairs the Presidential Task Force (PTF), which superintends all development activity in the Northern Province. Indeed, no public, private, or non-governmental organisation sponsored devel-opment activity can take place in the highly militarised Northern Province without the PTF's authorisation, which in turn is mainly the prerogative of its chairperson who engages more closely with the military in the Northern Pro-vince than with civilian authorities. The increased militarisation of the Northern Province has led to allegations that the state is systematically using Sinhalese Buddhists to Sinhalise Tamil areas as part of a larger strategy to keep down the already hagridden Tamils. The PTF's modus operandi when interacting with Tamil civilians, which is often based on capricious decision-making, merely adds to this belief.

Another brother, Gotabhaya, is the country's Defense Secretary who played a leading role in defeating the LTTE. In addition to superintending the armed forces, police, and coast guard, Gotabhaya Rajapaksa also oversees immigra-tion and emigration, the Land Reclamation and Development Corporation, and the Urban Development Authority. Gotabhaya is often referred to as Sri Lanka's most powerful man. He has refused to demobilise the military and is instead using it to supposedly develop the island. This has led to military personnel helping construct roads and bridges and refurbishing and building schools and temples – in addition to working in tea shops and barber salons along the A-9 highway, managing travel offices, overseeing whale and dolphin watching tours, running a canal boat service, superintending cricket stadiums, operating hotels and guesthouses, and growing and selling vegetables.[14] It is Gotabhaya Rajapaksa who instituted the policy of not tolerating criticism against the military, and he is most responsible for militarising Sri Lanka.[15] Gotabhaya is widely feared and journalists resist reporting on him negatively.[16] Some journalists, consequently, refuse to even write about him and newspaper editors freely admit that they resort to self-censorship whenever referring to him. Many in the opposition, media, and diplomatic corps consider him responsible for the paramilitary outfits that use white vans to disappear critics of the government.[17] Sri Lanka's former army commander has claimed that it was Gotabhaya Rajapaksa who ordered surrendering LTTE cadres carrying white flags be shot (Jansz, 2009), accusations that the Defense Secretary has vociferously denied (Sackur, 2010). Occasional reports also claim that he could be made prime minister, which is important because all presidents in Sri Lanka graduated to that perch following stints as prime ministers.[18]

A third brother, Chamal, is Speaker of Parliament, allowing him to block any attempt to impeach the president. Mahinda Rajapaksa has successfully engineered enough crossovers from opposition parties to ensure the SLFP-led UPFA coalition enjoys a two-thirds parliamentary majority and can amend the constitution at any time. Indeed, his government has 62 members who have crossed over from the UNP alone. Most UPFA members are cabinet ministers, senior ministers, deputy ministers, and project ministers – currently numbering 107 in a parliament comprising 225 members[19] – and they fear to challenge the president and his family lest they lose their sinecures. This combined with the all-powerful executive has led parliamentarians within the UPFA to be pliant and disengaged, which in turn has allowed the Speaker to get his brother's executive preferences easily rubber stamped and further vitiated the separation of powers between the executive and legislature.

Chamal's son, Shashindra, is the Chief Minister of Uva Province (one of the island's nine provinces), and the president's eldest son, Namal, is a member of parliament – as are two of the president's cousins. Nearly 130 Rajapaksa relatives are also said to have been provided prominent government postings.[20] The 27-year-old Namal is being groomed to eventually succeed the president,[21] and he currently controls the *Tarunayata Hetak* (A Tomorrow for the Youth) and *Nil Balakaya* (Blue Brigade) youth groups. Many members in these groups have been provided employment abroad while some others have been provided state employment.[22] Such patronage ensures the support of these youth during elections to mobilise against opponents.

The Rajapaksa brothers are said to control between 60 and 70 per cent of the country's budget through their portfolios. Mahinda Rajapaksa's father and uncle were prominent politicians in the country's south but the family's present status is due mainly to nepotism. Their stunning ascendance and widespread involvement in government affairs have marginalised and upset members of the SLFP old guard, although these elements fear to challenge the family at this stage. More importantly, Rajapaksa diktats have exacerbated political decay by making legitimate institutional actors irrelevant.[23]

For instance, decisions made by bureaucratic heads and ministers are summarily overturned, thereby confusing and compromising ministerial heads. This has contributed to ministers and their powerful secretaries at times abdicating their responsibilities, although overlapping ministerial portfolios have also assisted in this outcome. There is now also less transparency, with officials often relaying decisions by phone as opposed to in writing.[24] Even government circulars, which ought to be part of the public domain, are hard to locate and often times government agents (especially in the Northern Province) are forced to act on requests without access to the circulars. At the cabinet level memos and minutes fail to get distributed, so that cabinet ministers themselves are often unsure what they may have agreed to in past meetings. In short, most major decisions are based on directives by the president and his brothers, with the bureaucracy having become playthings of the First Family.[25]

Mediocre parliamentarians, who merely seek power and spoils and are disinterested in governance, have abdicated their legislative responsibilities and helped the executive monopolise power. Weak and divided oppositions have also helped the executive branch grow more powerful over time. The decline in standards and professionalism that have undermined state institutions has further allowed the executive branch to hold sway vis-à-vis entities that in the past provided a check against excessive and extraconstitutional executive power. But in the case of President Rajapaksa, an insidious patronage system (sometimes tied to intimidation) and a secretive operating culture within the executive branch have also eroded checks and balances.

Leaders inclined towards authoritarianism resort to a number of strategies (as noted above), and President Rajapaksa has done likewise by especially centralising governance and undermining the autonomy of ministries. A major reason for President Rajapaksa's success has been his ability to manipulate politics so as to ensure a weak opposition. At the time of writing in late 2013, the president's popularity shows signs of fraying. Yet the absence of a viable opposition has deprived people of an alternative to consider seriously. There are approximately 65 political partiers currently registered in Sri

Lanka. The next section focuses on the island's main parties and recent elections so as to highlight the quandary facing Sri Lanka's fractured opposition.

Political parties

The SLFP has overseen Sri Lanka's politics since Chandrika Kumaratunga became president in 1994, which also ended 17 years of UNP rule. President Rajapaksa currently heads the SLFP, which in turn heads the UPFA coalition. The manner in which the Rajapaksa family has arrogated power has not only undermined civil society, muzzled the media, and undermined the opposition; it has also weakened the SLFP. It is legal for parliamentarians elected through one party to cross over to another party and still keep their seat. President Rajapaksa has used ministerial portfolios to entice members of the opposition into government, and this has achieved three important outcomes: it has defanged opposition parties, disempowered SLFP seniors, and allowed the Rajapaksas to concentrate power among them while controlling the state's resources.

Indeed, the old guard within the SLFP has been marginalised because most in the group have been allocated less important portfolios while crossovers from the UNP especially have been elevated to relatively important posts. Some of the members of this old guard are urging former President Kumaratunga to run for a third term, which the 18th Amendment makes possible. This is a development that President Rajapaksa fears, and there is speculation that he may choose to hold a referendum that extends his and parliament's term in lieu of an election.[26]

South Asia is famous for its political dynasties (at both the national and state levels). Sri Lanka began this trend when Sirimavo Bandaranaike succeeded her husband S.W.R.D. Bandaranaike following his death in 1959. Chandrika Kumaratunga continued the Bandaranaike legacy by succeeding her mother. President Mahinda Rajapaksa and his wife are determined to create a Rajapaksa political dynasty by ensuring their oldest son Namal succeeds his father.

Namal's influence has been expanding because he is seen to represent the president's views. He has, in some instances, overruled the preferences of senior ministers; and Government Agents and senior bureaucrats in his Hambantota District especially do not seem to make major decisions concerning development and investment without consulting him. Ideally, the First Family hopes Namal could take over after Mahinda Rajapaksa completes a third term (when the president will be in his mid-70s and Namal in his mid-30s) or, even better, a fourth term (when the president will be around 80 and Namal in his early 40s). There has also been talk about how in the absence of Mahinda Rajapaksa the presidency could be handed over to one of his brothers until Namal can take over, although this is not the most preferred option for the president and his family – especially given that some in the military would like to see Gotabhaya Rajapaksa succeed his brother and others think that Basil Rajapaksa has designs on the presidency. Irrespective of whether the succession promoting dynastic politics is vertical or horizontal, it is clear that the Rajapaksas intend to rule for a long time and will not give up power without a major fight, which is bound to have drastic ramifications for politics in Sri Lanka.

The UNP's Ranil Wickremesinghe has refused to step down despite the party losing over a dozen elections at the presidential, parliamentary, provincial, and local levels under his leadership. Many party members accuse him of preventing necessary reform, transparency, accountability, and opportunity for changes in leadership. This lack of democracy within the UNP and the subsequent infighting, especially between Wickremesinghe loyalists and supporters of Sajith Premadasa, the son of former President Ranasinghe Premadasa, have prevented the party from mounting strong challenges to the government's malpractices – be it on corruption, favouritism, nepotism, militarisation, authoritarianism, rule of law, or the assault on civil society. Some in the UNP go so far as to argue that the government funds some of Wickremesinghe's travels and activities because President Rajapaksa considers him the perfect opponent who is unlikely to mount a serious challenge to the president.[27] The upshot is that the weak opposition in Sri Lanka has allowed the Rajapaksa government to further its authoritarian agenda.

The Janatha Vimukthi Peramuna (People's Liberation Front, or JVP), was allied with the UPFA but has since left the coalition and also split. The JVP and Tamil National Alliance (TNA), which comprises a few Tamil parties, are the only two entities in parliament that somewhat effectively challenge the government on legislation. While unable to change the course of proceedings, they at least provide counter-arguments to the government's stance.

The JVP has long combined extreme leftist politics with Sinhalese Buddhist nationalism. But Mahinda Rajapaksa, with his support for state-centric policies and proven Sinhalese Buddhist nationalist credentials, has stolen the JVP's thunder. The JVP fared best when it was allied with the SLFP. Split and on its own, it can mobilise a segment of the population but is now hardly a force when it comes to electoral politics.

The TNA, on the other hand, is currently the main representative of the Tamils. Considered a proxy for the LTTE during the war, the group continues to get vilified as separatist and a lackey of the LTTE-controlled Tamil diaspora. Some Tamils too criticise the group for being unduly sensitive to the Tamil diaspora's opinions than to the needs of the disempowered Tamils (especially in the north). Yet Tamils strongly support the TNA's demands for accountability for alleged war crimes, which the vast majority of Sinhalese strongly oppose. Tamils also support the TNA's demands for the military to disengage its personnel from the Northern Province, especially given widespread claims about sexual harassment involving soldiers and Tamil women (International Crisis Group, 2011). With the TNA having handily won the Northern Provincial Council elections, the party's popularity may depend on how well it succeeds on such difficult issues.

The Provincial Councils were mainly set up to provide the northeast with a degree of autonomy. While the system operated throughout the island, the civil war and the Rajapaksa regime's unwillingness to allow the Northern Province the right to superintend its affairs post-civil war led to elections there being postponed. Thanks to Indian and international pressure, elections were finally held in the Northern Province for the first time in September 2013. The TNA chose former Supreme Court Justice, C.V. Wigneswaran, as its chief ministerial candidate, and the party captured 78.48 per cent of the vote and 30 out of 38 seats. The president appoints the governor of a province, and the governor of the Northern Province is a former army general who commanded the security forces in the region. While the TNA provincial government in the north is bound to assert itself, the governor of the north will most likely seek to stymie its operations.

The government has supported the Sinhalisation of the northeast and reports of land grabbing by Sinhalese and the military are reported on a daily basis. The government has said it would not let any Northern Province government enjoy police and land powers, claiming that this would lead to Tamils reviving their claim for a separate state. This is bound to rile the Tamils and the international community, but the government's stance is popular among the majority Sinhalese and is likely to be carried out using an amendment to the constitution – especially if the TNA made demands in this regard.

The Eelam People's Democratic Party (EPDP) is a Tamil party from the north that is a part of the UPFA coalition. Its paramilitaries operate in the north together with the military. It opposed the LTTE and its leader Douglas Devananda narrowly missed being assassinated by the LTTE on many occasions. Successive governments have protected him and given sanctuary to his cadres, and they now have little choice but go along with the government. While the EPDP operates its own patronage network, the violence and extortion associated with the party is mainly responsible for its unpopularity in the north.

The Tamil Makkal Viduthalai Pulikal (Tamil People's Liberation Tigers, or TMVP) was formed by the LTTE's eastern commander Colonel Karuna after he broke away from the rebels in March 2004. With Karuna now a vice president of the SLFP, the party is led by another former LTTE fighter named Sivanesathurai Chandrakanthan alias Pillayan. Karuna's and Pillayan's forces have resorted to violence from time to time, which highlight the divisions among Tamils even from the same region. Pillayan was Chief Minister of the Eastern Province until September 2012 but was allowed little authority by the province's governor, also a retired military general. Factionalism and demographic changes continuing to take place in the east are likely to further weaken the TMVP.

The Sri Lanka Muslim Congress (SLMC) stood with the opposition until after the April 2010 parliamentary elections when the president engineered some crossovers within the party. Seeking to avoid a split, the SLMC's leader, Rauf Hakeem, reluctantly joined the UPFA. He was rewarded with the Justice Minister portfolio.

The past year has seen a few extremist Buddhist groups whip up anti-Muslim sentiment and attack mosques and Muslim-owned shops in Sri Lanka. There has long been an eddy of anti-Muslim feelings among both Sinhalese and Tamils, and many fear that the island's Muslims are bound to experience serious violence in the near future. Muslims, like Tamils and most other minorities, do not vote for the SLFP during presidential elections. At the same time, Sri Lanka has now reached a demographic stage where minority support is less relevant to forming a government (Uyangoda, 2011, p. 133). Minimising Muslim and minority participation during presidential elections especially suits the current regime, and many Sri Lankans believe that the extremist anti-Muslim Buddhist groups that have come to prominence in the past year are supported by elements within the government at the highest level. Post-civil war Sri Lanka may thus be heading for more ethno-religious violence.

A strong opposition is essential for democracy. Given the nature of Sri Lanka's current government, a strong opposition is all the more vital to push back against the country's authoritarian trajectory. Yet such an opposition is lacking in Sri Lanka. A major reason for it is the manner in which President Rajapaksa has manipulated the political process. Barring a serious economic crisis, he and the regime are likely to stay in power until opposition politicians get their act together.

Elections

Capitalising on the LTTE's defeat, President Mahinda Rajapaksa called presidential elections two years early in January 2010. A demoralised opposition supported Sarath Fonseka, the army commander who crafted the military strategy that vanquished the LTTE, as the candidate from the opposition. While Fonseka was – is – widely regarded a war hero, his crude campaign rhetoric certainly cost him votes.

In an election that may have been seriously rigged, Rajapaksa won 57.8 per cent of the vote.[28] What was also problematic were the tactics the president and his supporters adopted: state employees, media, and vehicles were used blatantly to promote the president's campaign; the opposition's supporters were threatened and harassed; posters promoting Fonseka were taken down no sooner they were put up; newspaper editors and journalists sympathetic to Fonseka were issued death threats; and Fonseka was widely pilloried as a traitor for impli-cating Gotabhaya Rajapaksa in the massacre of surrendering LTTE leaders. Fur-thermore, grenades were set off near some northern polling booths on the day of the election to discourage Tamils from voting, and Rajapaksa supporters also stuffed ballot boxes in a few areas. Ominously, troops were dispatched to Fon-seka's hotel even before the election results were announced, which suggests that the Rajapaksas are unlikely to give up power easily.

In the April 2010 parliamentary elections the SLFP won 118 seats, while the SLFP-led UPFA alliance won 144 out of 225 seats. The president thereafter easily engineered sufficient crossovers to ensure a two-thirds majority in parlia-ment. Two months prior to the elections Sarath Fonseka was arrested after being dragged out of his office. He nevertheless won a parliamentary seat while in detention, but was divested of it and other emoluments in an August 2010 court martial hearing that accused him of engaging in politics while in uniform. A month later a second military tribunal found him guilty of corruption and sentenced him to three years of hard labour. Fonseka was released in May 2012 after serving over two years in prison and he currently heads the Democratic Party. The manner in which Fonseka was treated was partly designed to send a message to the country's citizenry: if a war hero and highly regarded army commander could be treated in such humiliating fashion, then so could anyone else who tries to challenge the regime.

President Mahinda Rajapaksa and his UPFA coalition have, with the excep-tion of the Northern Provincial Council election held in September 2013, won all provincial council and national level elections held since the president was first elected in November 2005. The SLFP and its coalition partners have also been victorious in most local elections (municipal councils, urban councils, and divisional councils), with its most disappointing losses taking place in the Colombo municipality and the northeast. It appears that the president will take advantage of his relative popularity and the splintered opposition's woes and call for early presidential and parliamentary elections before mid 2015 – in addition to holding early elections in a number of provincial councils.

Accusations of election malpractice have compromised the government's success at the ballot box[29]; and many of those elected on the government's side at the national and local levels have serious criminal records. While Sri Lanka has long had dubious individuals in politics, the Rajapaksa adminis-tration especially has evidenced a troubling tolerance for politicians with crim-inal profiles.[30] What is especially disturbing is how these forces continue their venal and predatory practices with utter impunity (International Commission of Jurists, 2012). For instance, it is common knowledge that many among Sri Lanka's politicians are now engaged in the distribution of narcotics; and no less a figure than the Prime Minister recently bemoaned this development

(*The Island*, 2013). Ruling party parliamentarians also control gangs and some are said to operate prostitution rings.[31] Indeed, nothing exemplifies Sri Lanka's political decay than the now prevailing culture of impunity especially among politicians and their relatives. Such blatant disregard for the rule of law amidst growing authoritarianism have dashed the blithe hopes that many within and without Sri Lanka had for the country's post-civil war politics.

Conclusion

Sri Lanka has regressed from a relatively liberal democracy where the two main parties alternated in power amidst electoral rules that were respected to a situation where one family now dictates all politics. This political decay began with successive governments seeking to empower the Sinhalese Buddhist majority at the expense of especially the Tamils, and undermining impartial institutions in the process. The majority Sinhalese, bent on immediate gain, not only tolerated the manner in which institutions were compromised but considered this essential to move their community ahead. None seems to have associated such deinstitutionalisation with democratic regression and political decay because (it appears) malgovernance benefitting the majority community disproportionately was considered preferable to good governance benefitting all communities. The SLFP under Mahinda Rajapaksa and Sinhalese Buddhist nationalist parties especially continue to operate amidst such a mindset.

Ethnic conflict inevitably compromises democracy and also has a tendency to promote authoritarianism (Horowitz, 1993); and Sri Lanka represents a classic example of how ethnic chauvinism vitiated democracy and contributed to authoritarianism. Yet Sinhalese Buddhists who may grudgingly accept that anti-Tamil policies led to the civil war nevertheless have a difficult time connecting such ethnocentrism to democratic regression and the ongoing authoritarian milieu. Such an acceptance may be a prerequisite for meaningful post-civil war ethnic reconciliation between Sinhalese and Tamils.

While presidentialism and the civil war helped further political decay in Sri Lanka, the Rajapaksa regime has exacerbated the deinstitutionalisation that accompanied such decay by resorting to a combination of constitutional, extraconstitutional, and extrajudicial practices. With the Rajapaksas determined to further their authoritarian project and stay in power using any methods, this deinstitutionalisation is bound to continue. That augurs ill for Sri Lanka and its peoples.

Acknowledgements

The author thanks the journal's anonymous reviewers and his fellow panelists at the 2012 European Conference on South Asian Studies, Lisbon, Portugal, where a version of this paper was presented.

Notes

1. This is notwithstanding the Lessons Learned and Reconciliation Commission, which the government set up following the end of the civil war, bluntly stating that 'the root cause of the ethnic conflict in Sri Lanka lies in the failure of successive Governments to address the genuine grievances of the Tamil people'.

2. Politics, irrespective of how it gets defined, takes place within formal and informal institutions. Various authors refer to 'political decay' and 'institutional decay', both of which refer to institutions having a negative impact on political development.

3. This builds on Huntington's seminal argument that institutional decay ensued when economic and social modernisation failed to keep pace with political development.

4. This trend was especially true for Latin America, although it has since been adopted by leaders elsewhere (De la Torre, 2010).

5. In 1946 Sri Lanka's main ethnic groups stood at Sinhalese 69.41%, Sri Lankan Tamils 11.01%, Indian Tamils 11.73%, and Muslims 6.52%. In 1981, following thousands of Indian Tamils being coerced to move to India, the ethnic population stood at Sinhalese 73.95%, Sri Lankan Tamils 12.70%, Indian Tamils 5.52%, and Muslims 7.05%. See Department of Census and Statistics (1996).

6. A Buddhist monk murdered S.W.R.D. Bandaranaike in September 1959 and a rudderless SLFP enticed Mrs. Bandaranaike to take the helm, leading to her becoming the world's first woman prime minister.

7. Author interview with a retired CCS official in Toronto, Canada, 7 June 2010. This Sinhalisation has been so successful that today Sri Lanka's military is over 98% Sinhalese while the government service is over 95% Sinhalese.

8. The Constitution of the Republic of Sri Lanka (1972), section 106.

9. Thus a leading UNP member, whose party has been relegated to the opposition since 1994, bemoans that the concentration of power within the executive branch allows an individual to 'systematically undermine and destroy every other institution of governance'. Quoted in *The Island* (2012).

10. Mrs. Bandaranaike similarly appointed numerous relatives to positions within the state apparatus irrespective of their qualifications: her two daughters, son, and son-in-law were provided 'high appointments' within the government sector while three of her four brothers were made Director-General of the Export Promotion Secretariat, Chairman of the State Plantation Corporation, and a Supreme Court Judge. The other brother operated as her private secretary (Dissanayaka, 1977, pp. 58–59).

11. A common gripe among senior civil servants pertains to their powerlessness when dealing with low level ministerial employees (i.e. peons, clerks, tea boys, and janitors) who often happen to be the minister's constituents or relatives. Their intimate relations with the minister embolden these persons with a sense of immunity. As an official in the Ministry of Private Transport Services half-jokingly told this author, 'I dare not dictate to them because these fellows can get me fired in a jiffy'.

12. Author interviews with numerous individuals (including government employees), Colombo, October, November, and December 2012.

13. Interviews with former Sinhalese and Tamil civil servants in Sri Lanka and Canada paint an image of certain Sinhalese officials being so empowered by the new ethnocentric milieu that they operated with contempt and a sense of *schadenfreude* when dealing with non-Sinhalese.

14. Soldiers have also been used to clean drains when malaria and dengue were prevalent, demolish buildings and homes in Colombo that were constructed without the appropriate permits, and hang lanterns during Buddhist religious festivals. In November 2013 soldiers were used on a major scale to beautify Colombo in preparation for the Commonwealth Heads of Government Meeting. According to one businessman, soldiers sometimes even supervise workers collecting garbage and sweeping the sidewalks in Colombo. Author interview November 2012.

15. Retired military personnel have been appointed ambassadors and heads of state corporations. A new precedent now appears to be set with serving officers also being provided civilian posts. For instance, in October 2013 the serving Navy Commander was appointed chairman of the Ceylon Shipping Corporation. Similarly, following the civil war, General Daya Ratnayake was stationed at the Sri Lankan embassy in Germany before being made Army Commander. This feeding of the military appears related to the belief that security personnel and their families are the more patriotic and the most likely to stand by the regime.

16. See, for instance, his tirade and threats against the female editor of a prominent English newspaper – Jansz (2012). The media's fear of the defense secretary was evident when no newspaper (except for an op-ed in the *Daily Mirror*) dared comment on the incident.

17. Thus the phrase 'being white vanned' is now used in Sri Lanka to refer to someone who has disappeared. See, for instance, Blair (2013).

18. See *Lanka News* (2012). Some individuals close to the government also suggest that Basil Rajapaksa wants to be made prime minister, although others claim that the president's oldest son and wife disapprove of this outcome. Based on author interviews with various persons in Sri Lanka in October and November 2012.

19. This means that over two-thirds of the UPFA's parliamentarians are now ministers. This contrasts with Sri Lanka's first cabinet, which comprised only 14 individuals.

20. Some reports claim that people have changed their last name to Rajapaksa believing it lends them an advantage when seeking employment or trying to get a child admitted to a good school.

21. Some army officials, however, appear to want Gotabhaya Rajapaksa to succeed his brother as president.

22. Such employment has been arranged through various job agencies that specialise in sending Sri Lankans abroad to work, with South Korea recently becoming a prominent destination for these youth. According to one bureaucrat, some state employees suspect that youth associated with *Tarunayata Hetak* and *Nil Balakaya* monitor their political leanings. Author interview, January 2012.

23. As one newspaper complained,

> the [extant] breakdown of law and order is the culmination of the crumbling of most institutions that were put in place to maintain law and order. Independent public servants have been made to function like domestic servants. The police – the guardians of the law – are made to act like hired hoodlums and attempts are being made to convert a supposedly independent judiciary into a trained choir singing from the same hymn sheet.
>
> *Sunday Leader* (2013)

24. Author interview with a civil society activist, January 2012.

25. Foreign governments recognise this only too well. For instance, when India's National Security Advisor Shiv Shankar Menon visited Sri Lanka in July 2012 to discuss bilateral ties he only met with the president and his two brothers (Basil and Gotabhaya).
26. President J.R. Jayewardene extended the life of parliament via a referendum in 1982 and thereby extended the UNP's five-sixth majority for another six years, so President Rajapaksa could claim that there is a precedent for doing so.
27. When this author, in January 2012, talked to a high-ranking UNP member of parliament and inquired about the troubling nexus between the Rajapaksa family and military, the latter shot back saying the country should be more concerned about the nexus between the Rajapaksa family and the leader of the UNP.
28. Some prominent journalists, leading members of civil society, and some in the diplomatic corps were convinced that Sarath Fonseka would win the election and were surprised by the result.
29. This, in recent times, mainly has to do with government employees and state resources (especially in the form of vehicles and media) being used to promote government candidates. Government supporters resorting to violence with impunity has also tarnished elections, as have instances of marked ballot papers being found discarded. See, for example, *Sunday Times* (2010).
30. Thus a pro-government newspaper could bemoan that 'politics has become a haven for all anti-social elements such as drug dealers, fraudsters, murderers, rapists, bootleggers and cattle rustlers!'. See *The Island* (2013).
31. In October 2011 two leading SLFP parliamentarians (closely associated with President Rajapaksa and his brother Gotabhaya) and their gangs shot at each other in public, which led to the more senior politician being killed. *The Island* newspaper's claim that 'behind every criminal gang there is a powerful ruling party politician' is hardly hyperbole. See *The Island* (2012).

References

Acemoglu, D., & Robinson, J. (2012). *Why nations fail: The origins of power, prosperity, and poverty.* New York: Crown.

Barany, Z. (2008). Civil-military relations and institutional decay: Explaining Russian military politics. *Europe-Asia Studies, 60*(4), 581–604.

Blair, D. (2013, October 17). Scandal of Sri Lanka's disappeared. *The Telegraph.* Retrieved November 2, 2013, from http://www.telegraph.co.uk/news/worldnews/asia/srilanka/10387036/Scandal-of-Sri-Lankas-disappeared.html

Bromley, D. W. (2008). Resource degradation in the African commons: Accounting for institutional decay. *Environment and Development Economics, 13*(5), 539–563.

Commons, J. R. (1968). *Legal foundations of capitalism.* Madison: The University of Wisconsin Press.

Department of Census and Statistics. (1996). *Statistical pocket book of the democratic socialist republic of Sri Lanka.* Colombo: Department of Census and Statistics, pp. 15–16.

De la Torre, C. (2010). *Populist seduction in Latin America* (2nd ed). Athens: Ohio University Press.

De Silva, K. M. (1998). *Reaping the whirlwind: Ethnic conflict, ethnic politics in Sri Lanka.* New Delhi: Penguin Books.

Devendra, T. (2012, July 29). The myth of a [sic] independent public service. *The Island*. Retrieved August 20, 2012, from http://www.island.lk/index.php?page_cat=article-details&page=article-details&code_title=57886

DeVotta, N. (2004). *Blowback: Linguistic nationalism, institutional decay, and ethnic conflict in Sri Lanka*. Stanford: Stanford University Press.

DeVotta, N. (2007). *Sinhalese Buddhist nationalist ideology: Implications for politics and conflict resolution in Sri Lanka, Policy Studies 40*. Washington, DC: East-West Center.

DeVotta, N. (2011). Sri Lanka: From turmoil to dynasty. *Journal of Democracy*, 22(2), 130–144.

Dissanayaka, T. D. S. A. (1977). *J. R. Jayewardene of Sri Lanka*. Colombo: Swastika Press.

Dobson, W. J. (2012). *The dictator's learning curve: Inside the global battle for democracy*. New York: Doubleday.

Economist. (2012, March 3). Weighing the vote. *Economist*, p. 23.

Edirisinha, R., & Selvakkumaran, N. (2000). The constitutional evolution of Ceylon/Sri Lanka 1948–98. In W. D. Lakshman & A. Tisdell (Eds.), *Sri Lanka's development since independence: Socio-economic perspectives and analyses* (pp. 95–112). Huntington, NY: Nova Science Publications, Inc.

Fukuyama, F. (2011). *The origins of political order: From prehuman times to the French revolution*. New York: Farrar, Straus, and Giroux.

Harris, N. (1990). *National liberation*. London: I. B. Tauris.

Horowitz, D. (1985). *Ethnic groups in conflict*. Berkeley: University of California Press.

Horowitz, D. (1993). Democracy in divided societies. *Journal of Democracy, 4*(4), 18–38.

Huntington, S. (1968). *Political order in changing societies*. New Haven, CT: Yale University Press.

International Commission of Jurists. (2012). *Authority without accountability: The crisis of impunity in Sri Lanka*. Geneva: International Commission of Jurists.

International Crisis Group. (2011). *Sri Lanka: Women's insecurity in the north and east* (Asia Report No. 217).

Jansz, F. (2009, December 13). "Gota ordered them to be shot" – General Sarath Fonseka. *Sunday Leader*. Retrieved July 8, 2012, from http://www.thesundayleader.lk/2009/12/13/%E2%80%9Cgota-ordered-them-to-be-shot%E2%80%9D-%E2%80%93-general-sarath-fonseka/

Jansz, F. (2012, July 8). Gota goes berserk. *Sunday Leader*. Retrieved July 8, 2012, from http://www.thesundayleader.lk/2012/07/08/gota-goes-berserk/

Kearney, R. N. (1983). The political party system in Sri Lanka. *Political Science Quarterly, 98*(1), 17–33.

Kumarasingham, H. (2013). *The political legacy of the British empire: Power and the parliamentary system in post-colonial India and Sri Lanka*. London: I. B. Tauris.

Lanka News. (2012, June 18). SLFP seniors oppose move to appoint Gota as premier. *Lanka News*. Retrieved June 20, 2012, from http://www.lankanewsweb.com/news/2325-slfp-seniors-oppose-move-to-appoint-gota-as-premier

Levitsky, S., & Way, L. A. (2010). *Competitive authoritarianism: Hybrid regimes after the cold war*. New York: Cambridge University Press.

Levy, M. (1990). A logic of institutional change. In K. S. Cook & M. Levy (Eds.), *The limits of rationality* (pp. 402–418). Chicago: University of Chicago Press.

North, D. C. (1990). *Institutions, institutional change, and economic performance*. New York: Cambridge University Press.

Pierson, P. (2000). Increasing returns, path dependence, and the study of politics. *American Political Science Review, 94*(2), 251–267.

Rabushka, A., & Shepsle, K. A. (1972). *Politics in plural societies: A theory of democratic instability.* Columbus: Charles E. Merrill.

Sackur, S. (2010, December 27). HARDtalk 2010: A year on the road. *BBC News.* Retrieved July 8, 2012, from http://news.bbc.co.uk/2/hi/programmes/hardtalk/9313264.stm

Samarakone, P. (1984). The conduct of the referendum. In J. Manor (Ed.), *Sri Lanka in change and crisis* (pp. 84–117). London: Croom Helm.

Seneviratne, H. L. (1999). *The work of kings: The new Buddhism in Sri Lanka.* Chicago: University of Chicago Press.

Sunday Leader. (2013, March 10). Qualifications for premiership. *Sunday Leader.* Retrieved March 20, 2013, from http://www.thesundayleader.lk/2013/03/10/qualifications-for-premiership/

Sunday Times. (2010, March 21). CID still probing destroyed ballot papers. *Sunday Times.* Retrieved March 30, 2010, from http://www.sundaytimes.lk/100321/News/nws_22.html

Tambiah, S. J. (1986). *Sri Lanka: Ethnic fratricide and the dismantling of democracy.* Chicago: University of Chicago Press.

Tambiah, S. J. (1992). *Buddhism betrayed? Religion, politics, and violence in Sri Lanka.* Chicago: University of Chicago Press.

The Island. (2012, March 10). Living with ruling party terrorism. *The Island.* Retrieved March 10, 2012, from http://www.island.lk/index.php?page_cat

The Island. (2012, July 1). Karu's call. *The Island.* Retrieved July 4, 2012, from http://www.island.lk/index.php?page_cat=news-section&page=news-section&code_title=69

The Island. (2013, April 5). Justitia-requiescat in pace! *The Island.* Retrieved April 10, 2013, from http://www.island.lk/index.php?page_cat=article-details&page=article-details&code_title=76208

The Island. (2013, May 8). Trying to restrain the uncontrollable. *The Island.* Retrieved November 2, 2013, from http://www.island.lk/index.php?page_cat=news-section&page=news-section&code_title=42

Uyangoda, J. (2011). Sri Lanka in 2010: Regime consolidation in a post-civil war era. *Asian Survey, 51*(1), 131–138.

Weerakoon, B. (2004). *Rendering unto Caesar: A fascinating story of one man's tenure under nine prime ministers and presidents of Sri Lanka.* Colombo: Vijitha Yapa Publications.

Wilson, A. J. (2000). *Sri Lankan Tamil nationalism: Its origins and development in the nineteenth and twentieth centuries.* Vancouver: University of British Columbia Press.

Wriggins, H. W. (1961). Impediments to unity in new nations: The case of Ceylon. *American Political Science Review, 55*(2), 313–320.

Elite patronage over party democracy – high politics in Sri Lanka following independence

H. Kumarasingham

Institute of Commonwealth Studies, University of London, London, UK

When Sri Lanka became independent in February 1948 it lacked a well-established party system and instead relied upon patronage and elite social relationships. Though it had a long pre-independence history of constitutional development and evolving democracy, party politics was not deep-rooted and political power continued to be wielded by an elite that had an almost feudal relationship with the masses. The convention based Westminster model Sri Lanka adopted engendered a local system that relied more on relationships than rules. Political parties and institutions were often unable to check and balance the Executive's conduct of power. Sri Lanka's elite operated British institutions in an anachronistic eighteenth-century manner such as in having a patronage-based Cabinet dominated by its prime ministerial leader/patron rather than by collegial attitudes or values. The weakness of party institutionalisation and the ambiguity in the constitutional arrangements laid the foundations for future political conflict and marginalisation of segments of society. The continuity of affairs of state from the colonial era and the known and reassuring leadership of D.S. Senanayake and his 'Uncle-Nephew Party' masked the democratic tensions and institutional fragility within the Sri Lankan state that would come to the fore violently only years after what was then seen as a model transfer of power.

In contrast to the fissiparous tensions that characterised the colonial experience in India, the small island of Sri Lanka seemed to gently and courteously accomplish its own independence with the minimum of fuss on 4 February 1948.[1] Sri Lanka's cultural conditions at first seemed at variance with those of its vast northern neighbour. Not just Britain, but the Sri Lankan political elite, sought continuity for the new Dominion. In fact many 'dignified' elements of British culture remained. 'God Save the King' was retained as the National Anthem, the Union Jack flew next to the Lion flag on public buildings, Imperial Honours were still bestowed, Sri Lankan debutantes were still presented at Buckingham Palace – and there were also key personnel who stayed in their posts and thus ensured a smooth and reassuring transition. Along with senior military, judicial and civil service personnel, the Governor of the Crown Colony of Ceylon, Sir Henry Monck-Mason-Moore, was retained and translated on independence into the first Governor-General of the Dominion of Ceylon. Just over a year after independence the British High Commissioner at Westminster House, Colombo, drew to the attention of London

> [T]he transition from Colonial to independent status has taken place so smoothly. There have been no startling changes in the domestic political scene; there have been no disturbances among any section of the population; there have been no sudden or sharp alterations in any of the institutions of Government; there have up to the present been no untoward changes in the economic situation. On the contrary the skill with which the short-lived 'Soulbury' constitution was devised and the spirit in which it was accepted enabled Ceylon to slip into independence as easily as newly launched vessel slips from its yard into the sea ... Nearly all the public institutions, Governmental and other in Ceylon, are based on English models, laid down often many decades ago by the Colonial administration. The result is that an appearance startlingly familiar to English eyes is presented by the political scene. The Cabinet, the House of Representatives, the manner in which Parliamentary business is transacted and relationship of the Civil Service to the political executive all follow the English model. This combined with good relations prevailing between Europeans and Ceylonese has produced an atmosphere in which an English observer feels almost strangely at home.[2]

This article examines the Sri Lankan political context in the early years following independence and argues that the key features of parliamentary politics was patronage and personalities not parties. The 'game' of politics was confined to a small elite cadre of culturally related factions bound often by blood and interests instead of philosophy or policy. The peaceful and transactional nature of the transfer of power with its attendant continuity of institutions and state officers engendered a false confidence that masked the superficial depths of democracy in the island. Sri Lanka's *Eastminster* (Kumarasingham, 2013a, pp. 1–24) took British institutions, but without the conventions and polity-wide parties that make Westminster work effectively.

The pre-independent context

The first Prime Minister, D.S. Senanayake, and the Cabinet were seasoned politicians who were instrumental in the handover of power and with their long governmental experience and participation (and education) were actively conditioned and acculturated in the constitutional conventions required in British eyes for a successful and peaceful political future. The outward confidence and signs of peace and prosperity, bespoke-suited patricians at the helm, and the amicability of the transfer of power disguised the vast heterogeneity of people and tensions that would radically test the country in the years to come. The decade following independence demonstrated the constitutional and political pressures that called into question whether Sri Lanka really was a model state. Sri Lanka has for almost all its history been a multi-ethnic society. According to the 1953 census Ceylon had eight million inhabitants. The predominantly Buddhist Sinhalese comprised about 70 per cent of the population and lived in the south and centre of the island, while the mainly Hindu Ceylon Tamils made up 11 per cent, concentrated in the north and east. The Ceylon Tamils are distinct from the Indian Tamils, who were mainly brought in by the British to work on the tea plantations. Other smaller groups include the Muslims and the Burghers, descendants of Portuguese, Dutch and British marriages with native Sri Lankans (Wriggins, 1960, pp. 11–51).

The constitution that Sri Lanka *received* at independence was preceded by seven other constitutions drafted between 1801 and 1947, and was the 'product of colonial legal evolution' (Coomaraswamy, 1984, p. 8). The importance of this point is crucial in viewing and analysing the impact and accommodation of the British system in Sri Lanka as an implanted Westminster. Although British culture with its 'dignified' apparatus was foreign to the masses, it was familiar to and accepted by the political elite. The constitution of 1947, with few alterations, was the product of the recommendations of the Soulbury Commission of 1944–1945 and hence the first constitution of independent Sri Lanka, which lasted till 1972, was generally known as the Soulbury Constitution.

How Sri Lanka dealt with this constitutional legacy has been subject to enduring controversy. In comparing the three constitutions that Sri Lanka has had since independence De Silva noted that the 'most striking feature' of the Soulbury Constitution 'was that it came closer to the Westminster model than most other Commonwealth constitutions' and unlike India or Pakistan independence was legally conferred through 'a mere Order in Council' rather than through an Act of Parliament (De Silva, 1977, pp. 1–3). Sir Ivor Jennings, who advised the Ceylonese leadership and helped negotiate with Whitehall, explained that though the Sri Lankan leaders were concerned that an Order in Council 'would be represented as something less than full self-government', they were more worried about the extra time it would take to achieve independence by a full Act of Parliament.

If an Act of Parliament was required it would have to be prepared by Parliamentary Counsel to the Treasury. The whole Constitution would have to be examined by Parliamentary Counsel and perhaps numerous drafting amendments would be suggested ... It was therefore agreed to have an Order in Council which was subsequently approved as the Ceylon Independence Order in Council, 1947. (Kumarasingham, 2014)

Though it is understandable that Senanayake and the Sri Lankan leadership wished to expedite matters, it is interesting to speculate whether the 'deliberative democracy' application of further parliamentary and expert legal scrutiny to Sri Lanka's independence may have produced a version more democratically robust and better able to uphold the rights of all its citizens.

Though the sovereign reality of Sri Lanka's independence was in no way less than that of its larger South Asian cousins, there were distinct differences in the style and manner of independence such as the resistance to calls for a constituent assembly or any leaning whatsoever towards republicanism or anti-British sentiment among the political elites. The British Cabinet was represented at the Independence celebrations by Patrick Gordon Walker, who relayed back to London that

Everyone is most friendly and there seems to be a genuine and deep fund of friendship for Britain. On all official buildings the Union Jack flies with the Lion Flag and sometimes actually side by side on the same mast ... This would I think be quite impossible in India.[3]

Indeed, Senanayake had used the argument during independence negotiations that Sri Lanka should be rewarded for its courtesy and reasonableness towards Britain. The persuasive 'Grand Old Man' of Sri Lankan politics emphasised that Sri Lanka had stood behind Britain like few others in the non-white Empire, citing especially the indigenous leadership's support of Britain during the war and the fact that its negotiation methods were in stark contrast to India's. In language and a manner that would have astonished some freedom fighters Senanayake beseechingly declared

There has been no rebellion in Ceylon, no non-cooperation movement and no fifth-column: we were among the peoples who gave full collaboration while Britain was hard-pressed ... We cannot offer you a rebel general – the experience of South Africa and Burma seems to suggest that it would be easier if we could – but we do suggest that an act of faith and generosity ... will cement the bonds between our people. It will indeed do more. It will add to the powers of the British Commonwealth of Nations. (De Silva, 1997, pp. 40–42)

The British constitutional scholar Mansergh, in one of his surveys of Commonwealth affairs observed that ardent nationalists from other less peaceful lands might allude in tones of some condescension to Ceylon's fight for freedom, but the gentlemanly pressure for independence exerted by its conservative nationalist leaders upon Whitehall made up in good sense what it lacked in political passion.

Sri Lanka thus joined the Commonwealth, he explained, 'without bitterness, by orderly constitutional advance which made the manner of its attainment a source of unfailing satisfaction to British constitutional historians and status in the academic world that of a model dominion' (Mansergh, 1958, p. 246). With the violent riots of 1958, just months after writing these words Mansergh would probably have regretted calling the island a 'model dominion'. But until that point academics and Whitehall most likely did feel 'unfailing satisfaction' with their work and the rosy analysis on Sri Lanka. Recording his first impressions in early 1958 the new British High Commissioner to Colombo saw the following view:

> The same small westernised and predominantly wealthy class continued to dom-
> inate the scene as in the closing years of the British regime and in many aspects
> the Colonial era continued unchanged. (Even today, for instance, there are Euro-
> pean nominated members in the House of Representatives, or to take a more
> trivial example, it is possible to buy United Kingdom postage stamps over the
> counter at the General Post Office in this City.)[4]

Sri Lanka aimed to be a truly British Westminster and not an adapted West-minster as was the case in most transplanted and implanted countries. One of the reasons Sri Lanka developed a strong attachment to British culture and favoured the royal Commonwealth was out of fear of its large northern neigh-bour dominating the subcontinent. For Sri Lanka, and also Pakistan, in this era, if India was not countered by the Commonwealth she would be unrest-rained from pursuing hegemony in the region. The Sri Lankan Foreign Sec-retary, Sir Kanthiah Vaithianathan, said that 'Ceylon's real interest in the Commonwealth was to have the United Kingdom's support as a counter-weight to India' (Moore, 1987, p. 181). British Defence Chiefs appreciated Sri Lanka's loyalty to Britain and considered the country almost within the filial club of the 'Old Dominions' and critically central to British post-war geopolitical plans (Darwin, 2009, p. 218). Senanayake told the chiefs and the Colonial Secretary he believed that 'if the British Commonwealth was at war, India and Pakistan would be neutral, whereas Ceylon would fight with the other members of the Commonwealth'.[5] Like India and Pakistan, not only did British personnel remain in the posts of Governor-General, Chief Justice and other high public positions, but the first Commander of the independent Sri Lankan Army was a career British soldier, Brigadier Sin-clair, 19th Earl of Caithness.

The Soulbury Constitution succeeded the Donoughmore Constitution, which was in operation from 1931 to September 1947. The key features of the Donoughmore Constitution were that it established (in the year that the Statute of Westminster was passed in London) universal adult suffrage (Sri Lanka became the first Asian country to do so);[6] abolished communal representation, which was replaced by territorial representation; transferred substantial control over internal policy to elected representatives of Sri Lanka; and established a system of executive committees. Despite provisions for certain areas of legislative and executive power reserved for the Imperial power, the measures were substantial and as the Colonial Secretary eulogised at its passing in 1947, it was an 'experiment in adult suffrage and in responsible democracy, and it contributed much to the political maturity and drive for effective democracy of the people of Ceylon' (Namasivayam, 1959, pp. 12–13). The Donoughmore Constitution determinedly rejected communal representation and did not suggest any alternative (such as federalism) to contain communalism. This noble attempt to achieve national unity by means of the constitutional reform that entailed the abolition of communal representation stirred growing distrust and resentment amongst the communities. Interestingly, the Simon Commission and the Round Table Conference were formulating schemes for electoral and constitutional safeguards for minorities in India at the same period as the Donoughmore Commissioners were rejecting such a system of communal representation in Sri Lanka and pressing for national integration and territorial representation (Asaratnam, 1998, p. 297). Significantly, the minorities protested in the Legislative Council against the abolition of the electorates (Woodward, 1969, p. 35).

This distaste of the Donoughmore commissioners for communal representation was completely in line with Westminster axioms. However, the system of executive committees was not. Instead of the 'conventional' quasi-cabinet structure, which aspiring local politicians sought and expected on the path to self-government, these bureaucratic-legislative committees of the unicameral State Council were modelled on the London County Council and were explicitly meant to give experience in administrative and political affairs, through the seven committees of this difficult and novel system (De Silva, 2005, pp. 521–522). The Donoughmore Constitution was radical since it did not seek to replicate Britain's model, especially considering the 'non-existence of [the] party system' on which Britain's was based. Instead this constitution, by making parties an impotent force, concentrated powers in the inter-communal elite. As DeVotta explains, the Donoughmore Constitution by arresting the development of parties, instead 'afforded influence, largesse, and power without demanding sufficient accountability' (2004, p. 40). In a sense, this major development retarded Duverger's axiom that parties are 'bound' with the expansion of democracy (Duverger, 1959, p. xxiii). The Commissioners could 'detect few signs in the political life of the Island to make us confident that parties' would function as in Britain rather than being based on 'racial or caste divisions' (Colonial Office, 1928, p. 41). This contrast made the Commissioners agree that it 'must be our aim not slavishly to follow the forms and practice of the British model which was not designed to meet conditions similar to those obtaining in Ceylon'.[7] However, the Donoughmore Constitution, rather than fostering a national non-communal spirit, in fact served to intensify elite domination as the elite were the only actors capable of grasping what was a still a foreign concept to most of the population. The new constitution, though hardly Westminster, gave local leaders 'positions of authority unimaginable in most of Britain's colonial possessions' since they were a trusted westernised elite long competent as servants of the Crown. They resembled, the British believed, a 'Whig Oligarchy' who 'represent the power of family and wealth rather than the power of cohesive political judgment'.[8] In a sense Graham's proposition that parties for the optimist 'provided the essential bonds between citizens and the government' while to the pessimist they 'increased the dangers of oligarchic rule and destructive competition' (Graham, 1993, p. 16) was cynically apt in the Sri Lankan case.

The Soulbury Constitution that followed was the result of a commission headed by Lord Soulbury in 1944–1945 to consider a new constitution for the colony. Britain, after the fall of Singapore and the goodwill, wartime participation and effective delegations of Sri Lankan politicians, conceded that self-government would arrive after the war. The main constitutional tenets of the document which became with few alterations the constitution of Sri Lanka were universal suffrage; a bicameral legislature – consisting of a House of Representatives of 101 members of whom 95 were directly elected from territorial electorates and a Senate made up of 30 members – 15 elected by proportional representation by the Lower House and the rest appointed by the Governor-General on the advice of the Prime Minister; and the establishment of a Westminster Cabinet, i.e. a parliamentary executive spawned from the legislature though selected by the Prime Minister and appointed by the Governor-General as the King's Representatives.

Sri Lanka was a parliamentary unitary democracy and constitutional monarchy – a model of a British Westminster not of an adapted Westminster, which had conspicuously more safeguards and was generally federal in character. The constitution, as will be shown below, at the political executive level had little to condition itself to the Sri Lankan context. The premise was that 'the British and the Sri Lankan elites believed that the Constitution and political life would be animated and restrained by the customs and conventions which surround parliamentary democracy in Great Britain' (Coomaraswamy, 1984, p. 12). In the 16 years of the Donoughmore Constitution, though they had criticised the absence of political parties (and yet did little to foster their growth by concentrating power in committees, rather than a legislature) their Commission had at least recognised the difficulty in the mere replication of the British Westminster model. Just four years after independence and in contrast to the glowing High Commissioner's report of 1949 quoted at the beginning of the article, Britain's new representative in Colombo Sir Cecil Syers mordantly opined

> Ceylon must not be judged by Western standards. The political and social scenes are as treacherous to the European observer as the climate. Outwardly bright and gay, they have hidden and dangerous depths. To change the metaphor, the jewel of the East yet has its flaws.[9]

The Soulbury Commissioners, however, believed like the local elite that 'British is best' and that it was the most suitable model for Sri Lanka. The Soulbury Report could state that the Commissioners' British model-inspired constitution was recommended because 'the majority – the politically conscious majority of the people of Ceylon – favoured a constitution on British lines. Such a constitution is their own desire and is not being imposed upon them'. The report's conclusion continued with what in hindsight seems like constitutional and cultural carelessness in the approach to applying the British Westminster model to Sri Lanka. It hoped that the Sri Lankan elite's cognisance and affectation of British culture would mitigate the paucity of political appreciation amongst the Sri Lankans of the efficient operation of Westminster institutions:

> The Constitution we recommend for Ceylon reproduces in large measure the form of the British Constitution, its usages and conventions, and may on that account invite the criticism so often and so legitimately levelled against attempts to frame a government for an Eastern people on the pattern of Western democracy. We are well aware that self-government of the British Parliamentary type, carried on by means of a technique which it has taken centuries to develop may not be suitable or practicable for another country, and that where the history, traditions and culture of that country are foreign to those of Great Britain, the prospect of transplanting British institutions with success may appear remote. But it does not follow that the invention of modifications or variations of the British form of government to meet different conditions elsewhere will be any more successful ... At all events, in recommending for Ceylon a Constitution on the British pattern, we are recommending a method of government we know something about, a method which is the result of very long experience, which has been tested by trial and error and which works, and, on the whole, works well. (Colonial Office, 1945, pp. 108–109)

Independent realities

The Soulbury Report thus concluded that since it had worked well and for centuries in Britain it was more than good enough for Sri Lanka. But beyond the minority of the charmed circle of the island's political and social elite this was not accurate for Sri Lanka's path to independence. The constitution and the independence process had not captured the national imagination and thus its *new* negotiated constitution lacked populist and nationalist rapture to endear its contests to the wider population. S.W.R.D. Bandaranaike, a former secretary of the Oxford Union, acerbically captured some of that sentiment after he resigned from the first Cabinet:

> Then came freedom. But how did freedom come? It came not after a fight upon definite principled policies and programmes, but it really came in the normal course of events, that is, attempts to persuade Commissions sent from England to grant this little bit or that little bit extra, and, finally, in the wake of freedom that was granted to countries like India, Pakistan and Burma, our Soulbury Constitution was altered to extend to us the same type of Dominion Status. There was no fight for that freedom which involved a fight for principles, policies and programmes which could not be carried out unless that freedom was obtained. No. It just came overnight. We just woke up one day and we were told, 'You are a dominion now'. (Ludowyk, 1966, p. 204)

On the day the country achieved its independence from the British Empire, the first Prime Minister of Independent Sri Lanka, D.S. Senanayake, broadcast proudly to the nation that 'for the first time for a thousand years we have today become a free and united nation'. In contrast with the romantic nationalism that his counterpart, Nehru, had expressed in his address on India's tumultuous and fierce road to independence just months earlier, Senanayake's address was purposefully moderate and reassuring. No doubt with an eye to India, the avuncular Prime Minister continued that with Sri Lanka's path to independence 'there are no refugees crossing Elephant pass, the Ceylon Light Infantry is organising a party to welcome its Colonel-in-Chief, and the only explosions we shall hear will be those of the fireworks'. Senanayake accurately expressed Sri Lanka's status, from his point of view, when he stated happily that independence

> had been achieved without bloodshed and with no more controversy than was to be expected in so complicated and delicate a process as the framing of a new Constitution. That we owe in part to the British people. They have taken longer than we wished, and I for one have had to say hard things about them in the past, but they have lived up to the liberal traditions of a great people.[10]

Senanayake was proud that his country had achieved independence via a constitutionalist method with the British Westminster system that this implied, rather than adapting for Sri Lanka's peculiar circumstances. Sri Lanka maintained this constitutional concert with pride and diligence.

As the Prime Minister explained to his people, in the language that the former colonial power could only approve of, the King is no longer merely King of the United Kingdom, acting on the advice of his British Ministers. He has also become King of Ceylon, acting on the advice of his Ceylon Ministers. You will find that for the first time he and not the Governor or Governor-General is part of our Parliament and that executive powers are vested in him in order that they may be exercised by the responsible Government in office for the time being.[11]

The close relationship between the Governor-General and Prime Minister and the executive powers vested in their offices would be fundamental to all aspects of Sri Lanka's post-independence politics. This dualist relationship of duopolistic connotations would go far beyond the parameters of a Westminster 'efficient' operating culture and overshadow the Cabinet – which, similarly, was not operating according to collegial Westminster values and attitudes despite its 'dignified' Westminster façade.

[D.S. Senanayake was] to repeat the figure of speech so frequently used then, the architect of Ceylon's freedom. What he built, what he was responsible for constructing on behalf of the elite whom he represented so remarkably well, was a new façade with a burnished brass plate on the door: Free Ceylon. It was the outward and visible sign of all the elite had been pressing for since 1910. The structure raised by the British remained intact; inside there was some rearrangement. A number of Ceylonese previously relegated to rooms without a view moved higher up; they could stride the corridors of power with more confidence and even peer out of the commanding heights of the structure. The new façade was impressive; it delighted those who filed in and out of the building as the new VIPs ... The Ministers in the Cabinet of 1947 could feel ... that they had all they wanted and more. (Ludowyk, 1966, p. 204)

Rather than feeling some liberating cathartic desire to reform or recreate their implanted constitution, the new elite sought the Westminster embrace. The early Cabinets of Sri Lanka showed a definite inclination towards doing things the 'British way' in terms of ceremony and royalty; the new Dominion showed the Bagehotion 'dignified' British culture *par excellence*. The new independence Cabinet requested that Governors-General should wear the white colonial uniform and full decorations including the ostrich-plumed pith helmet. The young Queen herself during her first visit in 1954 was not only to open both houses of parliament with the 'ceremonial usually associated with the opening of Parliament in the House of Lords ... followed as closely as possible', but despite the blazing sun was requested by the Sri Lankan Cabinet to wear her heavy coronation gown for the occasion.[12] The new House of Representatives, which she opened, rejected communal representation as an unnecessary imposition and saw it to be worthy only of stirring Eastern parochialism for the new legislature. However, a communal group that did gain representation were the Europeans. The new constitution provided for six nominated members. By convention this meant in practice 'United Kingdom citizens have ... been nominated to fill three of these seats on behalf of the British businesses'. This extraordinary arrangement, which even the British High Commissioner called 'an odd and somewhat anachronistic set-up' allowed for British subjects to sit and vote in this fully sovereign *Eastminster* Parliament.[13] It shows another example of Sri Lanka's elite wanting to stay loyal to British Colonial practices and retain continuity. In sharp contrast to the rhetoric of modern Sri Lankan representatives a leading politician just after the end of World War II was able to impress Britain after independence with the assurance they should 'think of Ceylon as a little bit of England' and, with foolhardy confidence, gushed that 'Ceylon will rival Australia as the first Dominion to rally to the side of the Mother Country'.[14] Though not quite the feeling of the entire elite and Cabinet, it was not hyperbole either. The Cabinets at least until 1956 were dominated by the elite whose affluence, education and social backgrounds inclined them to find congruence with the British cultural way. The Soulbury Report recognised this:

> It must be borne in mind that a number of the political leaders of Ceylon have been educated in England and have absorbed British political ideas. When they demand responsible government, they mean government on the British parliamentary model and are apt to resent any deviation from it as 'derogatory to their status as fellow citizens of the British Commonwealth of Nations and as conceding something less than they consider their due'. To put it more colloquially, what is good enough for the British people is good enough for them.[15]

However, what the Commissioners and the elite blithely ignored was that what worked in Britain would not necessarily work in a country that lacked, for all its affection for British culture, a thorough working knowledge and participation of the 'efficient' mechanics of Westminster operational culture. Sri Lanka enjoyed the trappings of monarchy, which had always been part of its culture. D.S. Senanayake liked to claim that Elizabeth II was the latest in the long and ancient line of Sri Lankan monarchs. Sir Ivor Jennings commented:

> A good deal of ingenuity is required to prove the apostolic succession from Prince Vijaya to Queen Elizabeth, but nationalist history is not less influential through being romantic as the story of King Arthur and the Knights of the Round Table. (Jennings, 1956, p. 137)

Sri Lankans had a genuine affection for the Crown. British officials were amazed to find cut out pictures of the Royal Family in 'primitive' 'jungle' areas, but this does not mask the fact that to the masses the Queen was always Queen of England, not the Queen of Sri Lanka.[16] The trouble was that the idea of the Queen of Sri Lanka was almost entirely an elite conception.

Though legally correct, it was difficult to explain that an English Queen was actively part of the Sri Lankan constitution and not merely taken from a book of fairy tales demonstrating the dangerous fantasy of the Sri Lankan elite in thinking they were some latter-day Rajas of the Round Table.

The first four Prime Ministers all went to one of the two leading Colombo schools (both modelled on English public schools), St. Thomas College and Royal College, and were all wealthy landowners, high caste Buddhist Sinhalese[17] and all studied, with the exception of the first, at Oxford or Cambridge. They had all gained their political training through many years under colonial tutelage in the pre-independence legislature and all except the relatively youthful Dudley Senanayake had also had extensive tenure as ministers during the Donoughmore era. They all had a long apprenticeship in the legislature before gaining the seals of office as Prime Minister – S.W.R.D. Bandaranaike 25 years, D.S. Senanayake 23 years, Sir John Kotelawala 22 years and Dudley Senanayake the shortest, but still substantial period of 16 years.[18]

The Sri Lankan Cabinets between 1948 and 1956 also had many other things in common. More so than Britain and the transplanted *New Westminsters* (Kumarasingham, 2013c, pp. 579–596) the Cabinet in Sri Lanka in these years was ethnically 'somewhat federal', in deference to the plurality of the island. However, though consideration was given to the heterogeneity of nationality, caste, religion and region the Cabinet was, at least until 1956, remarkably homogeneous in terms of wealth, high social status, elite Christian denominational or government secondary schooling and often further education in Britain. Until 1956 there were generally nine low-country Sinhalese, two Kandyan Sinhalese, two Ceylon Tamils and one Muslim in Cabinet. Though this would seem to reflect an element of composite accommodation or consociationalism, in fact they all belonged to a common social elite and came from the same economic background, which belied their symbolic diverse representation. An example of this exclusivity was that, of the men who served in the first Cabinet, two were from Oxford, four from Cambridge, six from the University of London and four from the Ceylon Law College, while all but one had attended one or other of the country's leading secondary schools (Wilson, 1960, pp. 1–54). When D.S. Senanayake provided a memorandum on the high and 'dignified' cabinet doctrine of collective responsibility he furnished his paper, using the constitutionally ubiquitous Jennings's assistance, with laudable examples from the administrations of such ancient Westminster luminaries as Viscounts Melbourne and Palmerston and the Marquess of Salisbury, which would have found resonance with most of his Cabinet colleagues – especially the Oxbridge ones.[19] That said, no matter how often British Westminster traditions were voiced it was more to display erudition and comfort than to put them into practice or develop them to meet the unique needs of the Sri Lankan polity.

The Sri Lankan elite that composed the early Cabinets was very much like their settler cousins in Australia, Canada and New Zealand with the depth of knowledge, education in the British Westminster system and even the outward signs of dress and social niceties.[20] They happily acceded to the implant and admired the felicity and authenticity with which the British had planted their own institutions in Sri Lanka. This readiness to take on British conventions and constitutional tutelage made Ceylon a model transfer of power case for future independence negotiations. In colonial territories such as Malaya, Ghana, Sierra Leone and those in the Anglophone Caribbean, Ceylon's transactional transfer of power by the British elite and the indigenous elite negotiated without resorting to a constituent assembly or backing by a mass movement became the model to follow, however precarious this was for institutional and political democratic acculturation (see Lyon & Manor, 1983).

Sir Oliver Goonetilleke smugly proclaimed in the *New York Times* in 1952 that 'Ceylon is the best job the Englishman has done anywhere in the world, almost better than in his own country' (Woodward, 1969, p. 3). For elite figures like Goonetilleke, there was truth to this sentiment. Sri Lanka's peaceful path to independence and readiness to accept Britain's sponsorship was in contrast to India, and Sri Lanka's leading figures were happily cognisant of British Westminster. However, there were serious differences compared to transplanted countries with their well-established mechanics of a party system and the associated elite and mass awareness of how the formal Westminster institutions were 'efficiently' operated. The *New Westminsters* better understood the formal and informal conventions and the associated operating culture of attitudes and values. Even before the communal troubles that would inflame the Island Syers once again crushed any rose-tinted view that *Eastminster* was the same as Westminster

> We cannot expect to find Parliamentary democracy in the East in the developed form we know in the West. Although the result of the educative processes of 150 years of British rule, the outward forms of Parliamentary democracy are established and observed in Ceylon, democracy itself is in its infancy and pattern of government is more a cross between something very much like autocracy and oligarchy.[21]

The Westminster fixation on centralisation coupled with the nascent, urban and elite-dominated parties' failure to extend organisationally around the country disabled the ability to spread institutions and promote local knowledge of government. Manor has labelled this a serious 'failure of political integration' and argues that the 'elite/mass discontinuity, rather than the Sinhalese/Tamil discontinuity, is the principle cleavage in the polity in Sri Lanka' of that early period

(Manor, 1979, p. 22). Due to the absence of a cohesive national mass movement and the fragmentary nature of existing associations, most parties were formed in anticipation of the 1947 elections. The Donoughmore Constitution's State Council, as discussed above, did not engender cabinet or party loyalties or practices. As Jennings explains, the constitution, which Sri Lanka had until 1947 'was designed to suit a legislature without parties and therefore actively discouraged them' (Woodward, 1969, p. 43).

Parties of convenience

Sri Lanka could be characterised what Diamond, Linz and Lipset have termed 'low quality democracy' or 'low-intensity democracy' meaning though Sri Lanka was and is formally a democracy with open elections, independent organisations, free media, it 'nevertheless lack[ed] accountability, responsiveness, and institutional balance and effectiveness between elections' (Diamond, Linz, & Lipset, 1995, p. 8). The shallowness of party infrastructure and indifference to political mobilisation caused this imbalance between formal democracy and high quality or high intensive democracy. Instead important conditions for democracy in Sri Lanka such as 'meaningful and extensive competition' between established political parties that fostered 'a highly inclusive level of political participation in the selection of leaders and policies' with no major group excluded was clearly lacking (ibid., pp. 6–7). Unlike Britain or India, the parties that gained power did not have experience, were not well established and lacked party discipline, being dominated to a greater extent by their leaders. As such most parties at the time were 'stamped by the idiosyncrasies of their dominating personalities' since almost 'no party institution is well enough established to resist the characteristics and peculiarities of its leaders' (Wriggins, 1960, p. 105). The United National Party (UNP), for instance, was formed just a year before the 1947 elections, out of the rubble of ineffective organisations such as the exclusivist elite Ceylon National Congress. It essentially became the Senanayake family party and was known as the 'Uncle Nephew Party'. The conservative and intensely moderate Ceylon National Congress was founded in 1919, but waited until 1942 to advocate independence (Ashton, 1999, p. 453). The Sri Lanka Freedom Party (SLFP) was very much the personal creation of S.W.R.D. Bandaranaike and it was only constituted in 1951 on his disgruntled resignation from the Senanayake Cabinet.[22]

Most other parties were 'based on either communal or social divisions, though some were little more than cliques led by dominant personalities and most, including the UNP, offered little in the way of a detailed manifesto instead in concentrated on personal attributes' (Woodward, 1969, pp. 52–67). Despite being led by Senanayake, the UNP was unable to gain a majority in 1947 to govern alone, requiring support from minor parties including the Tamil Congress and Independents. Cabinet therefore was more a grouping of factions surrounding the leader than the vanguard of the majority party as in most *New Westminsters*. With minimal party institutionalisation Cabinet lacked the collegial, and yet disciplined, attitudes and values of Westminster Cabinet culture.

During the ten years after independence, cabinets and political parties were a collection of discernible followings and loyalties. Unlike India's post-independence cabinet there was no party oligarchy of well-established party leaders. The heterogeneity of Sri Lanka and shallowness of the party system in the early years meant that, in view of the cabinet's powerful representative function in Sri Lanka, the power associated with cabinet membership was often used to further the personal interests of the leader. As Wriggins has stated:

> In a country where personalities play such an important role, cabinet loyalty had been enhanced where the widespread popularity of the party's leader becomes, to some extent, a substitute for a party organisation and program. No doubt in the three elections in independent Ceylon, certain M.P.s had been brought to parliament on the coattails of the three elected prime ministers. This was true in the popular upsurge of emotion toward Dudley Senanayake in 1952 and S.W.R.D. Bandaranaike in 1956. There are relatively prominent men who are likely to be cabinet material in any event, but it is a significant fact that there are those who have entered parliament and even become ministers primarily because of their close association with the prime minister rather than from any other identifiable source of political strength. (Wriggins, 1960, p. 100)

With such use of patronage and personal followings, the politics of Sri Lanka was more akin to eighteenth-century Westminster than the twentieth-century Westminster. Two distinguished British visitors observed as much. On the day of independence, Patrick Gordon Walker wrote from Colombo to his Labour Cabinet colleagues that socially and politically 'Ceylon is a mixture of feudalism and eighteenth century landed aristocracy' with leaders who, in view of their wealth, local power and influence, were 'comparable to a Whig landlord in George III's time. They have much the same attitude towards politics. Public life is riddled with affable and open corruption, moral and otherwise' (De Silva 1997, p. 369). Ten years later, the Conservative Prime Minister Harold Macmillan noted in his diary from Sri Lanka that no regular Party system on modern British lines had developed there and instead 'in a curious way, the political life is more like that of Whig politics in the eighteenth century than one would suppose. The leading figures have a "following" (like the Bedfords or the Rockinghams)'. Ironically, and amusingly, considering Bandaranaike's language policy in contrast to the Indian Prime Minister's, Macmillan thought the Sri Lankan leader is a sort of local Nehru – except that he has only just got into office and had nothing to do with Ceylon obtaining independence. He clearly models himself on Mr N; dresses like an Anglo-Catholic priest at the altar, stole and alb; takes an interest in world politics; is a very rich man and son of a very rich man; is westernised (he was Secretary and Treasurer of the Oxford Union, where he was at Christ Church) [and] is partly Conservative and partly advanced Socialist, as is his Govt. (Catterall, 2011, p. 91)

Such analysis was in tune with the reality of the close confines of a parochial political class solidified by kinship and patronage rather than party and professionalism.[23] As one dissident Sri Lanka communist, himself a cousin of Bandaranaike, stated in 1968, the political power system in Ceylon was 'a game of musical chairs by which a Bandaranaike (SLFP) or a Senanayake (UNP) can alternatively come to power' (Jupp, 1978, p. 47). The game of musical chairs was also confined to almost exclusive ethnic parameters with Sinhalese parties competing for Sinhalese votes and Tamil parties doing the same with their community. As Stepan, Linz, and Yadav (2011, p. 152) note after 1956 Sri Lanka 'ceased to have any major polity-wide parties', which had dangerous ramifications for the future violent ethnic conflict ahead.

Such politics is natural when the cabinet and party system is embryonic and therefore prime ministers and leaders have to rely on their followings, which in such a society as Sri Lanka often comprise family members, rather than the Westminster leanings on cabinet and a rigid disciplined party. Westminster places the burden of power upon the prime minister, with the expectation that he or she will be supported through a party system by a cabinet of colleagues. This was not available in the early years in Sri Lanka as the party system was based essentially, as one substantial study puts it, on the premise that parties are based on 'a group of ambitious men who have chosen politics as a vocation and who seek personal success' (Woodward, 1969, p. 19), rather than the traditional disciplined loyalties of the twentieth-century Westminster model of organised parties. The defects in the system were already apparent in the first decade following, if not before, independence and as the years progressed the 'struggle to redesign flawed institutions' became de-incentivised since the baronial kin-based parties clung to these flaws for their political existence (Diamond et al., 1995, pp. 54–55). The British High Commission in 1955 at Westminster House, in an analysis that still rings true, assessed that elections 'are very largely a conflict of personalities over the distribution of Government patronage and services'.[24] Sri Lanka's *Eastminster* system of cabinet government functioned without the fundamental factor of an entrenched and comprehensive party structure, instead relying on personalist factions. This in turn led to the Cabinet as an institution operating in a culture of attitudes and values that differed markedly from the Westminster model and, as already observed, was more like that of the British Cabinets in the eighteenth century which predated the institutionalised party system that became a feature of most twentieth-century Westminsters.

Patronage and personalised power, rather than party authority, was the key to maintaining loyalty in this era. For instance, even during the relatively tranquil and unchallenged era of the first Senanayake ministry, 23 of 101 members of the elected lower house held government office. As Wriggins explains, this 'is no doubt excessive' considering Sri Lanka's size, and yet 'the extreme diversity of the island's people, the multiplicity of interests to be represented, and the tendency for followers to rally around an individual rather than a party suggests that it was an expedient move at the outset', which created a precedent followed by all his successors (Wriggins, 1960, p. 115). In the UNP and SLFP, leaders *emerge* as in the old British Conservative Party, without any consultation with lesser and lower elements of the party. Even the prominent smaller parties were very much the creations and creatures of their leaders, such as the Communists under Dr S.A. Wickramasinghe, Dr N.M. Perera's Lanka Sama Samaja Party, S.J.V. Chelvanayakam's Federal Party and G.G. Ponnambalam's Tamil Congress. These smaller parties existed mainly to further the goals of their leaders. This leader-centric approach often meant policy was secondary and party democracy an optional extra. Such conditions prevented durable collaboration between the smaller parties to further their common policy interests. For example distrust, ego and jealousy disabled a common Tamil political platform while for similar reasons the leftist parties, despite being among the best organised, never realised their potential of being a credible alternative governing force to the UNP.

Conclusion

This political tendency towards personalised, leader-follower factionalism often meant levels of disunity within the Cabinet and sometimes Parliament as well, especially after the death of D.S. Senanayake, whose stature as the independence leader clouded this feature. Dudley Senanayake's first ministry was dominated by disagreement with Kotelawala and his supporters over the succession; Kotelawala's abrasive personality angered many within the Cabinet; while Bandaranaike's coalition Cabinet was highly restive and divided over the many controversial policies and domestic crises that faced his brief government. However, though prime ministers may have had to make concessions to groups at times, due to the absence of true party accountability, theirs was a delegative democratic power direct from the people. This enabled them to go over the heads of their parliamentary colleagues and party members to the electorate, from which they derived real political power (they also became a prisoner of such expectations of the electorate, especially over issues like communalism). The system is leader-centric – a feature that the Westminster model encourages. The patronage-ridden and factional nature of cabinet and party government during this era meant that in Ceylon

> The role of *primus inter pares* is difficult to fill. Power and deference tend to be drawn away from the equals into the hands of the outstanding leader, a fact which makes it all the more difficult to succeed to his place. Disputes between colleagues could often be resolved only by the party leader himself. He became the dramatic focus of organisational loyalty and public interest. In all parties, whoever was conceded to be the leader was given a wide scope for policy initiative. The rank and file did not presume to have views that counted; by their competition, members of the entourage, including cabinet colleagues, ensured that the prime minister had the last word. (Wriggins, 1960, p. 149)

This lack of a Westminster culture of collegial attitudes and values based on shared institutional attachment to a party rather than personal loyalties to a leader meant a higher level of political instability and difficulty in making strong political and policy decisions. It also meant that there was minimal formal horizontal accountability within the Executive. Sri Lankan political leaders saw the cabinet as place of patronage and were not acculturated to the Westminster-style cabinet collegiality that was even evident in Nehru's India. In the formative years of Sri Lankan independence and beyond, patronage was the source of power; not the party.

Acknowledgements

The author is very grateful to the anonymous peer reviewers and to the Editor, James Chiriyankandath, for their helpful comments and suggestions. This article is largely drawn from chapters 5–7 of the author's book *A Political Legacy of the British Empire – Power and the Parliamentary System in Post Colonial India and Sri Lanka*, London: I.B. Tauris, 2013 and the author appreciatively acknowledges the permission of I.B. Tauris to reproduce parts of the book here.

Notes

1. For an analysis of the illusory nature of Sri Lanka's peaceful path to independence in contrast to India, see Kumarasingham (2013d).
2. High Commissioner to Noel-Baker, 17 May 1949, DO 35/3123, The National Archives, Kew, United Kingdom (henceforth TNA).
3. Extracts from Gordon Walker's diary, 6 February 1948 in DO 35/2195, TNA.
4. High Commissioner to Secretary of State for Commonwealth Relations, 6 March 1958, DO 35/8902, TNA.
5. Note of meeting of Prime Minister of Ceylon with Secretary of State for the Colonies, 8 October 1948, DO 121/154 and for further exploration of these issues, see Kumarasingham (2013b).

6. Sri Lanka had universal suffrage 20 years before its adoption in India and just 2 years after Britain itself.
7. Donoughmore Report, Cmd. 3131, pp. 45–46.
8. Hankinson to Noel-Baker, 17 May 1949, DO 35/3123, TNA.
9. High Commissioner to Secretary of State for Commonwealth Relations, 3 April 1952, DO 35/3127, TNA.
10. D.S. Senanayake's Broadcast, 4 February 1948, Sir Ivor Jennings Papers, Ceylon B3, ICS125, Institute of Commonwealth Studies, University of London.
11. Ibid.
12. High Commissioner to Secretary of State for Commonwealth Relations, 7 May 1954, DO 35/5144, TNA.
13. DO 35/8905, TNA.
14. The politician was none other than Sir Oliver Goonetilleke. Cited from Manor (1989, p. 199).
15. Soulbury Report, Cmd. 6677, p. 110.
16. High Commissioner to Secretary of State for Commonwealth Relations, 3 April 1952, DO 35/3127, TNA.
17. S.W.R.D. Bandaranaike, though brought up as an Anglican, had converted to Buddhism well before he became Prime Minister in 1956.
18. For further material, the most comprehensive analysis of the backgrounds of Ceylon's early Prime Ministers and Cabinets can be found in Wilson (1960).
19. Note by the Prime Minister on Collective Responsibility, undated, Jennings Papers, Ceylon B3, ICS125, ICS.
20. They even shared their names. In the 30 years that followed independence of the seven individuals that held the office of Prime Minister only Mrs Bandaranaike and W. Dahanayake had Ceylonese first names while Don Stephen, Dudley, John, Solomon West Ridgeway Dias and Junius Richard had such European names despite all seven being Sinhalese Buddhists.
21. High Commissioner to Secretary of State for Commonwealth Relations, 27 May 1955, DO 35/5362, TNA.
22. Bandaranaike, who had been a senior Minister under D.S. Senanayake, always thought he would succeed the 'Old Man' as leader and when it became apparent that this was not going to happen, he resigned. See Manor (1989, pp. 168–204).
23. For an interesting account of Sri Lankan family politics see Malhotra (2003, pp. 231–245).
24. High Commissioner to Secretary of State for Commonwealth Relations, 27 May 1955, DO 35/5362, TNA.

References

Asaratnam, S. (1998). Nationalism in Sri Lanka and the Tamils. In Michael Roberts (Ed.), *Sri Lanka – Collective identities revisited* (Vol. II, pp. 270–300). Colombo: Marga Institute.

Ashton, S. R. (1999). Ceylon. In Judith Brown & Wm. Roger Louis (Eds.), *The Oxford history of the British empire – The twentieth century* (pp. 447–464). Oxford: Oxford University Press.

Catterall, P. (2011). *The Macmillan diaries* (Vol. II). London: Macmillan.

Colonial Office. (1928). *Ceylon: Report of the special commission on the government of Ceylon*. Cmd. 3131. London: His Majesty's Stationery Office [Donoughmore Report].

Colonial Office. (1945). *Ceylon: Report of the commission on the constitution*. Cmd. 6677. London: His Majesty's Stationery Office [Soulbury Report].

Coomaraswamy, R. (1984). *Sri Lanka – The crisis of the Anglo-American constitutional traditions in a developing society*. New Delhi: Vikas.

Darwin, J. (2009). *The empire project – The rise and fall of the British world-system 1830–1970*. Cambridge: Cambridge University Press.

De Silva, K. M. (1977). A tale of three constitutions 1946–8, 1972 and 1978. *The Ceylon Journal of Historical and Social Studies*, *VII*(2) (published in 1979), 1–17 .

De Silva, K. M. (Ed.). (1997). *British documents on the end of empire series B – Sri Lanka, Part II, towards independence 1945–48*. London: Her Majesty's Stationery Office.

De Silva, K. M. (2005). *A history of Sri Lanka* (Special Sri Lankan ed.). Colombo: Vijitha Yapa.

DeVotta, N. (2004). *Blowback – Linguistic nationalism, institutional decay, and ethnic conflict in Sri Lanka*. Stanford: Stanford University Press.

Diamond, L., Linz, J. J., & Lipset, S. M. (1995). *Politics in developing countries – Comparing experiences with democracy* (2nd ed.). Boulder, CO: Lynne Rienner.

Duverger, M. (1959). *Political parties – Their organisation and activity in the modern state* (2nd ed., revised), London: Methuen.

Graham, B. D. (1993). *Representation and party politics – A comparative perspective*. Oxford: Blackwell.

Jennings, I. (1956). Crown and commonwealth in Asia. *International Affairs*, *32*(2), 137–147.

Jupp, J. (1978). *Sri Lanka – Third world democracy*. London: Frank Cass.

Kumarasingham, H. (2013a). *A political legacy of the British empire – Power and the parliamentary system in post colonial India and Sri Lanka*. London: I.B. Tauris.

Kumarasingham, H. (2013b). The 'Tropical Dominions' – The appeal of dominion status in the decolonisation of India, Pakistan and Sri Lanka. *Transactions of the Royal Historical Society*, Sixth Series, *23*, 223–245.

Kumarasingham, H. (2013c). Exporting executive accountability? Westminster legacies of executive power. *Parliamentary Affairs*, *66*(3), 579–596.

Kumarasingham, H. (2013d, June). *'The jewel in the east yet has its flaws' – The deceptive tranquility surrounding Sri Lankan Independence*. Heidelberg Papers in South Asian and Comparative Politics, No. 72.

Kumarasingham, H. (Ed.). (2014). *Constitution maker – Selected writings of Sir Ivor Jennings*. Cambridge: Cambridge University Press.

Lyon, P., & Manor, J. (Eds.). (1983). *Transfer and transformation: Political institutions in the new commonwealth*. Cambridge: Leicester University Press.

Ludowyk, E. F. C. (1966). *The modern history of Ceylon*. London: Weidenfeld and Nicolson.

Malhotra, I. (2003). *Dynasties of India and beyond – Pakistan Sri Lanka Bangladesh*. New Delhi: Harper Collins.

Manor, J. (1979). The failure of political integration in Sri Lanka (Ceylon). *Journal of Commonwealth and Comparative Politics*, *17*(1), 21–46.

Manor, J. (1989). *The expedient utopian – Bandaranaike and Ceylon*. Cambridge: Cambridge University Press.

Mansergh, N. (1958). *Survey of British commonwealth affairs – Problems of wartime co-operation and post-war change 1939–1952*. London: Oxford University Press.

Moore, R. J. (1987). *Making the new commonwealth*. Oxford: Oxford University Press.

Namasivayam, N. (1959). *Parliamentary government in Ceylon, 1948–1958*. Colombo: K.V.G. De Silva.

Stepan, A., Linz, J. J., & Yadav, Y. (2011). *Crafting state-nations – India and other multinational democracies*. Baltimore, MD: Johns Hopkins University Press.

Wilson, A. J. (1960). Ceylon cabinet ministers 1947–1959 – Their political, economic and social background. *The Ceylon Economist, 5*(1), 1–54.

Woodward, C. A. (1969). *The growth of a party system in Ceylon*. Rhode Island: Brown University Press.

Wriggins, W. H. (1960). *Ceylon: Dilemmas of a new nation*. Princeton, NJ: Princeton University Press.

Index

Page numbers in *italic* type refer to *tables*
Page numbers followed by 'n' refer to notes

accountability 156; horizontal 183; party 182
affiliation: political 144
aggregate voting 7, 10
agrarian bourgeoisie 57, 64, 67–9
Ahmad, S. 21–2, 28n; and Alavi, H. 22
Akali Dal *see* Shiromani Akali Dal (SAD)
Akram Ansari, M. 17
Alavi, H. 11; and Ahmad, S. 22
All India Anna Dravida Munnetra Kazhagam (AIADMK) 33–4, 38, 41, 51–2n
All India Congress Committee (AICC) 82–4
All-India Democratic Women's Association (AIDWA) 116
All-India Muslim League 2
Anandpur Sahib Resolution (ASR) 61–2, 66–7, 70n
Anbazhagan, K. (General Secretary) 36, 41
Andhra Pradesh (India) 44, 59, 125
Annadurai, C.N. 34
apathy: political 81–2
ape anduwa (our government) mentality 145
Archer, R. 15
armed conflict 57
Aruna, P.A. 44
assembly: elections 32–4, 37–9, *46*, 64–6, *76*, 115, 121–4; state 41, 46, 120

Association for Democratic Reforms (ADR) 4
authoritarianism 10, 14–15, 27, 139, 142–5, 148–51, 154–60; central 63–5; politics of 150–60; resisting 61–2; semi- 142; soft- 142–3
autocratic leadership 50
autonomy 35, 41, 49, 56, 68, 104–5, 157; regional 61
Ayub Khan, M. (President, Pakistan) 11–12, 17, 22
Azhagiri, M.K. (Minister) 35, 38–9

Baalu, T.R. 37, 43
Backward Class (BC) 33, 42, 45–7, 50, 88
Badal, M.S. 68
Badal, P.S. (Chief Minister, Punjab) 3, 61
Badal, S.S. 3
Bahujan Samaj Party (BSP) 63–4, 79–82, 87–90, 100–5, 116, 124, 129
Bandaranaike, Sirimavo (Prime Minister, Sri Lanka) 146, 155, 180–2
Bandaranaike, S.W.R.D. (Prime Minister, Sri Lanka) 140, 155, 174, 177–9
Bandaranayake, S. (Chief Justice, Sri Lanka) 151
Bangladesh Election Commission 2
Barany, Z. 143
Bari, S.: and Khan, H. 13
Basic Democracies 12, 17, 22
Baxter, C. 13

Beijing Platform for Action 111–12
Bharatiya Janata Party (BJP) 64–6, 78–82, 85, 88–90, 94–105, 109–16, 120–32; Mahila Morcha (women's wing) 121–2
Bhutto, B. (Prime Minister, Pakistan) 13, 19
Bhutto, Z.A. (Prime Minister, Pakistan) 2, 12, 17, 23
Biju Janata Dal (BJD) 118
Bille, L. 79–80, 90
biraderi 9, 16–20, 25–7, 28n; *Mekan* 8, 24–6, 28n
Bofors scandal 91, 104
bourgeoisie: agrarian 57, 64, 67–9; Hindu 65–6; industrial 64
Brahmanism 45
bribery 150
British High Commission 167, 170–3, 176, 181
Buddhism 158; Sinhalese 139–42, 145–52, 156, 160, 168, 177
bureaucracy 25, 144–8, 154; state 146
Burke, J. 14
by-elections 43, 88

cabinet ministers 154
campaigns: election 12, 18
candidates 79–81, 84–6; female 109–38; former 103–4; high-risk 119
capitalism 33, 55
caste 32–4, 40–1, 44–9, 86–9, 104, 112, 116; backward 33, 42, 45–7, 50, 88; dominant 46; forward 46–7; leading 36; low- 56; Scheduled Caste (SC) 41, 44, 47–50, 82, 87, 91, 114–16; upper 45, *46*, 88, 96, 105
catchall parties 81–2, 90, 105
Catterall, P. 181
censorship: self- 153
Central Election Committee (CEC) 82–3, 85–6
centralisation 78, 178
Ceylon: National Congress 2–3, 179, *see also* Sri Lanka
Ceylon Administrative Service (CAS) 146
Ceylon Civil Service (CCS) 146
Chandra, B. 57, 68
Chandra, K. 88; and Umaira, W. 49
Chandrakanthan, S. (Pillayan) 157–8
chauvinism: ethnic 4, 160

Chelvanayakam, S.J.V. 182
Chiriyankandath, J. 1–6
chit system 147
civil liberties 149
civil society 144, 148, 156
Civil War (Sri Lanka 1983–2009) 1, 139, 145, 148–9, 157, 160; post- 150, 157–60
class 22, 55–77; conflict 12; lower 33; middle 33, 69, 81, 105; urban 105; working 81, 110–11
clientelism 7, 10, 14–22, 27
coalition government 1–2, 67, 86–9, 96, 114, 151
Cold War (1947–91): post- 144
colonialism 11, 21, 57, 139, 147, 166, 176; post- 59–60, 66
colonisation 146
Commons, J.R. 143
Commonwealth of Nations 170
communal representation 171, 175
communalisation 60
communalism 83, 141, 171; Sikh 57, 68
communism 56, 140
Communist Party of India (CPI) 56, 60, 64, 70n, 116
Communist Party of India (Marxist (CPI-M)) 56, 64, 78–82, 86, 90, 96–105, 116
Communist Party of India (Marxist-Leninist (CPIML)) 56
Communist Party of Sri Lanka (CP) 140
community 86, 89; majority 62, 141, 146; minority 57–9, 145, 148, 158
competition 3, 24–6; electoral 144
confidence 168; self- 66–7
conflict: armed 57; class 12; ethnic 160, 181; ideological 15; political 166
conformity 145
Congress Legislature Party (CLP) 84
Congress Working Committee (CWC) 84
Conservative Party 182
consociationalism 177
constitutionalism 174
Constitutions: India (1949) 67, 110, 114; Sri Lanka (1972) 145–52, 155
convenience 179–82
Coomaraswamy, R. 172
corruption 4, 89, 150–1, 156, 159
coup d'état 1, 23

crime 4, 89, 159; war 150
crisis: domestic 182; economic 158; elections 90
Cross, W. 79
cultural rights 62

daaras (public meeting space) 8, 27n
Dagar, R. 112
Daily Times 13
Dalits 33, 36, 40–50, 63, 88–9, 116; female 110–11
De Silva, K.M. 168–9, 180
decay: political 139–65
decentralisation 79–81
decolonisation 139–41
defection 84, 91, 96, 101–5
degeneration 1; institutional 145; political 4
deinstitutionalisation 142–52, 160
democracy 4, 12–14, 27, 62, 65, 110–13, 160; controlled 28n; defending 61–2; deliberative 169; electoral 144; formal 179; internal 49, 79–82; liberal 142–4, 160; parliamentary 12, 172; party 166–86; representative 133; true 148; unitary 172
Democratic Party 159
democratic regression 139–65
democratisation 10
Devananda, D. 157
development 66, 141; constitutional 166; economic 81; social 81
DeVotta, N. 4, 139–65, 171
Diamond, L.: Linz, J. and Lipset, S. 179
diktat 150, 154
disadvantage: social 45, 48
disaggregation 34
discrimination 146; gender 111; racial 141
dissidence: internal 94
District Congress Committee (DCC) 82–6
District Councils 15, 24
district secretaries 35–6, 86
domestic crisis 182
dominance: party 18–20; political 11
dominant caste 46
domination: political 65–7
Donoughmore Constitution (1931–47) 140, 171–3, 177–9

Dravida Munnetra Kazhagam (DMK) 3, 32–56, 113; elite 34–7
Duraisami, V.P. 48
Duverger, M. 171
dynastic politics 32, 38–43, 49–50, 156

Eastminster system 167, 176–8, 181
education 45, 114, 120
Eelam People's Democratic Party (EPDP) 157
Election Commission of India (ECI) 2, 70n, 79, 114
Election Commission of Pakistan (ECP) 2
elections 7–14, 17–23, 35–8, 82–91, 100–2, 150, 158–60; assembly 32–4, 37–9, 46, 64–6, 76, 115, 121–4; by- 43, 88; campaigns 12, 18; crisis 90; democratic 12, 65; early 90, 104; emergency 90; flawed 65; general 90, 109–38; India (2009) 109–38; local 12, 22–4, 34–5, 88, 159; national 24, 85; non-party 25; parliamentary 78, 84, 159; plebiscitary 104; presidential 158–9; repeated 16; snap 90, 104; winning 49
electoral politics 15, 110–20, 125, 132–3
electoral success 115–19, 128–9
elite 18; party 50; patronage 166–86; political 32–54, 173–4; rural 14; Sinhalese 139; social 173–4
emergency elections 90
Emergency, The (India 1975–7) 61–2, 66–7
employment 45, 120; state 114
empowerment: female 121, 133; socio-economic 88
equality: economic 33; social 116
ethnic chauvinism 4, 160
ethnic conflict 160, 181
ethnicity 1, 4, 20, 82, 88–90, 104–6
ethnocentrism 139–42, 145, 148, 160
exclusion 148; ethnic 148; gender 133; institutional 125; political 116
exclusivism 141
extortion 157
extremism 63

factionalism 22–6, 83–4, 158, 182
Farooqui, A.: and Sridharan, E. 3–4, 78–108

favouritism 145, 156
Federal Party 140, 182
feudalism 8–14, 19, 166; anti- 21, 26
First Family 151–5
flawed elections 65
Fonseka, S. (General) 149, 158–9
foreign direct investment (FDI) 67
Forrester, D. 35, 40
forward caste 46–7, *48*
fragmentation 45; land 16
free-market system 140
Freedom House 144
French, P. 3
Fukuyama, F. 142–3

Gandhi, I. (Prime Minister, India) 61–2, 66, 90
Gandhi, R. 91
Gandhi, S. 115
gangs 160
gatekeepers 111, 119
Geetha Jeevan, P. 43
gender 32–4, 40–4, 56, 111–14; discrimination 111; inclusion 110, 132; quotas 133; recruitment 109–11, 128
general elections 90; (India 2009) 109–38
gerrymandering 145
Gilani, I.S. 19
Gilmartin, D. 17
Golden Temple (India) 63
Goonetilleke, O. 178
governance: centralised 61; good 141, 150; illiberal 141
government: coalition 1–2, 67, 86, 89, 96, 114, 151; minority 1–2, 96; self- 171
Graham, B.D. 172
Gramsci, A. 69, 71n
grassroots participation 80, 85–6
Guardian 14
Guha, S. 88
Gurdwaras 57–8

Hagopian, F. 15
Hakeem, R. 158
harassment: sexual 157
Harris, N. 141
health 120

hegemony 69, 71n, 170; post-Congress 96–100, 103
Herring, R.J. 11
Hindu bourgeoisie 65–6
Hinduism 58, 63–4
House of Representatives (Sri Lanka) 172, 175
human rights 149–50
hung parliaments 96
Huntington, S. 142, 161n
hybrid regimes 144

identification: party 7, 18–20
ideology 7, 90, 104–6
Illamvazhuthi, P. 36, 48
illiberalism 141–2
impeachment 151–2
impunity 159–60
incentives 82
inclusion 65–7, 148; gender 110, 132; political 116
incumbency 78–108, 128–30; anti- 18, 26
independence 139–40, 145; India (1947) 2, 59, 90, 112–14, 140; post- 90, 112–14, 140, 166–86; pre- 166–73; Sri Lanka (1948) 166–86
India 55–77, 109–38; independence (1947) 2, 59, 90, 112–14, 140
Indian National Congress (INC) 33, 47, 56, 59, 62–9, 78–105, 109–32
Indian Union Muslim League (IUML) 56
individualism 140
industrial bourgeoisie 64
inequality: functional 12; land 14; socio-economic 11
influence: economic 66; political 66
instability: constituency 105; political 183
institutionalisation 4, 104, 143, 180; party 166
interaction 143
internal processes 78–108
intimidation 144

Jaffrelot, C. 88
Jalal, A. 16
Jama'at-i Islami Pakistan 2
Janata Dal 118
Janatha Vimukthi Peramuna (People's Liberation Front, JVP) 156

Jayewardene, J.R. 148–9
Jennings, I. 168, 176–9
Jinnah, M.A. (Governor-General, Pakistan) 11, 17
Jones, P.E. 12, 16–18, 22, 28n
Judicial Services Commission (JSC) 150
Jupp, J. 181
justice: democratic 110; social 116

Kanimozhi, M.K. 43–4
Kant, S.K. 118
Karat, B. 116
Karunanidhi, M. (Chief Minister, Tamil Nadu) 3, 33–43
Katz, R.: and Mair, P. 81
Katzenstein, M.F. 112
Keefer, P.: Narayan, A. and Vishwanath, T. 13–14
Khan, H.: and Bari, S. 13
Khan, I. 13–14, 20
kinship 7–10, 16–22, 25, 44, 181
Kirchheimer, O. 81
Kitschelt, H. 14; and Wilkinson, S. 9
Kochanek, S. 83, 112
Kongu Vellalar Gounders 45–6
Kotelawala, J. 177, 182
Kumar, M. 110
Kumarasingham, H. 4, 166–86
Kumaratunga, C. (President, Sri Lanka) 149, 155

labour militancy 12
Lal, M.: and Narain, I. 83
land: fragmentation 16; grabbing 157; inequality 14; reform 11–12, 16
Land Reclamation and Development Corporation 152–3
landlords 9–12, 16–19, 20–4; candidate 8; powerful 7; wealthy 33
Lanka Sama Samaja Party 140, 182
leader-centrism 182–3
leadership 81, 156; autocratic 50; autonomous 82; central 59, 85; national 58, 80, 87, 119; nomination 133; party 36–40, 49, 61, 79, 90, 105, 121–2; senior 49; Shiromani Akali Dal (SAD) 61–4
Left Democratic Front (LDF) 86
Left Front 82, 90

left-wing politics 56, 63–4, 82, 116, 125, 182; extreme 156
legislature 109–10
liberal democracy 142–4, 160
Liberation Tigers of Tamil Eelam (LTTE) 141, 145, 148–53, 156–9
Lijphart, A. 82
linkages: party-voter 7–31
Linz, J.: Lipset, S. and Diamond, L. 179; Yadav, Y. and Stepan, A. 181
Lipset, S.: Diamond, L. and Linz, J. 179
lobbying 37–9
localism 40, 83
Lok Sabha (House of the People, India) 34–6, 39–44, 49–50, 109–10, 113–15, 118–25, 131–3
London County Council (LLC) 171
loyalty 45, 145, 170, 182
Ludowyk, E.F.C. 174–5

maaliks (owners) 21–6, 29n
Macmillan, H. (Prime Minister, UK) 180
Mahajan, S. 115
Mair, P.: and Katz, R. 81
majoritarianism 142
majority community 62, 141, 146
malgovernance 139, 144
Manikandan, C.: and Wyatt, A. 3, 32–54, 113
Manor, J. 178–9
Mansergh, N. 4, 169–70
Maran, D. 39
Maran, M. 38
marginal seats 128–30
marginalisation 22, 27, 114–16, 143–5, 155, 166
maulvis (caretakers) 22, 28n
Mayawati, K. (Chief Minister, Uttar Pradesh) 87–9, 116
mediocrity 145
Mekan biraderi 8, 24–6, 28n
Members of the Legislative Assembly (MLAs) 34–5, 40–9, 50–2n, 86–7
Members of Parliament (MPs) 34–5, 41–2, 86–7, 109–10, 113–15, 119, 128
middle class 33, 69, 81, 105
militancy: labour 12
militarisation 152, 156

minority: community 57–9, 145, 148, 158; government 1–2, 96; religious 36, 41, 46, 55
minority rights: protecting 61–2
Mishra, R.C. 113
mobilisation: local 82; political 179
mobility: upward 35; vote 16
Mohmand, S.K. 3, 7–31
monarchy: constitutional 172
Monck-Mason-Moore, H. (Governor-General, Sri Lanka) 167
Moore, R.J. 170
Most Backward Class (MBC) 45, *46–8*
munshis (managers) 21
Murugan, D. 36–7
Murugesan, V. 43
Musharraf, P. (President, Pakistan) 13, 17–19, 24–6
Muslim League 11, 17
Muslims *46–8*, 59, 88, 110–11, 158
Muthu, S. 33

Namasivayam, N. 171
Nanak, Guru 57
Narain, I.: and Lal, M. 83
Narayan, A.: Vishwanath, T. and Keefer, P. 13–14
Nasr, S.V.R. 2
nation 55–77
National Assembly 15, 20, 23, 26
National Commission for Minorities (NCM) 61
National Democratic Alliance (NDA) 89, 114–15
national elections 24, 85
National Labour Party 101
national parties 120–2
nationalism 59, 68, 139, 145, 174; competing 63–5; Hindu 63; Indian 63–5; Punjabi 60–3, 69, 71n; reactive 141; regional 55–6; romantic 174; Sikh 60–5, 69, 71n; Sinhalese Buddhist 139–42, 145–52, 156, 160, 168, 177
Nationalist Congress Party (NCP) 116
nationality 177
nazims (district mayors) 13
Nehru, J. (Prime Minister, India) 59, 174, 183
neoliberalism 67
nepotism 145, 154–6

New Westminsters 177–80
New York Times 178
Nil Balakaya (Blue Brigade) 153
nomination 78, 82–91, 104; calculated 89; candidate 79–81, 84, 120–2; central party 86; data 90–103; female 109–38; internal 89–90; intra-party 79; party 111–31; trends 109–38
North, D. 142–3
Northern Provincial Council (NPC) 157–9

Operation Blue Star 63–5
oppositionism 60, 66
Other Backward Class (OBC) 45, 82, 88
over-representation 46, 87
Oxford Union 174

Pai, S. 88
Pakistan 7–31
Pakistan Muslim League – Nawaz (PML-N) 8, 13, 16–21, 25–6
Pakistan Muslim League – Quaid (PML-Q) 19, 25–6
Pakistan Muslim League (PML) 2, 25
Pakistan People's Party (PPP) 2, 12–13, 16–26
Pakistan Tehreek-i-Insaaf (PTI) 13–14, 20–1, 26
Palmer, N. 83, 112
Palshikar, S.: and Yadav, Y. 57
Pandian, S. 36
parliamentary elections 78, 84, 159
parliamentary seats 50
Parliamentary Select Committee (PSC) 151
parliaments: hung 96; national 120, 125
parochialism 175, 181
participation 79; governmental 168; grassroots 80, 85–6
parties: catchall 81–2, 90, 105; ethnic 82, 90, 104–6; national 120–2
party-voter linkages 7–31
patronage 15, 26, 35, 88–90, 147, 151–4, 157; elite 166–86; interest group 105; political 144
People's Liberation Front (Janatha Vimukthi Peramuna, JVP) 156
Perera, N.M. 182
Periasamy, N. 43

personalism 181
Pierson, P. 145
Pillayah (Chandrakanthan) 157–8
pluralism 4, 78, 114; internal 32, 37, 50
political decay 139–65
politics: dynastic 32, 38–43, 49–50, 156; electoral 15, 110–20, 125, 132–3; high 166–86; left-wing 56, 63–4, 82, 116, 125, 156, 182; local 4, 21, 27; national 4, 7, 10, 132; personalised 9, 16–17; right-wing 9; rural 18; Shiromani Akali Dal (SAD) 55–77; Sikh 59–60, 63–5; state 125, 132; subnational 79–81; Whig 172, 180
Ponnambalam, G.G. 182
populism 45, 144, 174
post-Congress hegemony 96–100, 103
power 14, 166; devolution of 62–3; economic 7, 10, 14, 21, 27; executive 171; imperial 171; landlord 12; legislative 171; personalised 182; political 16, 21, 60–1, 182; rural 15; social 21; state 23, 88
Pradesh Congress Committee (PCC) 84
Pradesh Election Committee (PEC) 82–4
Premadasa, R. (President, Sri Lanka) 149, 156
presidential elections 158–9
Presidential Task Force (PTF) 152
Prevention of Terrorism Act (1979) 149
privatisation 68
privilege: social 45–6
professionalism 147, 181; declining 154
progression 37–41; political 50
propaganda: election 41
prosperity 168
protests: counter- 148
Public Service Commission 146
Punjab (India) 55–77
Purewal, S. 57

Racine, J. 45
racism 141
Rai, S.M. 113
Raja, A. (Union Minister) 35–8, 48, 52n
Raja, T.R.P. 43
Rajapaksa, B. (Economic Development Minister, Sri Lanka) 151–2, 156
Rajapaksa, G. (Defense Secretary, Sri Lanka) 149, 152–3, 156, 159

Rajapaksa, M. (President, Sri Lanka) 148–60
Rajya Sabha (Upper House, India) 34–5, 39, 43–4, 61, 110, 120
Ramachandran, M.G. 33
rank-and-file 79
Rashtriya Lok Dal (RLD) 118
Rashtriya Swayamsevak Sangh (RSS) 85
recognition: symbolic 44
recruitment 132; ethnocentric 147–8; gender 109–11, 128; political 34, 109–13, 128
reform 12, 156; constitutional 171; economic 33; homestead 12; land 11–12, 16; social 32–3; tenancy 12–13
regionalism 20, 56, 177
regression: democratic 139–65
regulation 147
religion 1, 4, 32–4, 45, 55–77, 87, 177
religious minority 36, 41, 46, 55
religious rights 62
renomination 78–108
representation 111–14; balanced 41; communal 171, 175; group 90, 105; over- 46, 87; symbolic 36; territorial 171
reserved seats 109–10
revisionism 148
right-wing politics 9
rights: cultural 62; economic 62; human 149–50; minority 61–2; religious 62
riots 148, 170
Rouse, S. 21–4, 28n
Roy, R. 82–3, 112

sabotage 149–50
safe seats 111, 128–30
Sahiwal (Pakistan) 10, 21–7
Samajwadi Party (SP) 79–82, 87–90, 100–6, 124, 129
Samarakone, P. 149
Sangma, A. 122–4
Scheduled Caste (SC) 41, 44, 47–50, 82, 87, 91, 114–16
Scheduled Tribe (ST) 41, 47–50, 91, 114–15
seats: female 109–10; marginal 128–30; parliamentary 50; reserved 109–10; safe 111, 128–30; unwinnable 109–11,

119, 128–31; vulnerable 129; winnable 119–22, 128–33
sectarianism 146
selection 84, 132; institutionalised 103, 106; internal 106
Senanayake, D.S. (Prime Minister, Sri Lanka) 166–70, 174–82
seniority 41, 49
separatism 4, 64, 141, 148, 156
Sharif, N. (Prime Minister, Pakistan) 2, 13, 21, 25
Shastri, L.B. (Prime Minister, India) 59
Shiromani Akali Dal (SAD) 3, 37, 101, 118, 124; anti- 64; leadership 61–4; politics 55–77
Sikhism 55–60, 63–5, 68
Simon Commission 171
Singer, W. 120
Singh, B. 65
Singh, G.Z. (President, India) 61
Singh, P. 3, 55–77
Singh, R. (President, BJP) 57, 121
Singh, S.F. 59–60
Sinhala Only Act (1956) 145–8
Sinhalese Buddhist nationalism 139–42, 145–52, 156, 160, 168, 177
Sinhalisation 157
sitting-getting rule 89–91, 94, 99–103, 106
Sivaraman, M. 33
snap elections 90, 104
social engineering 87–9, 105
socialism 12
society: civil 148, 156; strong 144
Soulbury Commission (1944–5) 168, 171–3, 176
Spary, C. 3–4, 109–38
Sri Chand 57
Sri Lanka 139–65; Army 170; Department of Elections 2; independence (1948) 166–86, see also Ceylon
Sri Lanka Freedom Party (SLFP) 2–3, 140–2, 145, 148–9, 153–60, 179, 182
Sri Lanka Muslim Congress (SLMC) 158
Sridharan, E.: and Farooqui, A. 3–4, 78–108
stability: regime 15
Stalin, M.K. (Treasurer) 36, 37–41

standards 147; declining 154
state: assembly 41, 46, 120; politics 125, 132; power 23, 88
State Council 140, 171
State Election Committee (SEC) 85, 122
State Services Advisory Board (SSAB) 146–7
State Services Disciplinary Board (SSDB) 146–7
status: economic 27; personal 14; social 46, 177
Stepan, A.: Linz, J. and Yadav, Y. 181
subnational politics 79–81
success 120; electoral 115–19, 128–9
suffrage 139, 145, 171
suicide bombings 149–50
support 39; outside 47; political 147
Supreme Court 150–2
Swaraj, S. (Opposition Leader, India) 115
Syers, C. 173

Talbot, I. 17
Taliban 20
Tamil Congress 140, 180–2
Tamil Makkal Viduthalai Pulikal (Tamil People's Liberation Tigers, TMVP) 157–8
Tamil Nadu 32–5, 45–6, 61, 68, 124–5
Tamil National Alliance (TNA) 156–7
Tarlochan Singh, S. (Chairman, NCM) 61–2, 70n
Tarunayata Hetak (A Tomorrow for the Youth) 153
tenancy reform 12–13
terrorism 1, 141, 149–50; counter- 149
trade unions 81, 140
tribe: Scheduled Tribe (ST) 41, 47–50, 91, 114–15

Umaira, W.: and Chandra, K. 49
Uncle-Nephew Party 166, 179
Union Territories (UTs) 12, 122, 125
Unionist Party 11, 58
United Democratic Front (UDF) 86
United Front Ministry 63
United National Party (UNP) 2–3, 140–2, 145, 148–9, 153–6, 179–82
United Nations (UN) 150

United People's Freedom Alliance (UPFA) 152–9
United Progressive Alliance (UPA) 35, 89, 114–16
United Women's Front (UWF) 118
unwinnable seats 109–11, 119, 128–31
Upper Caste 45, *46*, 88, 96, 105
Urban Development Authority (UDA) 153
Uttar Pradesh (UP, India) 64, 79, 82, 86–91, 105, 124, 129

Vaithianathan, K. (Foreign Secretary, Sri Lanka) 170
Vansh Sabha (house of dynasties) 3
Veerasami, A.N. (HQ Secretary) 36
Velu, E.V. 38
violence 144, 157–8
Viplavakari Lanka Samaja Party 140
Vishwanath, T.: Keefer, P. and Narayan, A. 13–14
voting 96, 112, 115; aggregate 7, 10; assured 106; party 19; urban 96
vulnerable seats 129

Walker, P.G. 169, 180
war crimes 150
Waseem, M. 17
wealth 4, 14–16, 177
Weerakoon, B. 146
welfare: social 65–8

welfare state 81
Westminster system 166, 168–75, 178–83
Whig politics 172, 180
Wickramasinghe, S.A. 182
Wickremesinghe, R. (Prime Minister, Sri Lanka) 156
Wigneswaran, C.V. (Supreme Court Justice) 157
Wilder, A. 16–19, 22
Wilkinson, S.: and Kitschelt, H. 9
winnable seats 119–22, 128–33
Wolkowitz, C. 44
Women's Reservation Bill (2010) 120–33
Woodward, C.A. 179
working class 81, 110–11
World Bank 15, 67–8
World War II (1939–45) 176; post- 81, 139
Wriggins, W.H. 141, 179–83
Wyatt, A.: and Manikandan, C. 3, 32–54, 113

Yadav, M.S. 87
Yadav, Y.: and Palshikar, S. 57; Stepan, A. and Linz, J. 181
Yahya Khan, A. (President, Pakistan) 18

Zaidi, A. 14
Zia-ul-Haq, M. (President, Pakistan) 13–19, 23–5

3 20